HERMANN BECKH (1875–1937) studied Law and later Sanskrit, becoming Professor of Oriental Studies at the University of Berlin. A master of ancient and modern languages, he wrote extensively on religious and philosophical subjects, including Buddhism, Indology, Christianity, Alchemy and Music. In 1911, he heard a lecture by Rudolf Steiner and was inspired to join the Anthroposophical Society, where he soon became a valued co-worker. In 1922, he helped found The Christian Community, a movement for religious renewal. His many books are gradually being translated from the original German and published in English.

The Buddha by Katrin Binder

BUDDHA'S LIFE AND TEACHING

Hermann Beckh

Translated from the German by Dr Katrin Binder
Edited with a Foreword by Neil Franklin

TEMPLE LODGE

Temple Lodge Publishing Ltd.
Hillside House, The Square
Forest Row, RH18 5ES

www.templelodge.com

Published in English by Temple Lodge 2019

Originally published in German under the title *Buddha und seine Lehre,* Berlin/Leipzig 1916

A CIP catalogue record for this book is available from the British Library

ISBN 978 1 912230 26 6

Cover by Morgan Creative featuring image by Daniela Ruiz
Typeset by DP Photosetting, Neath, West Glamorgan
Printed and bound by 4Edge Ltd., Essex

Contents

B. The historical Buddha

PART 2: THE TEACHING

A. General Viewpoints

B. The individual stages of the Path

Foreword

It is striking that in the midst of total European disaster (1915–16) Sammlung Göschen sought to publish a new book on Buddha for well-educated readers in general, and undergraduates in Indology in particular. The contract, offered to Hermann Beckh, was for a small volume to supersede their earlier booklet *Buddha* by Edmund Hardy, 1903.[1] Beckh was instructed, as were all contributors, not to exceed a certain length but a compromise was reached whereby the new publication could stretch to two volumes. This was unusual for S. G. but not without precedent.[2] No one could have guessed what Beckh was going to make of the opportunity.

With some hindsight it is now possible to come to some appreciation of what he wanted to achieve. If physical, social and economic structures were being torn apart by the war, then also religion and spirituality were under immense pressures. Neo-Buddhist groups were in their infancy; Theosophists in Germany were still wallowing in H.P. Blavatsky, Alfred Sinnett and Annie Besant; Tibet had established a romanticized appeal; prominent Professors of Indology could display Roman Catholic or Evangelical prejudices.[3] Given such distortions the first thing that was needed was absolute clarity, aided by accurate scholarship.

Here Beckh was very well equipped with his doctorate-level legal training (1893–1901). Some attention needs to be paid to his very first publication, *Die Beweislast nach dem bürgerlichen Gesetzbuch*, Munich 1899.[4] This highly technical study of the new Bavarian Code of Law is concerned with what does, and what doesn't constitute proof. A recent study of criminal cases in Bavaria during the nineteenth century[5] assembled convincing evidence to show that many trials rested only on verbal testimonies, that the word of a gentleman could be taken as proof over the words of illiterate farm workers, and that the conviction of the illiterate on such grounds was widespread. In 1899, aged only 24, Dr Beckh took the sharpest legal scalpel in hand and helped to lance the filthy boils and ulcers of nineteenth century practice, after which there was no going back for the privileged minority.

As with the law so it was with Beckh's academic studies of Tibetan, Sanskrit and Pali 1903–14.

After resigning his appointment as what one might call a circuit-judge[6] in Munich, Hermann Beckh spent a short time in three universities, probably sampling the Indology provisions. In the summer of 1903 (age 28) he stayed in Kiel for a term where the distinguished Hermann Oldenberg had held the Chair since 1898. This was followed by a similar short period in the Friedrich-Wilhelm Universität in Berlin where the Faculty was led by the newly arrived (1902) but equally celebrated Richard Pischel, a specialist in Kālidāsa and Vedic literature. The final trial was in the University of Bonn (1904) which had the distinction of having Hermann Jacobi as Professor of Sanskrit (since 1899). By autumn 1904 Beckh had decided that his future was with Richard Pischel and Berlin.

At the time it is worth remembering that Emil Bock was nine years old and Friedrich Rittelmeyer had just completed his D.Phil. in Würzburg entitled *Friedrich Nietzsche und das Erkenntnisproblem*, while taking up the appointment as Pastor in the (Lutheran) Heilig-Geist-Kirche in Nürnberg. While Bock was picking fruit berries and Rittelmeyer was responsible for sermons in Nürnberg, Hermann Beckh continued to astonish the Faculty in Berlin. Within three years he had achieved such a level of competence in Tibetan, Pali and Sanskrit as successfully to undertake a second doctorate (D.Phil.) under the supervision of Pischel. It appears as though he didn't really have to learn the languages, he seemed to remember them, thence in 1907 completing his dissertation 'Ein Beitrag zur Textkritik von Kālidāsas Meghadūta'[7] which allowed him to become a lecturer for the University. However, this academic study was no routine piece of research.

The task was to compare, for the first time, the well-established Sanskrit texts, which had also been translated several times into German and English, with a number of Tibetan versions of the *Meghadūta*, which had been little examined. Character by character Beckh studied the wood-block printed texts (red and black Tanjur) against the Sanskrit versions.

He found that what was required was no orthodox philology but a different kind of sensitivity, something very largely lacking at the time in the professional world of Indology. By now Beckh was so far advanced in Tibetan as to recognize or intuit its poetic speech rhythms, what one would expect in any given line or phrase. By calling on this faculty it became possible to establish exactly where the wood-block printer (printing by hand) must have made a slip. Once a suggested corrected text was established one could also come to more general conclusions: the Tibetan sources represent a free-flowing version of the older Sanskrit story, but one that is steeped in its own rhythms. When the final text of Beckh's study was published in 1907 he had been studying Tibetan for less than four years.

With the appearance of Beckh's edition of the *Udānavarga* in 1911,[8] again making detailed comparison of Tibetan and Sanskrit texts, Beckh had attained the position of being one of the very few scholars in Germany—indeed in Europe—who were qualified and sufficiently experienced to deal with primary sources in Tibetan. Full recognition of this fact was made abundantly clear some two years later by the request that he should inspect the substantial Kanjur holdings of the Königliche Bibliothek, Germany's largest and most prestigious library, within a stone's throw of the University. What was needed was a fully annotated index of the deposit of Kanjur texts. Beckh achieved this vast undertaking by 1914,[9] shortly before the outbreak of the Great War, and just as the library was moving a short distance along Unter den Linden.

What all of this indicates, apart from Beckh's truly extraordinary gifts and capacity for work, is that Sammlung Göschen in 1916 either made a very well-informed choice of their author for a new book on Buddha's life and teaching, or, as the event showed, were serendipitously blessed by good fortune beyond any reasonable expectation. In fact their only other realistic option (one can only make inferences here) had been Richard Pischel's other principal student, Karl Eugen Neumann,[10] who had found a Professorship at the university in Vienna but who had sadly passed away in 1915. As it was, Göschen must have congratulated themselves on agreeing a contract with Hermann Beckh that could allow for a double volume.

Nevertheless, it would be quite inappropriate to see Hermann Beckh between 1915 and 1916 as some kind of ink-bound philologist, albeit with a profoundly honed sense for the sounds of speech and its rhythms in sacred texts, and equipped with the sharpest legal eye for what does and what does not constitute acceptable evidence. Quite apart from his love for Wagner performances (note also Wagner's own involvement with Buddhism) and also for strenuous walks in Bavarian mountains in all weathers, Beckh had a deeply personal relationship to the Buddhist texts. Later in life he once became explicit on this, and on another occasion explained how he would spend *decades* with such texts as the *Mahāparinibbānasutta* trying to find an appropriate German expression that is both accurate and aesthetically in harmony with the original language.[11]

Gundhild Kačer-Bock's biography[12] and other sources paint a fascinating picture of the 36-year-old Hermann Beckh searching for something truly meaningful beyond comparative linguistics and the deciphering of the Tanjur. Again there is a significant contrast with Friedrich Rittelmeyer who, despite his own soul struggles, found it acceptable to remain at the Heilig-Geist-Kirche in Nürnberg for 14 years (1902–1916) and Emil Bock who, after 1914 (age 19) followed orthodox studies in Greek and Latin and then wished to compose a thesis on Christianity and Novalis.[13]

Hermann Beckh's encounter with Rudolf Steiner's public lecture at the Berlin Architektenhaus, quite close to his own place of work at the University, on 14 December, 1911 has been well documented.[14] So too his joining the brand new Anthroposophical Society ('Theosophical' still remained on the old paperwork), his acceptance into the Esoteric School, his letters to Steiner, his attendance at major lecture cycles, his friendships with Rittelmeyer, Michael Bauer and Else Kraus, and perhaps above all, his most serious attention to *Knowledge of Higher Worlds* and *Occult Science*. On many occasions it appears as though he was in his element within Anthroposophy between 1911 and 1916. As his biographer, Kačer-Bock is quite justified, too, in making a strong case for Steiner giving a number of lectures at this time in the knowledge that Beckh was in attendance and speaking especially for him.[15] One might be tempted to embrace the idea that one of Europe's leading scholars on Tibetan and Buddhism, strongly dissatisfied with the 'hostile materialistic science'[16] in the halls of the university, found great light, warmth and encouragement from Anthroposophy. This is certainly true, but it is not enough to penetrate *Buddha und seine Lehre* in a truly meaningful way. There needs to be an appreciation of something further.

Beckh joined the Anthroposophical Society at Christmas 1912, and being resident in Berlin (Steglitz) he was duly registered as a member of the Berlin Group. Yet despite records of his correspondence with Rudolf Steiner, and his journeys to Leipzig and Köln to attend lectures, so far nothing has come to light regarding a participation in the life of the Berlin Group. Later in life, once again, Beckh explicitly said that he never felt at home in Stuttgart and northern Germany, and often longed for München and the highlands of Bavaria. His quite substantial autobiographical writings insist on the fact that the general society of students at The Maximilianeum, where he originally studied Law, were remote to him. His later life within the Seminary of The Christian Community (again well-documented) clearly indicates that he felt himself increasingly to be an outsider, misunderstood by many.[17]

Early 1914 found Beckh away from the university in Berlin staying with his parents and sister in Nürnberg where he remained during the first months of the Great War.[18] As the initial euphoria wore off with the German advance becoming bogged down in trench warfare, we find him leaving the family home in order to complete the meticulous but eye-straining task of indexing the Kanjur papers for the Königliche Bibliothek. Not long afterwards he comes to terms with Sammlung Göschen for this book on Buddha and Buddhism.

Thus several powerful streams converged around 1915/6 when Beckh was writing *The Buddha and His Teaching*. Some of the most harrowing scenes that Europe had ever seen were taking place on both the western and eastern Fronts.[19] Beckh had become increasingly frustrated with the academic world of Indology, widely encountering religious prejudice and pedantic scholarship. He was, in the Buddhist sense, one of the 'homeless,'[20] one, in fact, whose vision and personal experience tended to set him apart from colleagues. Concerning his close personal affinity with Buddhism Beckh wrote in 1931:[21]

> For many years I was a lawyer before I took up an academic career as a Sanskrit scholar. Then, when starting from the University to *enter life and beginning to suffer some things*, I felt increasingly drawn to Buddha ... Not that I lacked the organ for the clear thinking of Buddhism which leads human beings in all higher development to the important 'inner zero-point'. In anthroposophy, too, this 'clarity of thinking' is indeed in the first place valued for everything. I did *always* have the organ for the consecrated and esoteric side of Buddhism very strongly precisely in the midst of all simplicity of thought. As the cool breath of the snow-covered mountains relates to the stuffy vapours of large cities and their sultry plains, so I *always experienced* the clarity and consecration of Buddhist thoughts in the midst of today's decadent and philistine materialism ... [trans. by A. Stott, my emphases].

While it is quite right to observe that Rudolf Steiner's publications, lectures and private teachings for the Esoteric School were absolutely essential to Hermann Beckh between 1912 and 1916, and that Steiner himself made considerable personal efforts to provide lasting encouragement and inspiration for him, one further factor should not be entirely overlooked. It was precisely during the Great War, as Beckh continued to study Steiner's *Knowledge of Higher Worlds* and *Occult Science* in particular, thus to foster his own meditational practice, that Annie Besant came to betray anything that might have been valuable in H.P. Blavatsky and the early *fin-de-siècle* theosophists. Her promotion of Jiddu Krishnamurti as the reincarnated Maitreya Buddha and world-saviour took concrete form in 1911 with the establishment of The Order of the Star of the East, and of course this could only mean the formal separation of the new-born Anthroposophical Society from the world of Besant and British India.[22] What is significant in this context is that the period 1911–16, leading up to the publication of *Buddha und seine Lehre*, saw the *continuing persistence* of this aberration representing *the high tide* of the O.S.E. Krishnamurti continued to wear the mantle of the Maitreya Buddha as chlorine gas swept over the second Yprès battlefield and the massive confrontation at Loos.[23] He was not to give it up until 1929.

Rudolf Steiner made every effort to counteract the viral growth of Annie Besant's error with numerous lectures on Buddha between 1909 and 1912.[24] It is very likely that Beckh read these (after Christmas 1912) and pondered the suggestions relating Christianity to Buddhism. Now, the very least that a new reader of Beckh might observe is that the author was well read in his subject, and this, of course, is to put it mildly. Time and time again in this 'Buddha book' as he came to call it, and later in most important publications, Beckh will take the time to refer to a vast array of scholarly works and adduce pertinent criticism, usually appreciative but sometimes otherwise. One needs to have the convincing impression that the author of the Göschen, *Buddha und seine Lehre* knows the Tibetan and Pali texts, the Sanskrit analogues, and the secondary literature probably as well as anyone lecturing and writing in Germany in 1915/16. Given this, one can only imagine his response to Annie Besant's, *Elementary Lessons in Karma* and *A Study in Karma*, both published in 1912. Did he ever bother to read Besant's early work, *The Myth of the Resurrection* (1886)?

This is all to suggest in conclusion that the book before us here is not some kind of dusty text or just another undergraduate-level introduction to Buddhism. It is nothing less than the still, clear, luminous centre of a hurricane, formed in the midst of the most violent forces which themselves led to unparalleled destruction and misapprehension. It is born, too, out of the author's commitment, in the midst of profound personal struggles, to set forth with the utmost clarity the Buddhist 'argument from suffering' and its resolution in mental or spiritual self-control.

Its value as such has not entirely passed-by later generations. After seeing several subsequent editions the Göschen text was republished by Verlag Freies Geistesleben, Stuttgart, 1958 with an insightful introduction and additional bibliography from Heimo Rau. This was followed by a Dutch translation and then a Japanese edition, both without further textual additions.[25] The first English translation here, by Dr Katrin Binder, celebrates the centenary of the 1916 publication and includes further notes and references in the attempt to clarify some uncertainties. The bibliography has also been updated to indicate some of the significant developments since 1958. Beckh's original notes are found at the bottom of the page, additional notes for this edition are located at the end of sections, and the occasional editorial additions in the text are marked with square brackets.

Translator's Introduction

Hermann Beckh: *Buddha and his teaching*—an appreciation

Like other works in Beckh's extensive oeuvre, his *Buddha* appears to be at once unique and typical. It is unique among his scholarly Indological works in its general appeal and accessibility. Although standing before his explicitly anthroposophical masterpieces, the work foreshadows these by its concern for humanity and its stringent coupling of rigorous historical-philological methods with the author's inner, meditative insights. And in this, it is 'typically Beckh' and may allow those of us who are just starting to discover his work to find an ideal starting point.

The earliest publications on Buddhism in European languages faced the problem of limited access to original sources and even to the necessary language skills. While this situation had improved markedly by the time Beckh studied Indology, academic approaches to Buddhism were still influenced by a nineteenth century bias for the search for the 'original'—i.e. the 'original' texts and oldest strata of the tradition in question. For many scholars at the time, this implied accepting only Theravāda (Hīnayāna) sources as valid and denouncing texts and commentaries from the Mahāyāna. Beckh does not accept such a limited approach but draws freely on several Buddhist textual traditions. He, too, is interested in capturing the Buddha and his teaching in their 'original' truth. Working from a sound philological basis, he is able to argue, however, that it is not necessarily the actual age of a text as it appears today that tells us all about the information we can obtain from it. 'Later' texts that appear full of interpolations and hagiographical material may rest on much older strata of tradition, and even 'overgrown' legends may contain pictures and metaphors that point us to 'original' facts and truths. Beckh argues all these points convincingly and in a scholarly way which at the same time reflects his warm-hearted interest and involvement.

What can be considered the lasting contribution of Beckh's work on Buddhism? Apart from those aspects already hinted at above, the most striking characteristic of Beckh's *Buddha* is the fact that in his delineation of the Buddha legend in particular he remains very close to his textual sources from within the Buddhist traditions. Bringing his inner connection with the subject fully to bear on his writing, he finds a beautiful, adequate language in German. The reader feels as if he is reading an original text. At the same time Beckh sometimes achieves a vividness that allows the reader to get very close to the events and teachings. Thus we may say that in a way unusual for the early twentieth century, he allows the sources and the associated tradition *to speak for themselves*. To me, this was not only a radical step then, but remains so now, making the publication all the more relevant.

In his thoughtful and well-placed comments, Beckh does not pass sweeping judgements or confront us with startling generalizations. Where necessary, he provides gentle aids to understanding for the general reader. Here again, we come across a unique characteristic of Beckh's writing on Buddhism. Not only does he work from a basis of inner understanding but indicates directions for accessing the *meditative truths* behind the Buddha legend. While the reader is left with the task to verify these truths for him/herself, pointing them out itself allows Beckh to assign the texts the legitimacy and value due to them. This also applies to his relentless but non-judgemental explanation of how to approach and understand even the most complicated aspects of the Buddha's teachings (notably his lucid analysis of the *pratītyā-samutpāda*, or the chain of conditioned arising). He very clearly notes the challenges posed to a 'Western' form of understanding, but convincingly demonstrates that within its own domain, the Buddha's teaching is not lacking in logic. While in this context Beckh very clearly outlines the kind of understanding which is needed to understand Buddhism in its own terms, he applies his almost radical approach also to the broader historical developments of Buddhism as a world religion, arguing that the later Mahāyāna does not constitute a decadent distortion of the original teachings, but a necessary development in the history of humanity based on continuities of crucial parts of even the earliest teachings.

As the above introduction by Neil Franklin suggests, Beckh significantly goes beyond the usual sectarian tendencies present in virtually all other works of his day—be they Christian, Theosophical or Neo-Buddhist. In this context, his outstanding analysis of what the 'memory of previous existences' actually means is remarkable indeed. Firstly, this memory is among the powers acquired through right meditation, and is closely linked to the ultimate penetration of the truth of suffering. But Beckh explains that according to Buddhism, this memory also serves as the connector between incarnations, and he leads the reader through a succinct delineation of the Buddhist teachings regarding the absence of a permanent part of being, or ego, i.e. the teachings of the non-I.

The section 'Buddha as a human being and spiritual teacher' also appears to be particularly important. Here Beckh gauges the extent of what we (are able to) know about the Buddha, and explores how we can approach his person ourselves. As Beckh draws our attention to the particular emphasis of Buddhism on the significance of a human birth for the goal of salvation, we begin to see his own life choices and later works casting their shadows. We also begin to understand that indeed Beckh's *oeuvre* is of one piece (as Alan Stott argues elsewhere). Throughout the Buddha book we find suggestions of thoughts more fully developed in his last MS, *Der Mensch und die Musik* (*The Mystery of Musical Creativity: The Human Being and Music,* Temple Lodge Press, forthcoming), for example in the discussion of the concept of *nirvāṇa* where in the linguistic analysis there appears the root *vā*, blowing, extinguishing. Especially details like this show how a single root is often allowed to grow and expand into cosmic dimensions over Beckh's *oeuvre*. From this it almost follows as a necessity that together with his translation of the *Mahāparinibbānasutta*, the Buddha book lays the foundation for his later contribution *From Buddha to Christ* (1925).

In these later works he returns again to a point made on the significance of the 'poetical element' in the Buddhist canon. Beckh's insight into the deeper meaning of seemingly superficial outer characteristics of these texts is unique indeed. In contrast to many other descriptions of the Buddha legend, Beckh allows this element to penetrate his own writing, and he knows how to justify his approach in academic terms. No other publication I know has taken the significance of the particular textual forms into account. Where we find elsewhere (e.g., with Oldenberg) an exasperated impatience with the seemingly endless parallelisms and repetitions, Beckh shows that this rhythmical element of the texts can actually offer an aid to find the appropriate forms of understanding they demand.

Finally, a technical remark may be in order at this point. Throughout this book, I have chosen to translate the German term '*Erkenntnis*' with 'realization'. This decision arose in response to Beckh's call for the above discussed forms of understanding. With Beckh I understand Buddhist '*Erkenntnis*' as knowledge or insight acquired in meditation. This inner process implies a 'making real' of the teachings, including the Buddhist 'truths' and imaginations. This is well illustrated by Beckh's discussion of the role of deities and supernatural beings in Buddhism. It also emerges from his discussion of the concept of '*schauendes Erkennen*'—'realizing vision (or 'seeing realization', *ñāṇa-dassanaṃ*). This term implies not only the gradual acquisition of supernatural powers of clairvoyance through the practice of meditation (for example with regard to the memory of previous existences). It also carries the Buddhist image (resting on much older Indian ideas) of the 'blind' person who is made seeing by his insight, or realization, into the Buddhist truth of suffering. After reading Beckh's *From Buddha to Christ* I felt even more justified in this choice as the central point there is that the Buddha contributed '*Erkenntnis*' to humanity and the course of history, and that in a sense I feel is best rendered as 'realization'.

Working on the translation of Beckh's *Buddha* for me has been one of life's amazing invitations to delve deeper into a dear subject while providing unexpected opportunities to learn and broaden the horizon. This translation has been worked from the heart. I have been fortunate to approach it on a background of a practiced Buddhist meditation coupled with a vibrant interest in anthroposophy, with a deep interest in Buddhist scriptures and traditions, and a direct experience of Indian culture and ways of life. As a 'colleague' of Beckh, having studied Indology to Ph.D. level and taught the discipline at several German universities, this has indeed been a labour of love.

Dr Katrin Binder, Michaelmas, 2016

Regarding the pronunciation of Indian words (Sanskrit and Pali)

Hermann Beckh, 1st Edition, 1916

Long single vowels bear the long stroke (ā, ī, ū) and should be spoken in a very long drawn-out way. e and o are effectively compound vowels and as such are always long (they only become shortened before a double consonant in Pali). All other vowels are short and are spoken as very short and muffled. ṛ is vowel-r, and comes close to being spoken today as ri (r with a short, muffled vocalized resonance). The word Ṛṣi (ṛṣi) is also pronounced as something like Rishi.

kh, gh, etc. are the so-called aspirated consonants, the h bound to the consonants is also heard as an independent breath. (Hence th is not pronounced as in English but as t-h, ph is not to be spoken as f but as p-h.)

c is the well-known palatal in Italian, also pronounced as something like tsh. ch is the similar sound strengthened by aspiration (also not to be spoken like German ch); j is the corresponding middle form (a soft dsh), also to be pronounced like j in English, not as in German. y in Indian words corresponds with the German j (as y in English). v is the semi-vowel w.

ḍ, ṭ, ṇ (so-called cerebrals or lingual) are distinguished from the dentals t, d, n through being pronounced higher on the gums (t, d, n are more forward on the teeth). ṅ is guttural n (as in [German] *Anker* [English spring], ñ is the corresponding palatal variation of n. In Pali ñ is pronounced as dorsal n, jñ in Sanskrit words as dny.

s is pronounced sharply, ś and ṣ are sh- sounds (ś pronounced as a palatal, ṣ as cerebral).

ṃ (the so-called Anusvāra) causes the nasalizing of a preceding vowel, in actual speech the pronunciation is usually as that for m.

h stands for a vocalized breath, distinguished from the non-vocalized ḥ (Visarga) in Sanskrit words.

The word-stress in Indian words results from a consideration of the length of the vowels (with regard to the syllables) which stems by itself from the initial remarks indicating vowel length and the great preponderance of the long syllables over the short in Indian. Where the penultimate syllable of a word is long owing to a long vowel or double consonant (the so-called prosodic or long by position) it bears the stress; in other cases the stress is drawn back to the third-to-last syllable; hence it may be that another position for the stress results, e.g. bhagavá.

Single examples of the pronunciation of important words: Mahāyā́na, Lálitavistara, Mahā́-parinibbā́na-sútta, Śuddhódana, Kapilavástu, Lúmbinī, Mahāprajápati, Ásita, Rúdraka, Nairáñjanā, Rājagṛha, *ámṛta,* Tathā́gata, Hiráṇyavatī (here the accent is on the fourth-to-last syllable).

Abbreviations

Hermann Beckh, 1916.

Aṅg.	Aṅguttaranikāya
Dīgha	Dīghanikāya
ed. Lefm.	Lefmann edition
L.V.	Lalitavistara
Majjh.	Majjhimanikāya
MPS	Mahāparinibbānasutta
PoṭṭS	Poṭṭhapādasutta
Saṃy.	Saṃyuttanikāya
SPhS	Sāmaññaphalasutta
YS	Yogasūtra

Unless otherwise stated, all texts have been quoted from the editions of the Pali Text Society (PTS).

Hermann Beckh's original footnotes are retained and set out at the bottom of the relevant page. End notes (2016) are presented at the end of the volume.

Introduction

From a noble lineage of the warfaring caste of the nobility (*kṣatriya*) came the greatest Indian saint of historical times and founder of that Eastern religion most widely spread to this day who is known to the world by the name of the Buddha. He was born in the North of India, not far from the snowy mountains [Himalayas]. Casting away the worldly good fortune that seemed to be due to him from his birth, he did when still young what many did in India at that time: he left his home in order to devote himself in solitude to the practices of spiritual concentration. Pious tradition recounts much about the time of his lonely strife, nothing of which may be proven by the means of historical research. But this much is certain, that after years of intense meditation and inner struggles he had spiritual experiences which he regarded as the decisive turning point of his life. He now called himself the Buddha, i.e., the 'enlightened one' or 'awakened one', the one who no longer sleeps, who has acquired a kind of knowledge and consciousness against which the everyday understanding and the consciousness of ordinary people is only a dream, a sleep of delusion, of 'not knowing'.

Even if the nature of that Buddha-experience cannot be accessible to external understanding and research, we have in front of us one certain fact, and that is the unique power to move the hearts of others that the Buddha had made his own through that experience. Rarely have such strong effects emanated from the personality of a single person, so in a certain way it is not entirely a myth when legend tells us how soothsayers prophesy from the signs on the Buddha-child's body that for one who carries on himself these marks of a world hero, a 'great personality' (*mahāpuruṣa*), there are only two paths: if he stays in his rank, he will be a king reigning over all the world, if he renounces the world, he will be a world-saving Buddha, a leader and enlightener of other souls. That characteristic which is implied in the term *mahāpuruṣa* and which a personality such as the Buddha shares with those who are called Great by world history is that power of the soul, that unique influence which they have had on their fellow men. But the Buddha did not exert this influence in the service of worldly achievement like Alexander and other great men of world history. He did it in deepest self-effacement, only concerned with leading others to the light of insight and through insight to salvation, to peace, to freedom from all that pulls the soul down into the lower regions of the soul, by indicating spiritual goals outside the sphere of material personal interests to them, always inspired by love and compassion—that compassion with all living beings which flowed from a heart otherwise detached from all earthly matters.

The effect of Buddha's teachings did not remain confined to his contemporaries and to India, but took hold of vast areas of Asia over the following centuries and thus decisively influenced the cultural development of an entire continent. The circle of students and followers that had gathered around the master, after the Buddha's death formed the nucleus of a comprehensive church, one of the large world religions, and the influence of the Buddha-thought has made itself felt even in the Occident in recent times.

If we now focus our attention on India while differentiating in this sense a three-fold effect of Buddhism on India, the remaining parts of Asia and the Occident, we find Buddhism at the height of its external expansion and power in the third century BC under the great emperor Aśoka, the Constantine of Buddhism, who united almost all of India (as well as areas in present-day Afghanistan, Beluchistan, Kashmir and Nepal) under his sceptre. Inspired by genuine Buddhist tolerance towards followers of all faiths and sects—a tolerance which received its characteristic expression in his rock inscriptions and column edicts—he was an ardent worshipper of the 'Saint of the Śākya-lineage.' Buddhism was not only elevated to a kind of state religion under him, but under Aśoka the entire internal and external aspects of Indian culture were pervaded and filled with Buddhist impulses. In this, it remains remarkable that no ruler of Indian blood has ever ruled over such a vast territory or elevated his empire to such external power as this 'monk on the throne'.

In the long run, Buddhism was unable to maintain this position of spiritual supremacy in India. Over the following centuries we find a resurgence of Brahmanism, and today Buddhism as an *external religion* has long lost any importance for India (even though recently movements exist which seek to recreate this prestige). And yet its Buddhist period did not pass without leaving a trace on India. This period stands between the older Vedic and the later Hindu culture and much in the intellectual and religious life of India has to be traced back to just that impulse (among others) which has gone into the development of

Indian culture through the Buddha. Even if Buddhism has achieved lasting importance outside of India, its entire connection with the Indian intellectual life must never be overlooked. Irrespective of all contrariness which it now occupies vis-à-vis the Indian religions in the context of church politics today, Buddhism in its original nature presents only one limb, one phase of the development of Indian thought, from which it originated and which has in turn been fertilized by it and received new impulses from it. And yet Buddhism is that form of Indian thought in which Indian thinking could be carried beyond the boundaries of India and which was able to fulfil a cultural mission outside India. Brahmanism as such could not and never wanted to become a world religion because it has, tailored entirely to the Indian way of life and the Indian caste system, declined any adjustment to non-Indian circumstances at all times. Whatever appears to us as intrinsically great in the teaching of the Buddha, namely that here the all-human thinking has broken forth for the first time in historical development, that here we are faced for the first time with a religion which is not simply folk religion—it is this circumstance that allows us to understand the fact that Buddhism as an external religion has not been able to maintain its importance, that it has over the course of time not only stepped back in the face of Brahmanism, but that another form of thought, the sect of the Jains which entered the scene at roughly the same time as that of the Buddhists, has met with a more lasting existence in its homeland than Buddhism.

Just as Palestine was a site of the spiritual search of man around the beginning of our era, we find that longing and searching which has always been native to India particularly strong and lively there during the time of the Buddha, and large sections of society were seized by it at that time. Individual personalities had an impact through their influence; they gathered pupils around themselves and won followers as spiritual teachers. In the Buddhist texts we find seven teachers as representatives of seven different movements. The most famous and influential and undoubtedly most significant among them was the Buddha. The names of the others (designated by the Buddhists as the 'six heretical teachers') are named by the texts as follows: Purāṇa Kassapa, Makkhali Gosāla, Ajita Kesakambalī, Pakudha Kaccāyana, Sañjaya Belaṭṭhiputta (i.e., the son of Belaṭṭhi), Nigaṇṭha Nātaputta. The latter, also called Vardhamāna Mahāvīra or Jina (victor) for short, is the founder of that Jain-sect which still has numerous and pious followers in India today. There are many similarities and points of convergence in details between Buddhism and Jainism, but Jainism is closer to the orthodox philosophical systems of the Hindus than Buddhism. Additionally, it complies more strongly with the Indian's inclination to asceticism, and outer formalities of all kinds play a more important role in Jainism—as in Brahmanism—than in Buddhism which is tremendously free-spirited in Indian terms. Precisely based on a consideration of the nature of these two directions of thought we may understand why Buddhism has not been able to maintain its external power in India and why the Jain-sect has been more fortunate in this respect.

Buddhism has fulfilled its actual mission outside its country of origin, among the peoples of Asia. In Ceylon [Sri Lanka], Burma and Siam [Thailand], in the countries of the Himalayas, in Tibet and Mongolia it has become the dominant religion, it has stretched its influence far into northern Asia, even in China and Japan it has numerous followers. Especially in China, Buddhism entered early on—probably in the first century AD—and even though it passed its zenith of outward power there long ago due to strong persecution, all true religious life in China is still under the sign of Buddhism, and according to the verdict of a renowned expert (J.J.M. de Groot)[1] religious piety, true religious life in China is only found in Buddhist circles. Buddhism has held a particular attraction for those peoples where certain mystic tendencies that are rooted in the dawn of humanity were alive in greater measure. This explains the peculiar organization and power Buddhism has received in Tibet especially. From a state of wild barbarism, those countries have been elevated to milder behaviour and higher spiritual life by the revelation of the Buddha of the compassion with all living beings. Just as Buddhism in the above-mentioned mystic element on the one hand carries something that points back to a distant past of the human race, in its characteristic as 'Gospel of compassion and love' it appears on the other hand like a precursor of Christianity.

Buddhism's influence on the Occident is shown for the first time in a very remarkable way in the novel of Barlaam and Josaphat (Joasaph) which was widely read in the Middle Ages and which contains nothing but a Christianized depiction of the Buddha legend. In 'Josaphat', the name of the Indian prince who then converts to Christianity, is hidden the Indian 'Bodhisattva.' If connections with Buddhist motifs are made in the most unmistakable way in all this, it should not be overlooked that the intention was not to show Buddhism to advantage in the

Occident, or to glorify it, but to show Christianity as the victorious power, able as it were, to absorb the Indian message of salvation, to transfigure it in a Christian sense and to shine through it with its higher light. In connection with this [classical] romance we can thus not yet speak of an actual Buddhist current in occidental culture. We only find such a current much later, in the nineteenth century. Schopenhauer who above all other occidental thinkers confessed a peculiar leaning towards Indian thought—a leaning that appears like congeniality—always places Brahmanism and Buddhism side by side, without conceding an actual preference to the latter. What he said about Buddhism is in many ways remarkable in spite of its onesidedness. This applies especially to the significance he attributes to a knowledge of Brahmanism and Buddhism for a deepening of the understanding of Christianity (*Parerga* II § 179). Another personality who has significantly influenced the cultural life in more recent times by his creations, Richard Wagner—who followed Schopenhauer's philosophical suggestions in many things—calls the teaching of the Buddha 'a world view in the face of which probably any other dogma must appear petty and narrow-minded' (to Mathilde Wesendonk),[2] and speaks about the profound impression the figure of the Buddha and the Buddhist mendicant, as ancient Indian life in general, awakened in him. His work 'The Victors'—which remained incomplete—addresses a Buddhist subject, the legend of Ānanda and Prakṛti (in Wagner's work: 'Sawitri'). In the actual completion of his life's work, in *Parsifal*, where Wagner outlines the picture of a spiritualized religion of the future of humanity as he imagined it, not Buddhism, but Christianity—although certainly not the Christianity of any confession, but the esoteric-Christian imagination of the grail legend—forms the spiritual background. It is however remarkable in this how Wagner slipped the Indian motif of rebirth (also important in Buddhism and known to him chiefly from that context) into this sphere of imagination.

Whatever has emerged in the Occident in recent and most recent years [sic] in terms of propaganda for Buddhism usually looks at—in as far as it is not connected with theosophical or related endeavours—Buddhism as a rational system, an 'atheist moral philosophy' (cf. on this strand Lehmann, *Buddhismus*, p. 263f.)[3] easily synchronized with dominant modern world views and which in this sense may be grafted onto the occidental intellectual development as a kind of substitute religion. It is probably in this conception that we find the deepest possible misapprehension of the nature of Buddhism, and the following description will sufficiently reveal that Buddhism is neither atheism in our sense, nor just philosophical rationalism, moreover that according to its nature it is something entirely different from a philosophy and that it does not have the least in common with modern materialism. Nor can true Buddhism as it presents itself to objective scientific enquiry be identified with modern theosophical endeavours from which it differs in nature in spite of certain common aspects. In this connection, the title of Sinnett's book, *Esoteric Buddhism* has created a confusion of terms. [Sinnett, Alfred Percy, *Esoteric Buddhism,* London: Trubner and Co. 1883.] Today, the term 'esoteric Buddhism' for the school of thought represented in that book has almost ceased to be in use even among its followers.

The opinion which wanted to see in Buddhism the religion of the future for the West does not require serious refutation today. Buddhism cannot be separated from the temporal and spatial circumstances of its emergence and spread. The cultural task it had to fulfil in Asia has already been pointed out. To entrust it with a similar mission for the Occident would be a complete misapprehension of its historical conditions. The cultural development of the West would have been impossible under Buddhist impulses. This development is rooted by its inner nature in the conviction that man has been assigned the fulfilment of earthly tasks by the very powers of existence that put him into this life on earth. And he has been raised to their fulfilment in an entirely different way by that religion which urges him to take on the cross, to carry and transfigure the burden of earthly existence as a different doctrine, which, as Buddhism does, only preaches the renunciation of suffering and everything earthly. The Christian 'Blessed are those who mourn' [the German '*Selig, die da Leid tragen*' is more evocative of the Buddhist '*Leiden*', or suffering] could not yet be thought, not yet be felt in Buddhism. The development of an individual personality, of an 'I', means something entirely different to a member of Western culture than to the Asian person: in the same way, Christianity is a religion of personality in an entirely different way from Buddhism which regards the I, the individual self, as something devoid of existence or at least as something ungraspable. Finally it has to be said that the form in which Buddhism has cast its 'truths' is one which cannot be understood by wider circles in the West. They are conditioned by thoughts and feelings separated from our occidental thinking by worlds. Just take that famous twelve-part formula of causal origination (*pratītyasamutpāda*) which contains the most difficult and disputed problems, even for scholars. It is impossible to translate many of the technical words and terms into European languages. Those sentences which created such a deep, overwhelming impression from the mouths of those who proclaimed them for the first time would not be able to give rise to the same resonance in our souls today. Even that which today may be felt by this or that person as correct, may be experienced as true in Buddhism, will be expressed much more emphatically and in a way that speaks to our hearts much more than any of the formulas and sentences of Buddhism by words such as those by Goethe (in the fragment 'Die Geheimnisse' [The Mysteries]): '*Von der Gewalt, die alle Wesen bindet, befreit der Mensch sich, der sich überwindet.*' ['Who conquers himself frees himself from the power that binds all beings.'] However close those words may be to the thought content of Buddhist 'truths' (as whose quintessence they might be regarded), it is different in nature in its inherent nuance of feeling—this must not be overlooked—from everything Buddhist.

If one can then speak about a Buddhist current, about an influence of Buddhism even in the Occident in an entirely justified sense, it cannot be a case of elevating any misunderstood Buddhism to a religion of the future, be it from a rational-materialistic, be it from a theosophical viewpoint—the creation or adoption of new confessional religions probably belongs to the past anyway. Our task in this age can only be to realize Buddhism in its nature and to gain from this insight a deepening of religious realization and the religious life in general. Like any work in the field of comparative religions, not least a truly scholarly study of Buddhism will lead us to a deepened perception of all religion, and in particular of Christianity.

The old formula, probably going back to the Buddha himself, by which acceptance into the community took place, is: 'I take refuge in the Buddha. I take refuge in the norm (*dharma*).* I take my refuge in the

---

* The word *dharma* (Pali *dhamma*), usually translated as 'law', 'teaching', 'religion', etc., has no corresponding term in European languages in the sense it is used in Buddhism. It means the nature of things in their universal cosmic lawfulness as realized by the Buddha, a lawfulness in which our terms of natural law on the one hand and moral law on the other coalesce in one word whose nuance is foreign to occidental thinking. The *dharma* is the true spiritual reality hidden behind the things (of which as something essential Buddhism does not speak at all) as it appears to the spiritual eye (*dharmacakṣus*) of the Buddha or saint, the highest spiritual truth as the Buddha saw it and which may be realized by the path of meditation.

community (*sangha*).' Buddha, *dharma* and *sangha* are as it were the cornerstones on which the entire edifice of the Buddha religion rests. With this 'holy trinity,' the 'three jewels' as they are also called in Buddhism, we have the most natural point of view from which a description of Buddhism may be structured. Here, too, we will follow this structure in so far as the discussion of 'the Buddha' will form the content of the first, the description of the 'norm' or teaching the content of the second part, while a closer consideration of the 'community' suggests an inclusion of church history which must be treated separately.

Part I

THE BUDDHA

General considerations

The meaning of the Buddha for Buddhism

It has been said (Oldenberg, *Buddha,* p. 379 of the 5th edition), that in everything essential the Buddhist doctrine could be everything which indeed it is and it could still be imagined without the concept of the Buddha. And it is certainly correct that the significance of the person of the Buddha for the Buddhist religion, especially for its older and more original phases, is not at all immediately equal to the significance of the person and life of Jesus for Christianity. A *doctrine* is at the centre of Buddhism—the doctrine of suffering and of the path of liberating realization. At the centre of the Christian religion is the figure of the saviour as the fulfiller of a *deed,* the act of salvation at Golgotha. Christ speaks to the disciples: 'lo, I am with you always, even unto the end of the world.' (Matth: 28, 20) and 'I will not leave you comfortless: I will come to you.' (John: 14, 18). In contrast to this, the Buddha speaks to his disciples before his passing into *nirvāṇa*: 'The norm I have taught you, that will be your master when I have passed away' (*Mahāparinibbānasutta*). To a theoretical consideration focussing only on the older phases of Buddhism it may thus indeed appear as if the *doctrine* is everything in Buddhism and that it may be imagined without the person of the Buddha. And yet it is on the other hand a self-evident fact that a Buddhist doctrine, Buddhism itself, would not exist at all if there had not been a Buddha. Even if every detail of that doctrine could be traced in other Indian systems nothing would be proven against this fact. For they owe entirely to the preaching of these doctrines by the Buddha, to the influence of his towering personality, the power which enabled them to provide that big impulse for the spiritual development of an entire part of the world and to become a world religion. Buddhism is special in comparison with other Indian schools of thought not through the creation of actual new terminology and sentences, but because the Buddha and his disciples carried 'truths' into the world as a gift to the general public breaking all barriers of caste and racial belonging. These 'truths' were until that point claimed as their own particular possession of knowledge by narrowly defined communities which kept themselves well apart from the rest of society—this applies especially to the Yoga school.

Still, what has been said regarding the receding of the figure of the Buddha in comparison with his doctrine applies in a certain sense particularly to those older strands on which Buddhism rests in the southern countries of Asia, in Ceylon [Sri Lanka] and in Indochina [Southeast Asia]. Over the course of time, strands have however developed which in principle allow for more importance of the personality of the Buddha. Those strands are called Mahāyāna ('large vehicle' or 'large track'), in contrast to the other strand, which is called Hīnayāna ('small vehicle', 'lower track'). Mahāyāna-Buddhism has assumed power in the wide area of the countries of central and eastern Asia. The majority of Buddhists thus—at least nominally—belongs to the Mahāyāna. The follower of the 'lower path' for himself only aspires to the level of saint or *arhat,* working only for his own 'salvation'. In the Mahāyāna the higher ideal of the succession of the Buddha prevails, the precept of taking on the suffering of the entire world, of working for the perfection and salvation of all beings, just as the Buddha did not content himself with finding the liberating realization but had through much internal strife wrested from himself the decision to reveal himself to the world and to sacrifice his entire life to the fulfilment of this task. In this the Buddha is thus not only the proclaimer of a doctrine which might exist without him, but he is an essential factor within this doctrine itself, he is the model whose emulation is to be the highest ideal to the disciple of this doctrine. It is not correct, as it still often happens, to see in this Mahāyāna doctrine a distortion of the 'ancient and original' Buddhism. On the contrary, it has developed from seedlings already quite present in the original Buddhism and which have merely receded in those strands designated as Hīnayāna. The main thought of the Mahāyāna, that of the working towards the salvation of the world and all beings, thus contains that formula with which we already meet frequently in the old Pali texts and which is not only used for the ministry of the Buddha but also for that of the disciples: 'for the benefit of many people, for the happiness of many people, from compassion with the world, for the wellbeing, the benefit, the happiness of gods and men' (*bahujanahitāya bahujanasukhāya lokānukampāya atthāya hitāya sukhāya devamanussānaṃ*). In the Pali canon (e.g. Mahāparinibbānasutta 37, ed. Childers) it is already explicitly stated that the saintly life of the disciples not only serves their own salvation, their own perfection, but—in the sense of the above formula—the world, the salvation of many beings.

From that which has been said regarding the nature of the Mahāyāna doctrine it is easy to grasp that the most important texts dealing with the life of the Buddha, in particular the story of the Buddha's becoming, have flowed from this Mahāyāna strand or are at least close to it. These texts tell the life of the master in the images of myth and mysticism, they are thus far from what we would regard as historical accounts. This means that in the following the historical discussion is to be distinguished sharply from that which legend has to say about the personality and the story of the Buddha's life in such mythical-mystical pictures. For an occidental methodology, setting the historical approach in the foreground seems to suggest itself. But quite apart from the fact that not too many historical details of that life can be ascertained with scientific certainty, what matters much more is to acquire a full picture of Buddhism as a religion, and in this full picture that mythical-mystical account of the life of the Buddha constitutes an essential part. Furthermore, as a scholar who has rendered services to Buddhist problems (Windisch in '*Buddhas Geburt*' [Buddha's birth] p. 4)[4] has rightly pointed out, in particular with regard to the Buddha legend the mythical is often the cover for profound thoughts. That which constitutes Buddhism in its innermost nature has probably found its most profound expression in that legend. Buddhist art, whose depictions are important for the study of the Buddhist religion, in many ways has sourced from it its principal stimulus.* We can say that Buddhism speaks to us about its nature in two ways: once in the texts containing the teachings and terminologies in the abstract pallor of the thought, and then lively and concrete in the colourful pictures of legends. It has already been emphasized that merely due to their language and strange technical expressions the abstract teachings of Buddhism can easily appear cold and austere to us today and do not exercise the same effect they had directly from the Buddha once upon a time. But in an entirely different way the Buddha legend, the *life* of the Buddha, as it is told in the sacred texts may still affect us today. This story, which ranks among the most beautiful and profound creations of

* It is important to keep in sight this stimulus which this 'legend' has provided to the visual arts. Kern (*Buddhismus*, vol. 1, p. 304) speaks finely and fittingly about the 'not minor artistic sense which always shimmers through in the entire legend'. [1st edition Henrik Kern, *Geschiedenis von het Buddhisme in Indië*, Haarlem, 2 vols., 1881–1883].

world literature, not only contains an abundance of humanly and poetically moving traits but it also puts before us—clothed in outer events—the quintessence of the Buddha's *teaching,* that which Buddhism is in its innermost nature, in a much more magnificent way, a way which speaks to our mind and feeling much more immediately than it is the case with the bare doctrinal texts. This is why the main content of the legend will be related in the following according to the sources; this will be followed by an independent discussion of the historical problem.

A. The Buddha of the legend

a) The sources of the legend

According to the sacred texts the biography of the Buddha—which according to Buddhist doctrine at the same time is in principle the typical biography of any Buddha—falls into twelve main events. The *Lalitavistara* has (in the fifth chapter, p. 44, ed. Lefm.) the following enumeration:

1. descent from the gods; 2. entering into the mother's womb; 3. birth; 4. youth (other texts emphasize here the competition for the bride as the main event); 5. marriage and life in the women's quarters; 6. the great separation/leave-taking; 7. asceticism; 8. entering into the circle of enlightenment (*bodhi*); 9. fight with Māra, the tempter; 10. awakening to the enlightenment of the Buddha; 11. setting in motion the wheel of the norm (i.e. the first preaching of the doctrine); 12. *parinirvāṇa*. (Other sources omit the 'entering into the circle of *bodhi*' in their enumeration and mention instead the burial of the mortal remains as the twelfth main event after the *parinirvāṇa*. The decades of public ministry as a spiritual teacher then lie between the eleventh and twelfth of these events. Numerous tales and legends (which may in some details contain a few historical truths) exist in various texts about this time as well. However, we understand as the actual Buddha legend, the 'legend' κατ' ἐξοχήν, the main narrative comprising those twelve events. Certain ancient texts which, it appears, contained the narrative of the entire life of the Buddha, have come down to us only in the fragments of occasional quotes. The *Lalitavistara* itself which, as pointed out, in one place calls the twelve events as that which together constitutes the biography of the Buddha, continues the narrative only up to the eleventh of these events, the preaching of the norm. Other texts (especially from the Pali canon) exclusively devoted to the relation of the twelfth main event, the *parinirvāṇa*, then provide a supplement. These texts do not have the purely mythical-legendary character the story of the early life of the Buddha has, but appear to contain much that is historical. We can thus call the narrative of the first eleven events, as it is provided to us by the *Lalitavistara* and elsewhere, the story of the Bodhisattva becoming the Buddha, the 'legend *sensu stricto*'.

If Mahāyāna texts (or at least northern texts close to the Mahāyāna) are our main source for this legend *sensu stricto*, while for the *nirvāṇa* it is older Pali texts, the obvious reason of this appearance lies in that which has already been said about the difference between the two main strands of Buddhism. Because for the strand of the 'great path', the path which leads to Buddhahood, the narrative about how the most recently appeared Buddha himself trod this path, rose from Bodhisattva to Buddha, had to be of particular importance and forms as it were the main gospel. However, for the follower of the Hīnayāna (the lower path) who aspires only to *arhat*-hood, the personal rejection of everything earthly, the individual *nirvāṇa*, the interest naturally turns more towards the doctrine than to the biography of the master and, as far as a biography is possible, the eleventh and twelfth of the events (first preaching of the doctrine and *nirvāṇa*) are in the foreground. Just as for the Mahāyāna the legend in the strictest sense, the story of the Bodhisattva's becoming the Buddha, the most important thing for the Hīnayāna—next to the doctrinal texts—is the gospel of his dying. It is thus quite appropriate and suited to the provision of a correct and full picture of Buddhism if in the following the 'legend' is told according to Mahāyāna, the 'gospel of his dying' according to Pali sources. It is for these reasons that in the first part Mahāyāna Buddhism, in the second part, which is devoted to the description of the doctrine, Pali Buddhism will have to be in the foreground. To begin with, a short summary of the main sources of the legend is given here.

In this respect it is useful for external reasons to distinguish three parts of the legend: 1. the story up to enlightenment, the narrative of how the Bodhisattva became the Buddha (i.e., from the first to the tenth event), 2. the time after the enlightenment until the first preaching of the doctrine. 3. the narrative of the 'great', the gospel of his dying (twelfth event). For the first of these three parts the main source is the Mahāyāna text *Lalitavistara*, according to which the essential contents of the legend are to be recounted in the following (Sanskrit text edited by Lefmann [Halle 1902, 1908], Tibetan text by Foucaux [Paris 1847]). If this text, as it is now before us, belongs only to one of the Christian centuries, the material treated in it, the legend itself, is yet much older, and of the metrical passages woven into the prose narrative some belong to the oldest of Buddhist tradition preserved for us. For example, the story of the temptation of the fasting and self-mortifying Bodhisattva by Māra in the eighteenth chapter of the *Lalitavistara* exists also as a fragment in the *Suttanipāta*, one of the oldest poetic texts of the Pali canon. The correspondence is almost literal (here Sanskrit, there the related Pali), and philological comparison reveals that the original text of the ancient legend is transmitted more faithfully in the *Lalitavistara* than in the *Suttanipāta.* Even where we have, such as in the narrative of the events following the enlightenment, parallels in old texts from the Pali canon (Mahāvagga of the *Vinayapiṭaka*), *Lalitavistara* corresponds to the older Pali texts in every essential detail. One must thus not infer from the later composition date of the *Lalitavistara* that the legend related in it was only invented in that later time. The legend as such is old, perhaps very old, and it is particularly, or so it seems, in the *Lalitavistara* that it is on the whole more faithfully transmitted than elsewhere. The style alone (especially that of the prose narrative) bears the imprint of a later age. The language of the *Lalitavistara* is Sanskrit, namely pure Sanskrit in the prose passages and Sanskrit mixed with dialect in the metrical paragraphs (so-called Gāthā-dialect). Another Sanskrit text, the 'Sutra of the great parting' (Abhiniṣkramaṇasūtra, translated in fragments from the Chinese by Samuel Beal, *The Romantic Legend of Sākya Buddha,* London 1875) which is available to us in Tibetan and Chinese translations only, is not counted with the Mahāyāna, but is close to the *Lalitavistara* in content. It treats not only the episode of which it bears the name (the sixth of the main events), but the legend in general. A larger number of so-called Jātakas or stories of previous births have been woven into the main narrative (i.e., stories which are put into the Buddha's mouth and which deal with his fate in a previous life or that of persons close to him). In an even larger measure this is the case in the *Mahāvastu* (Senart, Paris 1882–1897, 3 volumes), entirely composed in mixed Sanskrit (Gāthā-dialect), which also does not belong to the Mahāyāna proper. Here, the story of the life of the Buddha is only a so-called frame story, the Jātaka-tales take up the larger space, they appear as the main thing. The *Mahāvastu* is considered to be older than the *Lalitavistara,* but the legend is hardly transmitted more faithfully in it. The text contains much valuable detail, even poetically beautiful (here we will only point out the charming story of Buddha's encounter with his little son, Rāhula), but overall, the composition is a confused one and the individual parts are of unequal value. The *Buddhacarita* of Aśvaghoṣa, the contemporary of King Kaniṣka (according to recent scholarship in the first century AD) and follower or at least preparer of the Mahāyāna, contains an epic adaptation.

In the Pali canon the story of the life of the Buddha of a previous world period, of Vipaśvin (the 'clairvoyant') is narrated in the Mahāpadānasutta ('*sūtra* of the great legend') of the *Dīghanikāya*. Since the biography of a Buddha is a typical one, this *sūtra* may be counted among the sources of the 'legend' with a certain justification. Apart from this piece we do not find the story of the future Buddha future in the Pali canon in its entirety, but only as individual fragments randomly preserved, like the story of the temptation in the *Suttanipāta* or the story of Asita, the Buddhist Simeon, in the same text. Nothing would be more mistaken than to draw from this fact the conclusion that during the time of the origination of these works from the Pali canon the legend did not exist in its entirety but only those fragments. On the contrary those fragments are narrated in such a way that they quite take the larger context of which they form a part as their prerequisite, just as certain myths are transmitted in such a way in the *Rigveda* that the entire way they are related points everywhere to something else which is not also told, but which the composers assume to be known. We also meet with references to individual traits of the legend in the different parts of the Pali canon so frequently, they all prove that the legend in its entirety already existed in its essential traits in ancient times.

The actual Pali version of the Buddha legend (*sensu stricto*), the so-called *Nidānakathā*, does not belong to the canon, but to the later literature, it forms the introduction to the collection of Jātaka tales and probably has the commentator Buddhagoṣa (fifth century AD) as its author. This version of the legend has so far been the most well-known and best loved in the Occident and it is true that it contains many a poetical beauty, but it is by no means closer to the ancient, original legend than *Lalitavistara*, rather it clearly bears the imprint of a later compilation, a creation by a second hand, and the composition is not very consistent. If the *Nidānakathā* in the scene of the great parting arrestingly pictures how the Buddha enters the night chamber once again before his escape from the palace at night, where his wife rests on a bed scattered with flowers, holding her hand over the head of the newborn child, how he then suppresses the wish to take his child into his arms in order not to awaken his wife from her sleep and thus be prevented from carrying out his decision, and how he leaves the palace silently, it is doubtlessly poetic, but it is in these cases that it is particularly clear that we are confronted with the work of a later poet, not with the original legend. As a whole the

Lalitavistara as one of the most significant creations of the entire Indian literature outshines the *Nidānakathā* by far and thus has to be taken into account first and foremost if we are to gain the right picture of the true legend.

For the second part of the legend, the events after the enlightenment until the first preaching of the doctrine, the narrative of the Mahāvagga, which forms the beginning of the *Vinayapiṭaka,* the first and oldest of the three parts of the (*Tripiṭaka,* i.e., called 'three baskets') Pali canon, joins the texts which also address this part mentioned thus far. The narrative of the Mahāvagga corresponds in all essential points to that of the *Lalitavistara,* a circumstance of more than slight significance for the overall evaluation of the *Lalitavistara.*

For the last part of the legend, the gospel of dying, the story of the great *nirvāṇa,* our main source is a work from the Pali canon, the Mahāparinibbānasutta of the *Dīghanikāya.* Works from the Northern canon with the same or a similar title (here in Sanskrit: Mahāparinirvāṇasūtra) cannot measure up in age and value with the Pali text mentioned. The *Lalitavistara,* the story of the becoming Buddha, is complemented chiefly by the Mahāparinibbānasutta, the story of the vanishing or 'blowing away' of the Buddha. We can regard both texts as the Buddhist gospels κατ' ἐξοχήν, *Lalitavistara* as the gospel story of Mahāyāna Buddhism, the Mahāparinibbānasutta as that of the older strand of Buddhism. In style, the two works are however quite different. The mysticism of the *Lalitavistara,* rich in images and colours, is opposed by the plain simplicity of the ancient Pali texts in the Mahāparinibbānasutta. The *Lalitavistara* relates spiritual processes acquired in visions of sensual images, in this sense being quite legend, the Mahāparinibbānasutta relates external reality in a much higher measure and in its detail certainly contains much that is historical. It has been emphasized that no Buddhist text is so close in style and in its entire mood to the Christian Gospels as the Mahāparinibbānasutta. This of course is only to be taken entirely relatively. The Mahāparinibbānasutta is undoubtedly one of the most important and moving Pali texts and one of the most beautiful products of Indian literature. 'One will', Oldenberg judges (*Buddha,* p. 227), 'sense in this Sutra a warm breath otherwise foreign to the impersonal coldness of the Buddhist ecclesiastical language as it may well have poured forth from the memory of the solemn last days of community between master and disciples'. In no other work does the spirit of ancient Buddhism approach us so immediately and lively as here. It thus also serves the intention of getting to know Buddhism from its different sides, if in the following the story of the becoming Buddha to be related according to the *Lalitavistara* is followed by the narrative of the gospel of dying according to the Mahāparinibbānasutta. In all this it has of course to be taken into account that in such a shorthand rendition as we are able to give here only a poor impression of the spirit of the original texts can be aroused. Just as little as we can provide an idea of the flourishing abundance of colour of the narrative style of the *Lalitavistara* can we provide an idea of the power of the sounding rhythms of the language which gives the ancient Pali texts and not least the Mahāparinibbānasutta their unique imprint.

b) The story of the Buddha's Becoming (according to the *Lalitavistara*)

1. *Descent from the gods.* Prior to his earthly incarnation the Bodhisattva (the future Buddha) exists as a spiritual being among the gods of the Tuṣita heaven, into which he has been elevated as the result of his *karma,* the fruit of the actions and sacrifices of previous lives. Out of the sounds of heavenly music the admonition is sounded to him that it was time to descend to the earth and to become the Buddha in order to conquer age, sickness and death and to let the water of immortal salvation (*amṛta*) flow to the thirsting beings (Chap. 2).

It is decided in the council of the gods to prepare the imminent descent of the Bodhisattva to the earth in a worthy manner. Divine beings appear on the earth, dressed up as Brahmins, in order to instruct the Brahmins there about the signs through which the 'great being' (*mahāpuruṣa*) will be recognized, whose destiny it is to become a universal ruler (*cakravartin*) with the seven attributes of world sovereignty or, if he renounces the world, a Buddha who liberates the world.

From his heavenly abode, the Bodhisattva casts his fourfold view over the earth to realize the time, continent, country and race of his imminent earthly incarnation. A consideration of the moment is necessary since Bodhisattvas may only appear on the earth at certain times. They do not appear in the beginning of the evolvement of a world (*ādipravṛtte loke*) but only when, during the progress of the development of the world (*yadā vyakto lokaḥ*) humanity has come to know birth, age, sickness and death.* The search for the continent and country centres on India (*Jambudvīpa*), because the law of the world stipulates that there, more precisely in the central country, the incarnation of the Bodhisattva has to occur. The race in which the Bodhisattva incarnates himself can only belong to the Brahmin caste or the caste of the military nobility (*kṣatriya*). Since the *kṣatriya* caste is in power at the moment in question, the incarnation of the Bodhisattva has to occur in this caste. In the selection of the race there is an in-depth consultation among the gods. The princely families of Magadha, Kośala, Vatsa, Vaiśālī, Ujjayinī, Mathurā, Hastināpura and Mithilā are each suggested in turn, however against all of them certain objections are raised. Upon a question by the gods the Bodhisattva himself enumerates all the requirements the lineage into which he is to be born has to satisfy. It must, it is said among other things, be a powerful lineage, a lineage of great forefathers, a fearless race, a race which honours the teachers of the past (*ṛṣi*) and fears the gods. The mother of the future Buddha has to be adorned by virtues of the highest kind: she has to be of perfect physical beauty, with a smiling countenance, intelligent, without falsehood, not prone to anger, 'free from the faults

*According to Buddhist doctrine, this is not at all the case from the beginning. The Aggaññasutta of the *Dīghanikāya* (ed. of the Pali Text Society vol. II, p. 80ff.), which contains a kind of Buddhist myth of paradise, teaches how in the distant past mankind still lived as beings of streaming light in purity, innocence and bliss in the air around the earth, when sun and moon were not yet visible in the sky, when no separation into male and female gender had yet occurred and a need for substantial nourishment did not yet exist, but these beings, radiating their own light, lived off pure bliss. A kind of sweet cream formed on the initially watery earth. Individual beings taste this cream, due to which sensual desires (*taṇhā*) awakens in them. Following their example, others succumb to the temptation. With the increasing consolidation of the earth, cruder and cruder food substances appear. By being led to these food substances through their sensuality, the beings never experience a hardening of their corporeality themselves, they are transported into more and more dense elements. In this way they leave the air around the earth and descend to the solid ground of the earth, their inherent light disappears, instead the sun, moon and the other lights of the sky become visible. Through this, day and night, months and seasons develop. With the entanglement into the cruder element, the separation into male and female gender also occurs. Lowly desires lead to actions of which the beings are ashamed. In this way, the entire suffering of the world gradually develops from sensual desire. In the Aggaññasutta the emergence of social inequality, the caste distinction and the creation of by-laws are connected with an increasing entanglement with the earthly element.

of her sex'. It is also demanded that she should not have given birth to a child yet. Their circumspection leads the gods at last to the race of the Śākya at Kapilavastu where King Śuddhodana is a noble and powerful prince and his youthful wife, Māyā, daughter of the Śākya prince Suprabuddha, of divine grace, the epitome of fair virtues, has not yet given birth to a child. She is distinguished especially by a smiling countenance, a beautiful forehead, lovely voice, irreproachable built, friendliness and sweet temper. The gods recognize in her the mother* suitable for the earthly incarnation of the Bodhisattva (Chap. 3).

Before he leaves his heavenly abode, the Bodhisattva speaks once more to the gathering of the gods. His instruction refers to the most essential basic terms of the norm which he is called to proclaim as the Buddha on earth later on (Chap. 4).

He then takes leave from the heavenly spirits, appoints the Bodhisattva Maitreya, the Buddha of the future world era, as his successor as teacher of the gods by putting his own tiara on his head, and decides to enter his mother's body as a white elephant with six tusks.

In the face of his imminent earthly incarnation the Bodhisattva then effects various different wonderful signs in the palace of king Śuddhodana: everything in the house and the court becomes shining and clean by itself, all harmful creatures avoid the place, wild birds arrive from the Himalayas and sing out from the gables; trees flower at the wrong time, all lakes cover themselves with lotus flowers; in the pantries the supplies remain inexhaustible; musical instruments begin to sound of their own; containers shimmer in heightened lustre and a wonderful radiance which outshines the sun and the moon fills the entire house.

Queen Māyā, too, feels the influence of the Bodhisattva who is preparing himself to descend to the earth from heavenly heights. She appears in front of the king with a smiling face and introduces her resolution to take up a vow of chastity. She thus asks him not to direct any desire towards her during this time. She asks for a bed of flowers to be made up for her on the highest roof terrace; she wants to spend the hours there in seclusion, withdrawn from all unpleasant sensory impressions, devoted only to lovely pictures, listening to soft sounds,

* In the esteem shown towards women a characteristic difference between Buddhism and Christianity is revealed. The glorification of the mother of the Buddha as we find it especially in the Mahāyāna texts is thus all the more remarkable. However there can be no question of a direct influx of Christian motifs.

breathing sweet scents. Words of dispute or anger shall not be raised near her. The king concedes to all her requests.

The gods decide to accompany the Bodhisattva on his earthly track and to be by his side during every important moment. They scatter flowers in Śuddhodana's palace and heavenly virgins (*apsaras*), who have descended to earth full of curiosity in order to see the mother of the future Buddha, float around Queen Māyā as she rests on her flower bed. They intone songs in her praise and scatter heavenly flowers onto her bed.

In this way, the time for the Bodhisattva to enter his earthly mother's womb draws near. Under the homages of countless Bodhisattvas and heavenly *apsaras* who have hastened here from all the corners of heaven he leaves the abode of the gods. Just at the moment when he starts to move in order to descend to earth, there is such a strong radiance emanating from his body that the entire, wide compass of the worlds is illuminated by it and the light of the sun and the moon pales against it. 'Even in those spaces between the worlds which are filled with the densest darkness, where those two great and powerful stars, the sun and the moon, cannot reach with their light, with their radiance, the great and exalted radiance was visible at this moment.' And the earth shakes and trembles and rocks to all sides, into all heights and depths, and thunder is heard rolling. At the same time, no being anywhere feels any anxiety or unease. The ray of light reaches as far as the underworlds, and the damned in the hells and the inhabitants of Yama's realm of the dead are free from their ordeals for a moment. Among the inhabitants of the earth, all low emotions—passion, hatred, conceit, jealousy, anger, pride, cruelty—are silenced, all beings are filled by friendliness and love towards one another like father and mother towards their children. Heavenly music fills the air and the singing of heavenly *apsaras* surrounds the Bodhisattva with sound as he descends from the heavenly heights to the earth (Chap. 5).

2. *Entering the mother's womb.* In the merry month of Vaiśākha,* when the earth is adorned with carpets of flowers, on the day when the full moon stands in conjunction with the *Puṣya* (Cancer) constellation, the Bodhisattva enters his mother's womb from the right side as a young white elephant with six tusks in calm consciousness (*smṛtaḥ saṃprajā-*

* April-May (the Indians counted in lunar years, thus their start of the month did not correspond to ours). The time of the event given in the *Nidānakathā* is the day of the full moon in the month of Āṣaḍhā (June–July).

nan). Queen Māyā, who had peacefully fallen asleep on her bed of flowers, sees the entire proceedings in a dream.* During her dream experience she is permeated with a hitherto unknown bliss; she feels as if she were transposed into the highest states of consciousness of yoga meditation (*dhyānasamāhitā*). Upon awakening she betakes herself to the Aśoka† grove in the garden of her palace and orders the king to be called to her. As if bound by earth's gravity, the king is unable to enter the Aśoka grove at first. Divine voices from the air then elucidate to him what has happened, and Māyā relates her dream to him. The Brahmins called to interpret the dream pronounce that joy has happened to him. A son with auspicious signs who is pre-ordained for world leadership is going to be born to him. However, if he renounces the kingdom, he will become a Buddha, a mercy to all the world, who will give joy to all beings through immortal salvation. The Brahmins are sent away after receiving lavish gifts from the king.

The gods offer Queen Māyā their abodes for her to reside in until the birth of the Bodhisattva.‡ By way of his magically effective concentration, the Bodhisattva causes Māyā to be seen in all those divine abodes at the same time. He himself rests in the womb in the position of yoga meditation (*paryaṅka*). So that no earthly impurity may tarnish him, a shell of radiating beryl lustre surrounds him (*ratnavyūhabodhisattvaparibhoga*) which is transposed into Brahmā's heaven by the gods after his birth and kept as a sacred relic there. In that night when the Bodhisattva enters his mother's womb, a lotus grows from the earth reaching up to Brahmā's heaven. Only Brahmā himself is able to see this lotus. Whatever is available as powerful essence in the wide compass of the worlds is present as a drop of honey in this lotus.

* The *Nidānakathā* relates poetically how Māyā in her dream is taken to the Himalayas by the gods and wafts away into higher and higher realms, and then, after she has been bathed and adorned with heavenly flowers and garments by the goddesses, meets the elephant. The *Nidānakathā* describes the entire scene merely as a dream, the *Lalitavistara* at the same time treats it as an objective event. Elsewhere, too, in Mahāyāna texts events thought of as supernatural are told as if they were physically real.

† A tree (Jonesia Asoka Roxburgii) with orange-coloured, night-scented flowers which, according to the verdict of an expert (Roxburgh, *Flora Indica*. Calcutta 1874, p. 313), has no equal in the entire plant kingdom.

‡ Whose supernatural form of being in the *Lalitavistara* is thought of as the spiritual self as it were, which through consciousness follows and guides all experiences of the child after and before its earthly birth.

Brahmā himself offers this drop of honey to the child in the womb in a bowl of beryl, and the Bodhisattva accepts the refreshment in order to show himself gracious to the deity. Nobody would be able to tolerate this drop of power, except the Bodhisattva in his last earthly existence since over innumerable former existences he has never tired of bestowing refreshment and soothing balm to suffering beings. Indra, the four guardians of the world and scores of other deities hover constantly around the child resting in the womb, and Bodhisattvas from the spheres of all the worlds come to pay homage to it. They bow reverentially before the child before they return to their heavenly abodes in obedience to a cue by the Bodhisattva.

Immersed in meditation, Māyā herself has a vision of the Bodhisattva resting in her womb. The child never causes any pain to the mother. She never feels any heaviness of the body in her condition, but instead a heightened lightness and wellbeing; she is free from all low impulses of the soul, of desire and passion. She is not aware of any unpleasant sensory impressions, she does not have any bad dreams. Wonderful healing powers emanate from her during this period: all men and women, boys and girls in the area who are possessed by all sorts of demons, are freed from their trouble at the sight of Queen Māyā and the demons depart from them; sick people of all kinds are healed when Queen Māyā puts her right hand on their head or offers them a blade of grass torn from the earth. And if the Queen looks down on her right side while doing so, she beholds the Bodhisattva in her body in the same way as one beholds one's own countenance in a clear mirror, and the sight fills her with great joy. Day and night, heavenly music sounds for the Bodhisattva resting in his mother's womb, and heavenly showers of flowers rain down on him. All this happens by the supernatural power (*ṛddhiprātihārya*) of the Bodhisattva (Chap. 6).

3. *Birth.* After the Bodhisattva has spent ten months* in the womb of Queen Māyā wonderful portents occur once again at the court and in the country of king Śuddhodana: a deep silence descends on nature, flowers remain unopened, the winds are silent, rivers hold back their course, the fire does not burn, all business in the country comes to a halt; women have easy births; from the Himalayas young lions come running into the town, but they do not harm anyone and lie down peacefully in front of the doors of the houses. The moon stands in the

* This is the amount of time, as different texts mention explicitly, that lies between conception and birth of a Bodhisattva.

constellation of Cancer (*Puṣya*) again. Queen Māyā then knows that her time has arrived. She feels a desire to spend time in the open countryside and speaks to the king about her wish. A few miles away from the town of Kapilavastu is the pleasure grove Lumbinī which she wants to seek with her friends. Māyā moves to the Lumbinī grove with great pomp and the gods and other supernatural beings mix invisibly with the visible following. It is just the time of the first spring* and the Lumbinī grove is resplendent and scented with the lushest spring panoply, all trees are in bloom even if it is not the time of their flowering, and gods have adorned the grove with heavenly flowers. Queen Māyā enters the garden and walks from tree to tree. When she steps towards a Plakṣa fig tree, the tree bends towards the ground through the supernatural power of the Bodhisattva. Māyā stretches out her right arm and takes hold of a branch; she is standing there in this way in a graceful pose (*salīlam*) looking up towards the sky with her mouth slightly open. In this moment countless heavenly damsels (*apsaras*) approach in order to attend to the queen with their services, and the Bodhisattva emerges from the right side of the mother's womb, in mindful consciousness, unsullied by earthly impurity.

Gods pay the Bodhisattva the first assistances: Indra and Brahmā personally take the child into their arms with reverence and clothe it in robes of heavenly silk. The snake kings, Nanda and Upananda, give rise to two streams of water, one cold and one warm, and offer the first bath to the Bodhisattva. Scores of heavenly beings drip perfumes and let flowers rain down.

Just born, the Bodhisattva steps onto the earth and directly the earth opens and a large lotus grows from it. Standing in this lotus the Bodhisattva looks into all cardinal directions with the lion's gaze (*siṃhāvalokitam*) of a great being (*mahāpuruṣa*). Overlooking all world spheres with his divine clairvoyant eye and penetrating the thoughts of all beings he realizes that there is not his equal anywhere. He then executes seven steps into all cardinal directions and says: 'I am the first in the world, I am the greatest in the world, this is my last birth, I will end the suffering of birth, old age and death.' And everywhere the Bodhisattva puts his foot a lotus grows from the earth. The earth

---

*The calculation of the *Lalitavistara* leads to the month of Phālguna (February-March). According to the *Nidānakathā* Vaiśākha (April–May) would be the birth month of the Buddha, the time into which the *Lalitavistara* puts the entry into the mother's womb.

trembles, heavenly and earthly string instruments sound of their own accord, flowers bloom at the wrong time, there is the rolling of thunder in spite of a clear sky and a light rain drizzles down, gentle winds blow, laden with heavenly scents of sandalwood, darkness retreats from all areas of the world and an immeasurable radiance penetrates the entire world, joy and delight fill all beings, all low emotions are silent, all dishonest behaviour ceases, the sick get well, the drunken sober, madmen are brought to reason, the blind become sighted, the deaf hearing, hunchbacks straight. Even the damned in the lowest hell are relieved from their tortures for a moment, animals lose the desire to eat each other and the souls in Yama's realm of the dead feel freed from the tortures of hunger and thirst.

After the Bodhisattva has been born divine virgins venerate Queen Māyā with heavenly flowers, scents and garlands, adorn her with heavenly robes and jewels and anoint her with scented water and balms. The Bodhisattva's future wife is born at the same time, as well as Chandaka, the charioteer, and the horse Kaṇṭhaka which carries the Bodhisattva in the night of the great parting.

King Śuddhodana names the prince Sarvārthasiddha, which means: 'the one through whom all my aspirations have come to fruition'.

The body of Queen Māyā is entirely unharmed after the birth of the Bodhisattva and shows no marks of the birth whatsoever. Day after day divine virgins are still busy with services of all kinds to mother and child. They bring food to the child and heavenly hosts strike up a song in praise of the Bodhisattva on high. However, seven days after the birth of the Bodhisattva Queen Māyā dies and is elevated into the heaven of the 33 gods.*

The splendid processions with which Māyā proceeded to the Lumbinī grove seven days ago now accompanies the prince back to Kapilavastu. Thousands of virgins walk in front of the procession and

---

* At this point in the *Lalitavistara* the Buddha himself interrupts his biography, the narrative which is put into his own mouth here, with the following words: 'It may be, oh disciples, that the thought enters you: through the fault of the Bodhisattva Queen Māyā has died. But you should not look at it like that. For she had fulfilled the full measure of her life. With each Buddha of the past, too, the mother died seven days after the birth. This has to be this way, because if she were to witness the parting (i.e., the renouncing of the world) of the son when he has come of age, the mother's heart would break.' According to the *Nidānakathā*, the reason for the early death is that the mother is too exalted after the birth of a Bodhisattva and may henceforth no longer be touched by earthly love.

heavenly *apsaras* draw the chariot of the Bodhisattva, which has been decorated by the gods, and mix with the earthly following. By the supernatural power of the Bodhisattva it is effected that the earthly humans are not blinded by the heavenly damsels and that the *apsaras* are not harassed by human smells.

After entering his father's house, Mahāprajāpatī Gautamī, the sister of Queen Māyā, takes over the care of the motherless prince. The king however, who thinks of the prophecies made by the Brahmins, is already filled with concern for the future of the child.

At this time, an aged holy eremite (*ṛṣi*) by name of Asita who is endowed with clairvoyance (*abhijñā*) and supernatural power (*ṛddhi*) lives in the Himalayas, the 'king of mountains'. With the clairvoyant vision of his 'divine eye' he beholds the different miraculous phenomena which occur at the birth of the Bodhisattva and hears the jubilations which this joyful event awakens in the heavenly worlds where the gods call out 'Buddha' and flourish their robes. By casting his clairvoyant vision towards India in order to learn the reason of this heavenly joy, he sees how a prince with the 32 signs of the great being (*mahāpuruṣa*) has been born in the palace of King Śuddhodana. Accompanied by his youthful sister's son Naradatta he uses his magical powers (*ṛddhi*) to take the path through the air to Kapilavastu. Having reached it, he renders himself on foot, like an ordinary mortal, to the palace of King Śuddhodana. 'An old *ṛṣi* stands at the door,' the doorkeeper announces. The king commands to let him enter and asks him filled with reverence about the purpose of his visit. When the *ṛṣi* makes his wish known to see the newborn child, the king asks him to have a little patience, for the child was just sleeping. But the seer responds: 'It is not the habit of such great persons to sleep for long, their natural condition is waking,' and directly the Bodhisattva effects his own awakening in order to pay his respects to the *ṛṣi*. The king offers the child to the seer. As the latter beholds the '32 signs' of a *mahāpuruṣa*, he falls at the feet of the Bodhisattva, calling out: 'Verily, a wondrous being has arisen for the world' and he venerates him in reverent awe. He then suddenly breaks into tears. The king, fearing a calamity for the child's future, asks the seer worriedly why he is shedding tears. Asita responds that he was not crying over the prince, but over himself because he was now an old man and aged. The prince Sarvārthasiddha however would certainly become a Buddha and 'initiate the movement of the wheel of the norm' (i.e., proclaim the doctrine) for the salvation of gods and men. 'Just as, O great king, a flower of the Udumbara fig tree only arises over a long course of time, a holy Buddha only arises in the world after long world periods. The prince however will certainly awaken to this highest enlightenment of a Buddha and then save innumerable beings from the ocean of the cycle of rebirth (*saṃsāra*) and lead them across to the other shore, to the place of immortal salvation (*amṛta*). Because I will now, O king, no longer behold this gem of a Buddha (i.e., no longer witness the moment when the Bodhisattva becomes the Buddha), I am crying now and feeling sorrowful in my heart.' The king, highly filled with joy, allows the *ṛṣi* to part from him after entertaining him lavishly. Divine visions also confirm to him the words of the seer (Chap. 7).

4. *Youth.* Following the advice of the family elders, King Śuddhodana decides to take his son to the temple of the gods soon after his birth. The town is decorated festively for this purpose and Mahāprajāpatī Gautamī puts festive garments and jewels on the child. As the prince hears 'to the temple of the gods' in answer to his question where he was to be taken, he says to his foster mother with a smile: 'How can any deity be greater than myself, to whom gods were bowing down even at birth; I am exalted above all gods.' And when the child enters the temple, the lifeless idols rise from their pedestals and fall at the feet of the Bodhisattva; they begin to speak and offer their venerations to the child (Chap. 8).

On another occasion, a delicate jewel, wrought for him upon the advice of the Brahmins, is put on the prince in the garden early in the morning. But all shimmering emitted by gold and gemstones in the radiance of the morning sun fades in the face of the radiance which emanates from the body of the Bodhisattva, and a forest goddess appears and scatters flowers for the Bodhisattva (Chap. 9).

When the prince grows up, the time arrives that he attends school together with numerous youths of his own age. When he enters the scriptorium, the teacher Viśvamitra falls to the floor in the face of the radiance of the Bodhisattva. A Tuṣita-deity raises him up again. It is revealed that the Bodhisattva already knows all types of writing, even those of whose names the teacher has never heard, thus making the latter burst into admiration. In the recitation of the alphabet by the pupils, the power of the Bodhisattva effects that each letter becomes the beginning of a word which is connected to the saving doctrine of the later Buddha. The minds of those pupils are thus prepared to receive the doctrine itself when the time comes, and 'that is the reason why such a wise person as the Bodhisattva attends school at all' (Chap. 10).

The prince is still in the years of childhood when suddenly he feels the desire to go into the countryside with friends of his own age. After watching the work in the fields for a while, he seeks the reclusiveness* of a garden, and sitting under a rose-apple tree (*jambu*) in the position of yogic meditation with crossed legs (*paryaṅka*), he sinks into reflection. By fixing his thoughts steadfastly onto a point, he rises in mindful consciousness from the first level of meditation (*dhyāna*) – which is still connected with concrete perceptions – to the highest, fourth level where the mind rests in unmovable tranquillity and seclusion. At this moment, five holy seers (*ṛṣi*), endowed with supernatural powers, move through the air from south to north. As they find themselves on that point where the Bodhisattva sits immersed in meditation, they suddenly feel as if stuck and are unable to proceed. Astonished they ask themselves who created this impediment for them, and a forest deity whispers to them that it was a prince of the Śākyas of the radiance of dawn who, immersed in solitary meditation, broke the point of their magic powers. The seers then turn their gaze towards the earth and see the child surrounded by the radiance of his sublimity as if by the glow of fire. At first they take him to be a deity. Descending to the earth, they recognize the Bodhisattva and venerate him as the one who has appeared as a light into the world shrouded in the night of the darkness of delusion. When they have offered their veneration to him, they depart again through the air.

Meanwhile, the king, for whom there is no joy in the world without his son, misses the sight of the prince. He sends a large following to search for the prince, and they find the Bodhisattva sitting in deep meditation in the shade of the rose-apple tree with crossed legs. And while the shadows of all other trees have advanced according to the movement of the sun, the shadow of the rose apple tree still spreads over the body of the meditating Bodhisattva. When the miracle is reported to King Śuddhodana, he, too, makes his way to the tree, and when he beholds the Bodhisattva engulfed by the radiant glow, he bows down at his feet in veneration and says: 'Twice I have clasped your feet in veneration: when you, O Holy One, were born, and when I found you in the radiant light of meditation.' And the following sent by

*In a different source of the Buddha legend, the Abhiniṣkramaṇasūtra (Beal, *Romantic Legend of Sākya Buddha*, p. 74) [Samuel Beal, 1st ed. 1875, Trübner & Co., London] it is described how it is the sight of the suffering of man and animal and the fighting in nature which makes the prince thoughtful and causes compassion to arise within him.

the king is anxiously worried that the prince's playmates should not disturb the silence of the meditation by loud noise (Chap. 11).

5. *Marriage and life in the women's quarters.* After the prince has reached the age of maturity, the elders of the Śākyas remind King Śuddhodana of the prophecies of the soothsayers. They hold that it was for the prince to marry; for in the enjoyment of the pleasures of love he would certainly renounce all thoughts of withdrawing from the world and fulfil his fate as a world-reigning king, not as a Buddha. It was difficult to influence the prince, the king says, but he makes the plan known to his son. The prince asks for seven days to consider. The dangers of sensual desire stand before his soul; the prospect of devoting himself to meditation in the silent solitude of the forest is already an enticing prospect to him. But the Bodhisattvas of previous world eras, his inner knowledge tells him, also chose a wife before entering the path to Buddhahood. He thus shows himself content with his father's proposal and names the advantages with which the woman who is to be his wife must be adorned. She is to be noble, young and beautiful but without conceit regarding her beauty, kind to all beings like a loving mother and sister, generous, without falsehood, without jealousy, faithful and true, without pride, pure in thought, words, and deeds, without inclination to complacency, wise and deft, an early riser. Not caste and descent, the prince explains, but solely virtue and inner value are decisive for him. After a prolonged search, a girl who appears to correspond to the prince's wish is found in Gopā, the daughter of the Śākya-prince Daṇḍapāṇi. But in order to be on the safe side, the king comes up with still another plan. He has baskets made of Aśoka-flowers (see footnote on p. 38), lavishly decorated with precious jewels. The prince is to distribute these to the girls of the country. He wants to choose that girl as a wife for his son upon whom the prince's eyes will rest. By a public announcement the king calls all girls of Kapilavastu to the palace for the seventh day, so that they may receive the gifts from the prince's hand. And on the appointed day, the girls all walk past the prince who, sitting on a throne in the reception hall of the palace, distributes the flower presents to them. None of the girls is able to bear the radiance emitting from the prince; silently, with their eyes cast down each accepts her gift and quickly walks away from there. At last Gopā appears, the daughter of Daṇḍapāṇi and she is the first who dares to look fully into the prince's eyes. The prince, however, has given all of the flower presents away already. 'Prince, what have I done that you should disregard me like this?' she smilingly addresses him.

He replies: 'I do not disregard you, you have just come too late,' and gives her the precious ring he wears on his finger. But she says: 'I am only worth this much* to you?' He then wants to give her all his jewels, but she opposes him with the following words: 'I do not want to rob the prince of his jewels, rather, I want to adorn him myself,' and leaves quickly. The king learns from secretly placed scouts that the prince's eyes have rested on Gopā, and that words were exchanged between the two of them.

Upon this the king has someone woo for his son with Daṇḍapāṇi and Gopā. However, it is the custom in the race of the Śākyas to only give a daughter to a suitor tried in chivalrous arts. Daṇḍapāṇi thus has reservations to obey the king's request. The rejection makes the king thoughtful because his son's withdrawn nature has long been a cause of concern to him. His son's peers among the sons of the Śākyas avoid him, because they take him to be a weakling. When the prince hears about the affair, he asks his father to give him an opportunity to try his mastery. The king, who smiles doubtfully at first, shows himself acquiescing to the request in the face of the prince's self-confidence and causes it to be publicly announced that on the seventh day from today the prince would give proof of his abilities. All those experienced in chivalrous arts were called to the contest. 500 Śākya youths appear for the contest which takes place outside the gates of Kapilavastu in the open fields, and the Śākya princess Gopā is put up as the prize for the winner. The king and a large crowd of people attend the contest as an audience. The prince Sarvārthasiddha is victorious in all contests. He defeats his hostile cousin Devadatta with ease who, inflated by the pride of the Śākyas, enters the ring filled with pretension and certainty of winning, and he presses him down to the earth in a friendly gesture. Finally, Daṇḍapāṇi invites them to try their skilfulness in archery. At a far distance, each of the five applicants puts up an iron drum as their aim; the Bodhisattva puts his up at the furthest distance of all, ten calls (shouting distances) away. Behind his aim, there are seven palm trees and the image of an iron boar. Each of the fellow contestants shoots his arrow into the aim set by himself, but not beyond it. When the turn comes for the Bodhisattva to shoot, every bow he takes up breaks in his hand. Then he asks the king if there was no other bow which would be

* In the *Lalitavistara* the meaning here is not entirely free from doubt. In the *Mahāvastu* however, where the episode is told in a similar way, Gopā's words have this meaning. It is narrated there how she had shown herself dissatisfied with the Bodhisattva already in a previous existence.

strong enough for his strength. The king: Yes, my son, Siṃhahanu, your maternal ancestor, had a bow which is now solemnly kept in the temple, and no-one is able to tauten it. The Bodhisattva: The bow is to be brought to me so that I may get to know it. The bow is brought and none of the youths has the strength to tauten it. Even Daṇḍapāṇi can only move the bowstring a little, not tauten it fully. What nobody else can do, the Bodhisattva achieves as if it was child's play. Without rising entirely from the ground, sitting in half-*paryaṅka* (the pose of yoga meditation), he grasps the bow given to him with the left hand and tautens it with the tip of a single finger of his right hand. The sound of the bowstring penetrates through the entire town of Kapilavastu and soon the news travels from one mouth to the other: prince Siddhārtha has tautened the bow of his ancestors, from that the sound rang far. And divine voices from on high celebrate the Bodhisattva: 'As he, without rising from the ground, has tautened the bow, in the same way he, the Holy One, will reach his aim with certainty and vanquish Māra, the tempter, and all his hosts.' After the Bodhisattva has thus tautened the bow and put the arrow on the string, he shoots it off with so much power that the arrow cuts through the targets of all his fellow contestants and finally his own target and beyond the seven palm trees and the iron boar to drill itself into the ground in the far distance out of sight. And where the Bodhisattva's arrow splits the ground, a well springs up which is still called 'the well of the arrow' (*śarakūpa*) today.* The gods' applause again mixes with the jubilations of the crowd, and the gods shower heavenly flowers for the exultation of the victorious Bodhisattva and let their voices sound thus from their heights: 'He, who, resting on the ground in the position of the previous Buddhas, has proven himself as a skilled archer, he will bring down the enemy of sinful passion with the non-substantial arrows of selflessness and will attain the blessed, sinless, highest Buddha enlightenment (*bodhi*) free from suffering by cutting through the net of what is visible.' Gopā however, Daṇḍapāṇi's daughter, becomes the wife of the Bodhisattva. She proudly walks around with her head uncovered while otherwise courtly custom demands the veiling of the face of the young woman, and the king lovingly defends the wife of his son in this (Chap. 12).

In this way, time passes with earthly enjoyments for the prince who has received a following of 84,000 wives for his pleasure. Then the gods

* This motif has been used by Kipling in his book 'Kim' in a strange fashion. The 'well of the arrow' is turned into 'the river of the arrow' by Kipling.

think the Bodhisattva is staying in the palace too long already, and it might be that all those beings who have ripened and been prepared through his influence for the future reception of the doctrine will pass away before he has become the Buddha; when are we going to witness the great parting of the Bodhisattva, when are we going to experience that the Bodhisattva becomes the Buddha? While the women delight the prince who is resting in the palace on soft cushions with song and strings, the power of the Buddhas of the ten regions of heaven causes the tune of the music to sound to him like an admonition for parting, for the great renunciation. 'The time has come for you, O Holy One, let the waters of immortal salvation (*amṛta*) rain down for the refreshment of the thirsting beings. The joys of youth are moving quickly like a torrential mountain stream, they vanish into themselves like a cloud in the autumn, unsubstantial like a mirage in the desert, like an echo, like a dream.' And by the supernatural power of the Bodhisattva himself it happens that the strings plucked for songs of love sound of the meaning of the highest salvation, of *nirvāṇa*. A deity of the Tuṣita heaven, who appears towards the end of the night, also reminds him to part (Chap. 13).

After the Bodhisattva has received such admonitions, he sends a dream to his father at night showing how he leaves the palace at night, surrounded by hosts of gods, and how he puts on the yellow robe of the ascetics. Starting up from his sleep, the king asks the chamberlain if the prince was still in his room. The servant affirms; the king, however, 'is pierced by an arrow of pain in his heart'. It is certain, he thinks, that the portents will fulfil themselves and the prince is preparing for the great renunciation. He still hopes to keep him from this step by earthly pleasures. He has three palaces built for the prince, a cool one for the summer, a warm one for the winter, a temperate one for the rainy season. All precautions are taken to avert an escape of the prince. At the 'gate of the auspicious omen' (*maṅgaladvāra*), through which according to the prophecy the riding out of the prince was going to happen, strong bolts are put in place, which require 500 men to be moved. And women have to entertain the prince with the playing of string instruments, song and dance unceasingly.

Then the prince utters the wish to go for a ride. Since the king out of love for his son, in spite of his worries, does not want to deny him anything he asks for, he issues a decree for everything to be removed from the streets which may be unpleasant for the prince on the seventh day, the one appointed for the ride. The town is decorated festively, the paths are strewn with flowers, and the Bodhisattva rides out through the eastern town gate in splendour. Directed by the higher power of the Bodhisattva, the gods thus arrange it that the prince beholds an old man with all the infirmities of old age by the wayside, with swollen veins, missing teeth and wrinkles, tottering on a stick and shivering in all limbs. The prince, to whom the sight of the infirmity of old age was unfamiliar thus far, asks the charioteer what the matter was with the man, and receives the answer corresponding to the facts. He then asks further, whether old age was only an institution (*dharma*) reigning in the family of this particular man, or if everyone succumbed to it. When the charioteer affirms the latter, all enjoyment in the ride is taken from the prince and he orders their return. In the same way on a second ride, this time through the southern gate, he beholds a seriously ill man groaning and rolling in his own filth, and again this impression and the information given by the charioteer on the nature of the illness cause the prince to turn back. On a third ride, which is undertaken through the western gate, the prince beholds a dead man on a stretcher, surrounded by mourning relatives. Unfamiliar with death he asks the charioteer who was lying motionless like that on the stretcher, and when he hears: 'a dead man who has left mother and father, son and wife to pass over into the other world', the prince is so deeply moved by the information that he breaks into lamentations on the transience of youth and of life, on the suffering of old age, illness and death, and orders the charioteer to turn back.*

The prince's fourth and last ride out leaves through the northern gate. Here the gods, again driven by the higher power of the Bodhisattva, show the prince a mendicant monk (*bhikṣu*) full of mild tran-

---

*Thus according to the *Lalitavistara*. The narration of this episode is most impressive in the Mahāpadānasutta of the *Dīghanikāya* (where Vipaśyin, a Buddha of the past, is the hero of the narrative, and all the other essential circumstances are the same): During a ride, the prince beholds a crowd of people in mourning dress and asks the charioteer who was present here. 'A dead man, prince.' 'What does that mean, a dead man?' The charioteer: 'He is dead—that means, mother and father and the other relatives of the blood will not see him anymore, nor will he see mother and father and the other relatives.' 'Am I, oh charioteer, also subject to the law of dying? Will the king, my father, the queen and all the relatives not see me anymore, will I not see them anymore?' 'You, too, oh prince, are, like all of us, subject to the law of death; the king, the queen and all the relatives will not see you anymore, either, nor will you see them anymore.' The prince then bursts into lamentations: 'Woe over birth, if everything that is born has to experience old age, illness and death.'

quillity and self-restraint who has dedicated his life to holy chastity (*brahmacarya*) and who, his eyes cast down to the ground, is standing by the wayside in his ascetic's robes and with a begging bowl, fair and majestic in all movements and gestures. The prince asks again who it was who was standing in front of them like this, and when the charioteer explains: a *bhikṣu* who, shunning sensual desire, lives in discipline and who, free from passion and hatred, longing for the tranquility of the soul, aspires to the spiritual life—the prince is highly pleased and praises that renunciation which not only leads to personal salvation, but also to that of other beings (*hitam āmanaś ca parasattvahitaṃ ca*) and whose fruit was a blessed life in immortal bliss (*sukhajīvitaṃ sumadhuram amṛtam*). He then gives the charioteer the sign to turn back.*

After receiving knowledge about these events the king has his son watched even more closely. Ramparts and moats are built, gates strengthened and an entire army is deployed in order to prevent the prince's flight. But portents already point to the parting of the Bodhisattva: birds' voices fall silent, lotus flowers wilt, on the trees the leaves dry and the flowers fall off, strings plucked for music tear, all playing of string instruments falls silent and a profound melancholy falls over the entire town. Gopā, resting at night on the bed shared with the Bodhisattva, is frightened by visions. She dreams that the earth was shaking, trees were uprooted, stars fell from the sky, her pearl necklace was ripping, the feet of her resting bed broke off, her jewellery lay scattered on the floor, a fire meteor left the town which is left shrouded in deep darkness. She who woke up from her sleep with gestures of fear is comforted by the prince with kind words; auspicious, he tells her, are the signs of her dream and portents of future salvation. To himself, dreams reveal his imminently becoming a Buddha (Chap. 14).

6. *The great parting*. The Bodhisattva knows that the hour of parting has come. But wrong, he thinks, and ungrateful it would be without his

---

*According to the *Nidānakathā*, the prince does not, as after the previous rides, return directly home, but stays in the garden that had been the destination of the ride until evening. He is then overcome by the desire to put on royal jewels for the last time before the great parting, and upon Indra's orders the god Viśvakarman also adorns him with divine jewels. Thus adorned he enters Kapilavastu and the eyes of the girls rest with admiration on the appearance of the prince. At home he then learns of the birth of his son Rāhula. In the *Lalitavistara*, Rāhula is not mentioned at all; the birth of the son before the great parting is foreign to the original legend.

father's consent. Thus he appears in his father's chamber before daybreak.* The glow of light emanating from the appearance of the Bodhisattva illuminates the entire palace so that the king asks the chamberlain in astonishment if the sun had already risen. The chamberlain however informs him that only the first half of the night had passed. The king's eye then falls on the Bodhisattva standing before him in the glow of light. The son declares to his father that the time of parting for him had now arrived. In tears the king tries to hold him back and promises the fulfilment of his every wish if he stayed. The prince then says to the king with a soft voice: 'Four requests, oh father, I have to make of you; if you can give me these four things I will stay with you forever and from now on not think of parting. This is what I ask of you: eternal youth not followed by old age; unfading beauty; health not threatened by any illness and eternal life without death.' When the king has to admit that it is not in his power to give such things, the Bodhisattva asks him if he could not at least grant him this one thing: not to be born again to a future life when he had passed from this life. The king then realizes his powerlessness, and, overpowering his paternal love in himself, he declares himself willing to let his son go for the salvation of the world. But during the day, he reconsiders and seeks to thwart the prince's flight by keeping a closer watch.

But the gods know that the hour of parting has now arrived. Just as they were the ones who had given the Bodhisattva the first thought of renunciation from the world, they now decide to support the success of the plan with their help. Indra himself takes on the opening of the gates for the one who parts and to show him the path, to others falls the task of pouring out sleep over the entire town and to dampen all sounds, to others the honouring of the Bodhisattva with heavenly music and to scatter flowers on his path. To give the Bodhisattva's inner being the final impulse, one of the 'deities of pure sojourn' (*śuddhāvāsakāyikadeva*) effects that the women's quarter shows itself in repulsive deformation. The prince sees the women as they display all kinds of weaknesses and afflictions of their bodies. The sight awakens in him the impression of a cremation ground, and in deep meditation he devotes himself to the contemplation of the impurity and impermanence of earthly life.† He

* This episode is told in the *Lalitavistara* more like a vision than an external event.

† This is illustrated in the *Lalitavistara* with a rich abundance of images. Meditation on the impurity of earthly existence, especially of the earthly body as a site of decay, plays an important part in Buddhism.

sees his own body as a site of impurity and decay. The vision of the cremation ground then gives rise in him to another picture: looking up to the heavens he beholds hosts of gods who offer their veneration to him with flowers, perfume and garlands. Standing at his left and right sides he sees the deities of moon and sun. It is midnight and the moon again stands (cf. above p. 37, 40) in the sign of Cancer (*Puṣya*).

The Bodhisattva then orders his charioteer, Chandaka, (Pali *Channa*) to saddle the horse Kaṇṭhaka without delay. All counter proposals by the consternated charioteer—it befitted young people to enjoy the pleasures of life, later, in old age, there was enough time to consider renunciation—he refutes.

> Enough, Chandaka, impermanent are these pleasures; they are like the quickly running mountain stream, like the autumn clouds that gather one moment and then dissolve again into nothingness, like the fleeting [bolts of] lightning in the firmament, the foam in the water, the mirage in the desert, the magical illusion of a Yogi, a dream. From an inversion of consciousness (*saṃjñāviparyāsa*), from a fault in our vision they originate. They are difficult to cross like the ocean, they cause thirst like salty water, they are dangerous to touch like the head of a snake.

Chandaka bursts into tears. But all his speeches are in vain. During countless existences, the Bodhisattva replies, he had tasted the pleasures of the senses and yet found no satiety. As steadfast as Mount Meru was his decision taken for the salvation of the world. At this point, the gods let a shower of flowers fall and heavenly spirits spread out sleep over the entire city and dampen all sounds. Finally obeying the urgent orders of the prince, Chandaka brings the horse and when the Bodhisattva mounts it, the earth shakes, gods appear from all directions to venerate the Bodhisattva and to scatter flowers on his path and heavenly *apsaras* strike up a song of praise in veneration of the parting Bodhisattva.

His nightly ride leads the prince through the areas of the Śākya, Kroḍya, Malla and Maineya [clans]. Near the hamlet of Anuvaineya the day dawns. The Bodhisattva then dismounts his horse and gives leave to the deities who had escorted him until this point. Chandaka receives the order to return to Kapilavastu with the horse Kaṇṭhaka and the prince's jewellery. A shrine erected in this place is still called Chandakanivartana ('Chandaka's turning back') today. Then the thought comes to the Bodhisattva that parted hair does not suit a mendicant monk. With his sword he cuts his hair from his head and hurls it into the air where the gods receive it and keep it as a relic. Of his silken robes, too, which he had worn as a prince, the Bodhisattva wishes to be rid in order to put on the yellowish-brown [ochre] bark garment which befits life in the forest. Then one of the 'gods of pure sojourn' appears to him, dressed as a hunter; with him the Bodhisattva exchanges his robes. Thus the robes the prince had worn also come to the gods as a relic. On the earth, two shrines indicate the places of the cutting of the hair and the exchanging of robes.

There is rejoicing in the worlds of the gods over the Bodhisattva's step, but sorrow and misery in Kapilavastu when the absence of the prince is noticed. He is looked for at the 'gate of auspicious omen,' but only the flowers which the gods scattered on the path for the parting one are found there. Chandaka's return brings certainty of what has happened, and the king voices his desperation with the outcry: 'O my only son!' At the sight of the horse returning without its master Gopā falls unconscious to the ground. Having regained consciousness, she clings to the horse's neck and breaks into the lamentation: 'Woe, Kaṇṭhaka, noble-born horse, to where have you carried my husband off? Woe on the separation of what is dear to us!' Mahāprajāpatī's (see above, p. 42) grief is also deep. When Chandaka hands the prince's jewellery over to her, she thinks: as long as I look at these jewels, sorrow will be in my heart. And she sinks the jewellery in a lotus pond which is still called 'jewellery pond' today (Chap. 15).

Wandering from place to place as a mendicant monk, in between accepted as a guest by male and female Brahmins in different hermitages, the Bodhisattva reaches Vaiśālī. At that time, the Yogi, Ārāḍa Kālāpa, (Pali *Aḷāro Kālāmo*) is dwelling there with a circle of 300 disciples whom he leads to the level called 'ascending to the sphere of nothingness' (*ākiṃcanyāyatana,* Pali *ākiñaññāyatana*) by instructing them in meditation (Yoga). Ārāḍa, who sees the Bodhisattva coming from a distance, draws his disciples' attention to him. The Bodhisattva approaches the Yogi with the request to be instructed in the sacred conduct (*brahmacarya*). He is then soon able to rise to the level of meditation taught by Ārāḍa. The Yogi then makes him an offer of sharing the leadership of the disciples with him. But the Bodhisattva has realized that 'ascending to the sphere of nothingness' is not the final goal, it does not lead to the cessation of suffering, and the necessity to search further is before him. He thus leaves Ārāḍa and moves on to the country of Magadha. After spending some time in solitude there by the Pāṇḍava mountain near the capital Rājagṛha, only surrounded by hosts of gods, he takes himself to Rājagṛha on his alms round. His sight appears so noble to the inhabitants of Rājagṛha that they take him for a divine being. Under the influence of his personality they even abstain from enjoying intoxicating drinks. King Bimbisāra of Magadha also takes notice of the ascetic and seeks him at the Pāṇḍava mountain with his following. After a reverent salutation he asks [the Bodhisattva] to dwell in his kingdom where he wants to give him all that his heart desires. But with a mild voice, the Bodhisattva replies to him that his desire was not aimed at worldly pleasures which have never given satiety to those who attained them. When the king, who does not yet know him, asks him, he gives his name and lineage and declares his intention to become a Buddha. Bimbisāra feels this to be an honour for his town and his entire kingdom and is highly pleased. In deep awe, the king takes leave of the mendicant monk (Chap. 16).

7. *The time of asceticism (duṣkaracaryā)*. At that time, the Yogi Rudraka Rāmaputra ('son of Rāma') with 700 disciples lived in Rājagṛha. The spiritual meditation taught by him is called 'ascending to the sphere beyond conscious and unconscious' (*naivasaṃjñānāsaṃjñāyatana*). The Bodhisattva now turns to Rudraka with the request to be accepted as a disciple and led to the said level. Following the instruction by Rudraka he then practises, sitting in solitude with crossed legs, that meditation which—thanks to the favourable *karma* of previous existences and the spiritual concentration practised then—soon leads him to the desired success. Rudraka has to answer the question whether he knew a higher level in the negative. Like Ārāḍa, he also offers the Bodhisattva to share the instruction of his disciples with him. Alone, the Bodhisattva realizes that the path taught by Rudraka does not lead to enlightenment, not to *nirvāṇa*. He takes leave of Rudraka and continues on his path. Five disciples of Rudraka (*pañca bhadravargīyāḥ* 'the five of the blessed host') leave their master and follow the Bodhisattva in whom they see the great teacher of the world (*śāsta loke*) of the future. They had been impressed by the fact that the ascetic Gautama—as the Bodhisattva is called in those circles—has effortlessly and in a short time reached the spiritual goal which they themselves have been striving for in vain for such a long time already, and still strives for something higher. Together with these five the Bodhisattva arrives in Gayā in the country of Magadha and devotes himself to spiritual exercises (*prahāṇa*) on the mountain Gayāśīrṣa. While doing so, the following thought appears in front of him in the form of a parable. There are, he realizes, ascetics (*śramaṇa*) and Brahmins who in their

physical actions and in their thoughts are submissive to sensual pleasure (*kāma*) and in their entire inner soul still full of sensual desire. Even if these practise strict and painful austerities, they remain unable to realize within themselves the superhuman (*uttaramanuṣya*), noble clairvoyant knowledge. These are like a man who tries to light a fire by rubbing moist sticks together in water. Others have freed themselves in their actions and thoughts from sensual pleasure, but at the bottom of the souls sensual desire still lingers.* If these practise austerities, they are like a man who tries to light a fire on dry ground with moist sticks. They, too, are thus unable to reach the higher vision. Finally there are ascetics and Brahmins who are not only free from sensual pleasure in their actions and thoughts, but who have also eradicated all sensual desire at the bottom of their souls. They are, when they practise austerities, like the man who lights a fire on dry ground with dry sticks, and they succeed in realizing within themselves the superhuman, clairvoyant knowledge. Realizing that he himself has overcome all hidden propensity to sensuality in his soul and thus may expect that austerities will lead him to the goal of supernatural knowledge, the Bodhisattva walks from Gayā to Urubilvā (Pali *Uruvelā*) on the river Nairañjanā (Pali *Nerañjarā*). At the sight of the clear water running between pleasantly overgrown hilly riverbanks he thinks: This is a delightful spot of land, just made for one striving for perfection in silent withdrawal; well then, here I will stay.

As the different forms of austerities (*tapas*) prevalent in Jambudvīpa (India) are before him, he decides to surpass these methods by an austerity raised to the highest level. In that way he wants to 'force down to him the deities of the realm of forms presiding over the sphere of Yoga meditation'. To this end he takes on a six-year practice—*āsphānaka* meditation—which is so difficult that 'no human or extra-human being would be able to fulfil it, except the Bodhisattva standing in his last life on earth'. He starts by sitting down on the ground with crossed legs (in the '*paryaṅka* seat'), forcing down the body with the mind. 'Like a stronger wrestler wrestles down the weaker one by grabbing him by the neck, he wrestles, he tortures down this body with his mind until sweat breaks from his armpits and on his forehead and the drops of sweat that fall to the ground freeze into frost in the cold

* In the Yoga system relevant to the understanding of Buddhism a difference is made between that which consciously affects the soul (*vṛtti*) and that which is eliminated from consciousness but is still present latently (*saṃskāra*) in the subconscious, in a subtle condition (*sūkṣma*). Details on this in the second part.

winter nights and steam rises from them.' The meditation to which he then proceeds includes a complete restraint of the breath. As a result from the closing of all airways, a loud sound transpires from the opening of the ears. When the Bodhisattva in a further deepening of the meditation also closes the ears, the wind in the body pushes upward and hits the skullcap. 'As if it was hit with a blunt lance the upward pushing flow of breath hits the skullcap when mouth, nose and ears are closed.'

With this, the Bodhisattva has advanced extremely close to the margin of death and some of the gods already take him for dead and announce the news to Queen Māyā dwelling in Indra's heaven. The anxious Māyā then descends, surrounded by hosts of heavenly *apsaras*, to the river Nairañjanā at midnight, and when she sees the Bodhisattva with withered limbs lying on the ground as if dead, she breaks into crying and lamentations and says: 'When you, my son, were born in the Lumbinī grove, and did the seven steps like a lion, what you said then, looking up to the cardinal directions: 'This is my last birth,' this word now has not come true. And in vain was the prophecy of Asita, that in you a Buddha would arise for the world; since now you have neither enjoyed the happiness of world sovereignty nor have you partaken of the enlightenment of a Buddha, but you have perished lonely in the forest. To whom shall I entreat now for my son, to whom shall I call out in my pain? Who will give a spark of life to my only son, my life?' The Bodhisattva then wakes from his rigor mortis and says: 'Who are you who is thus lamenting, and who weeps for her son excessively, writhing on the ground with loosened hair and disfigured beauty?' And Māyā says to him: 'The one who carried you in her womb like a bolt of lightning for ten months; it is me, your mother, who now mourns you in deep anguish, my dear son.' The Bodhisattva then comforts his crying mother:

> You shall not be anxious in longing for your son, your suffering shall not have been in vain, not in vain the renunciation of a Buddha. I will bring to fulfilment Asita's prophecy; for the earth would rather burst into a hundred pieces or Mount Meru tumble into the sea or the stars fall to the earth than that I should die in this worldly existence without having attained Buddhahood. Thus abandon your sorrow, after a little while you will behold the perfection of the Buddha.

Māyā is filled with the highest joy through these words. Scattering heavenly flowers on the head of her son, she bows before the Bodhisattva three times in awe and returns to her abode of the gods amidst the sounds of heavenly music.

With his meditation the Buddha combines strict fasting which he continually increases. Initially he restricts the measure of his daily food to a kola berry, then to a single grain of rice, then to a sesame seed, finally he proceeds to complete abstinence from food. His formerly beautiful body loses all lustre in this and withers like a cut-off pumpkin. During the entire six-year practice he stays in the *paryaṅka* seat, always maintaining a joyful disposition. He never steps from the light into the shadow, from the shadow into the light; he remains unprotected against heat and cold, rain and wind. All bodily eliminations recede in him. Tempests erupt over his head, he does not mind it; he no longer notices the objects of the external senses. The youth of the village and all inhabitants of the countryside who are watching him play their pranks on him and throw soil on him. And deities and supernatural beings from all world spheres come as spectators and pay their veneration to the Bodhisattva who is mortifying himself.

During the entire six-year austerities, Māra, the evil one, attaches himself to the Bodhisattva's side and waits in vain for an opportunity to get at him. Once he approaches him during his fasting and tries to divert him from his practices: 'As you are now, a thousand parts of you belong to death and only one part to life; full of suffering is the path of serious striving (*prahāna,* Pali *padhāna),* difficult the mastery of the mind.' But the Bodhisattva replies to the visitor that it was better to fall in battle than to live ingloriously; his decision could not be shaken. Spiritual exertion leads to the highest consciousness (*utammacetanā*), in which the spiritual becomes independent from the body (*cittaṃ nāvakṣata kāyam*). All ordinary asceticism was in Māra's grip, but he knew how to face the visitor calmly and with understanding. Upon this, Māra realizes the futility of his efforts and withdraws in a cast-down mood.*

During the course of the practices the Bodhisattva realizes that the self-mortification to which he has devoted himself is not able to lead to the goal of the highest super-human realization, not to the end of birth,

* This episode can also be found in the *Suttanipāta,* one of the oldest works of the Pali canon. In the *Nidānakathā* the first temptation already happens at the point of the 'great parting'. Māra approaches the Bodhisattva as he is riding into the night and promises world sovereignty to him within seven days if he renounces his intention to become the Buddha.

old age and death, and he asks himself if there could not be another path. In his contemplation he remembers how he had found the right path, the path of pure meditation, quite on his own in his early childhood: 'As I then, in father's garden in the shade of the rose-apple tree, reached the first level of meditation (*dhyāna*) and raised myself through all intermediate levels up to the fourth, in that way I now want to awaken to the enlightenment of a Buddha (*bodhi*) which ends the suffering of birth, old age and death by following the path of spiritual meditation.' And the thought becomes certainty to him: this is the path to enlightenment. At the same time he realizes that for a successful following of this path the unabated strength of the body is necessary. He thus decides to take full food again. Gods realizing his thoughts draw near with the offer of instilling heavenly nourishment through the pores of the skin. But the Bodhisattva tells himself that he would then still give rise to the impression of fasting and he does not want to become guilty of this untruthfulness. He thus rejects the food of the gods to have prepared earthly fare from vegetables for him. The five disciples of Rudraka who had followed him until now, then think that if austerities were not able to lead him to his goal, he would succeed still less by this new path to reach clairvoyant realization. They thus leave him and take themselves to Benares where they stay in the animal park Ṛṣipatana.

Ten country girls, Balā, Balaguptā, Supriyā, Vijayasenā, Atimuktakamalā, Sundarī, Kumbhakārī, Uluvillikā, Jaṭillikā, Sujātā, who had been bringing the Bodhisattva the meagre food which he was then still taking in the beginning of his fasting also prepare the vegetable dishes desired by him now. Through these, the body of the Bodhisattva gains strength and beauty again, and the girls call him the beautiful ascetic.

Sujātā, one of the ten, has long taken on a sacrificial vow in order to become worthy of handing that food to the Bodhisattva which he will consume before the night in which he will awaken to a Buddha. In a dream she receives the afflatus from the gods that the time has now arrived. She starts to work and distils the sevenfold intensified cream from the milk of a thousand cows. To this exquisite cream she adds fresh rice. During the preparation of this dish, auspicious signs appear in it, which are interpreted by a passing soothsayer as [pertaining] to the gaining of immortal salvation (*amṛta*). Sujātā then sprinkles flowers and fragrant water over the rice pudding dish and hands it to the Bodhisattva in a golden bowl. Realizing the significance of this dish, the Bodhisattva says to the girl: 'Sister, what is this golden bowl supposed to be to me?' 'May it be yours.' 'But it has no purpose for me.' 'As you wish; but I will not hand any food without a bowl!' The Bodhisattva then receives the bowl in order to show his benevolence to the offering girl. After cooling his limbs in the water of the Nairañjanā, into which the gods have poured divine fragrant essences, he enjoys Sujātā's dish on a throne-seat made of precious stones which snake maidens have caused to rise from a sandbank in the river. After finishing his meal, the Bodhisattva throws the golden bowl into the river. The snake king Sāgara catches it there and brings it to his abode as a relic. Indra, nearing in the form of Garuḍa (Viṣṇu's eagle), makes vain attempts at stealing the bowl. Only when he takes on his true form, Sāgara gives him the bowl upon his friendly entreating, and Indra brings it to the heaven of the 33 gods where it is kept as a sacred object.

Soon after the Bodhisattva has consumed the dish, the former luminous colour again shows on his body, the 32 signs are visible on him again, and an aura of light rays surrounds him. In this way he strides like a lion with the walk of a 'great being' (*mahāpuruṣa*), sure of his victory, towards the bodhi tree (Chap. 18).

8. *Entry into the bodhi circle.* Between the river Nairañjanā and the circle of enlightenment the gods have scrubbed everything shiny and bright, and all trees in the far perimeter of the worlds bend their tops towards the *bodhi* circle. On both sides of the path that leads from the river to the *bodhi* tree, the gods have erected seven altars made of precious stones, and hosts of heavenly *apsaras* scatter divine flowers onto the path, pour fragrant water on it and let heavenly songs sound. Auspicious signs accompany the entry of the Bodhisattva into the *bodhi* circle. In the world of the gods, Brahmān celebrates the significance of this moment and requests all gods to venerate the Bodhisattva. In all world spheres the (mystical) Buddha fields (*buddhakṣetra*) are visible in full festive decoration by the radiant light emanated by the Bodhisattva. In the *bodhi* circle, which is marked out by the deities of the *bodhi* tree, all kinds of heavenly and earthly flowers, flowers of the earth and of the water, are brought to light, and the Bodhisattvas of all world regions become visible therein.

Again the powerful glow of light emanates from the Bodhisattva through which for this moment all suffering of the world is allayed: the sick are healed, the frightened breathe a sigh of relief, prisoners are released, those feeble from old age feel new strength, women have an easy birth, no being dies in this hour. All lowly feelings—passion, hatred, illusion, anger, greed, violence, envy, jealousy—are silent, all beings are filled with love and friendliness towards each other, like father and mother for their children. Even the agonies of the damned are appeased for a moment, and wild animals become friendly and tame, met by the rays of love from the great saint.

Seven times the Bodhisattva circles and pays his respects to the *bodhi* tree. On a self-prepared grass mat in the manner of the Buddhas of former world eras he then sits down in the position of Yoga meditation with crossed legs, upright body, the face turned towards the East, and makes the firm resolve not to get up until he had awakened to *bodhi*, the highest enlightenment of a Buddha: 'May my body dry up, may skin, bones and flesh disappear, I will not stir from this seat until I have attained the enlightenment of a Buddha which is difficult to find in the world eras.' (Chap. 19).

Around the Bodhisattva sitting in the *bodhi* circle deities gather from all cardinal directions so that nobody should cause an obstacle to his meditation. The Bodhisattva lets a ray of light depart from himself through which the Buddha fields in the ten different world spheres (*dhātu*) are illuminated and the spheres of the Bodhisattvas working in these worlds are stirred up. They all appear, perform manifold acts of magic and venerate the Bodhisattva who is now going to become a Buddha (Chap. 20).

9. *Fight with Māra*. But the Bodhisattva now has the thought: 'Here in the world of sensuality Māra the Evil One is Lord and Ruler. It would not befit me to awaken to the highest enlightenment of a Buddha without his knowledge. Well then, I will challenge Māra the Evil One.' Together with him, all beings of his world sphere are going to be defeated and turn their mind towards enlightenment. The Bodhisattva then lets a ray of light emit from the point between his brows through which the entire circumference of the worlds is illuminated and Māra's abode is stirred up. From the glow of light a voice sounds to Māra which announces his imminent defeat. In dream visions he sees himself in flight, his coronet has fallen off, the flowers have withered in his gardens and the lotus ponds have dried up, musical instruments fall to the ground with torn strings, his daughters mourn for him, his sons turn to the Bodhisattva, his head is covered with dust, in fighting he is unable to draw his sword from the sheath, his generals flee and all the gods bow before the Bodhisattva.

Upon this, Māra positions his army in battle formation and leads it into the field against the Bodhisattva. With horrible weapons, spitting out poisonous snakes, breathing fire and smoke, the hosts charge towards him. Even fire-spitting mountains roll towards the Bodhisattva. Darkness diffuses, and the field-cry of the nightly army sounds horribly. But because the heart of the Holy One is entirely clothed in love and friendliness, no weapon can harm him, fire and poison cannot harm him, the hurled missiles remain hovering over his head and transform into flower garlands by the power of his love which is noble beyond the world (*maitrī lokottarabhāvī*). Hurled mountains become flower palaces, masses of fire remain hovering over the Bodhisattva as a wreath of light rays.

Meanwhile, Māra has to contend with difficulties in his own camp; some of his sons counsel against the fight and turn to the Bodhisattva. When he realizes the impotence of his missiles, which, transformed by the love of the Holy One, cover the earth everywhere as scattered flowers and adorn the *bodhi* tree in wreaths of flowers so that the Bodhisattva sits as if under a flower canopy, hatred and jealousy rise in the heart of Māra, the Evil One. Pondering other means to snatch the victory from the enemy, he now tries to dissuade him from the path of salvation by offering him royal rule. But the Bodhisattva only refers to all those sacrifices made by him in previous lives which secure his claim to the honour of Buddhahood. Countless times in repeated existences he had offered body and life, wealth and possessions for the benefit of other beings, while Māra had acquired his dominance in the kingdom of sensuality only by a single sacrifice. Māra replies: 'You yourself are witness to my sacrifice, you have no witnesses for yours. Thus you are overcome by me.' The Bodhisattva then calls the earth as witness by stroking with the right hand over his entire body and then touching the earth lightly. And when the Bodhisattva touches it, the earth trembles and attended by countless earth spirits the goddess of the earth appears in visible form and confirms the sacrifices made by the Bodhisattva by her testimony.

After he has been defeated in this contest as well, Māra asks his daughters to try their arts of seduction on the Bodhisattva. But the saint remains unmoved and his countenance radiates like the sun. The daughters meet their father's reprimands with the excuse that nobody on the earth and in the world of the gods had the power to pierce through the mysterious spiritual nature of a Bodhisattva. They, too, counsel Māra to abandon the futile fight.

The deities of the *bodhi* tree already celebrate the Bodhisattva as the victor. But Māra does not want to be considered defeated yet. After he has been unable to gain anything against the Bodhisattva with words, he sets his army once more in a last assault against the enemy. But the Bodhisattva defies the onslaught unshaken: 'And if the whole world was full of devils (Māra), and each of them had a Mount Meru as his weapon, they still would not be able to lay a finger on me, let alone fatally strike me.'

And in the middle of the horrors that assail him he realizes that Māra and his army are merely an illusion and deceit (*māyā*), like the mirror image of the moon in the water. And this time it is the power of his truthfulness through which he transforms all missiles hurled towards him into flower wreaths. Māra's elephants, horses and chariots lie defeated on the ground and his hosts flee in a stampede. Now Māra finally has to declare himself defeated and hosts of gods celebrate the Bodhisattva as victor and offer rejoicing venerations to him.

10. *The enlightenment* (*bodhi*). After the victory over Māra the Bodhisattva raises himself from the first level of meditation (*dhyāna*) to the fourth, where the mind is above joy and pain and all perceptions of sensuality, and where it remains in complete seclusion after freeing itself from all memories. In this state he turns his inner organ towards visionary perception, and three-fold knowledge dawns in him.

During the first wake of the night, he first beholds, with the divine, clairvoyant, supernatural eye, all *beings* on their journey in the cycle of births; how after the disintegration of the body they sink down to dark places of pain (*naraka*) through their bad thoughts, words and deeds, [and how they] rise up to bright heavenly worlds (*svargaloka*) through good thoughts, words and deeds.

In the second wake of the night, the Bodhisattva turns the gaze of his spiritual eye to the clairvoyant vision of previous lives. And he beholds his own past embodiments and those of other beings through innumerable world eras, with all their changing experiences of joy and pain, of high and low fates, remembering what name he bore in each of these embodiments, to which lineage, which caste, which circumstances of life he belonged, and what his lifespan in each embodiment was.

In the third wake of the night, before dawn, the Bodhisattva turns his mind towards the cause of *suffering* and the turning of suffering. The world appears to him sunken into bad distress, where beings are subject to birth and old age, to death and rebirth, and he does not yet see the way out from the intertwined connection of suffering. He then asks himself: what is the cause from which *old age* and *death* (*jarāmaraṇa*) originate? And he realizes: the cause of old age and death is birth (*jāti*).

And tracing back the chain of causes further, he realizes how birth originates in the entering into physical being through conception (*bhava*), conception in the grasping of the sensual in satisfying sensual desire (*upādāna*, lit. the 'grasping of the fuel'), just as the grasping of the sensual originates in sensual desire (*tṛṣṇā* 'thirst'), desire in feeling (*vedanā*), feeling in touch (*sparśa*), touch in the (superphysical) substrate of the six senses (*ṣaḍāyatana*), the senses in the substrate of personality (*nāmarūpa* 'name and form'), the personality in the substrate of consciousness (*vijñāna*), consciousness in the forces of imagination (*saṃskāra*) working in the sub-conscious, and how these forces of imagination (which contain the seed to all physical being in themselves) are a product of ignorance (*avidyā*).

Thus the following realization stands before him: from ignorance originate the forces of imagination in the subconscious, from subconsciousness consciousness, from consciousness name and form, from that the senses, from the senses touch, from touch feeling, from feeling sensual desire, from sensual desire the grasping of sensuality, from that conception to physical being, from conception birth, from birth old age, death, sorrow and mourning, suffering, grief and despair. And from this realization follows the other one for him—that, as through the origin of one the origin of the other is dependent, so is the non-existence of the one dependent on the non-existence of the other, so that in the destruction of ignorance he realizes the path which leads through the destruction of the forces of imagination and all phases of sensuality originating from them finally to the destruction of old age, death, and suffering. He thus sees the truth of ignorance, of the cause of ignorance, of the destruction of ignorance, of the path which leads to the destruction of ignorance; likewise, the truth about the forces of imagination, their origin and their destruction, and in the same way through all the links of the chain of causation, until he finally realizes: this is death, this is the cause of death, this is the destruction of death, this is the path which leads to the destruction of death; this is suffering, this is the cause of suffering, this is the destruction of suffering, this is the path which leads to the destruction of suffering.

After the saint has found the 'highest perfect enlightenment' (*anuttarā samyakṣasaṃbodhi*) before dawn and has reached the three-fold knowledge (*traividyā*) of a Buddha, the gods say: 'Let us scatter flowers, the Noble One has awakened to a Buddha.' And they shower him with heavenly flowers up to his knees. Joyful feelings in all beings, vanishing of the darkness of the world, glowing light and earthquakes accompany the awakening to Buddhahood, and all Buddhas greet the one who has trodden the same path (*tathāgata*) like them and who has now become a Buddha (*abhisaṃbuddha*). In all the parts of the heavens, Bodhisattvas join in the jubilations: 'The Knowing One has risen among beings, the lotus flower in the sea of realization, untainted by earthly nature, who will pour forth the rain of compassion as healing balm for all beings.' Heavenly *apsaras* celebrate the Awakened One (Buddha) as the hero who defeated Māra's army without the force of weapons, as the highest physician and god over gods, as the giver of the fruit of immortal salvation (*amṛta*). Gods descend down to earth, trees bend their tops towards the *bodhi* circle—'a world era would not be sufficient to describe all the various kinds of magic which accompany the awakening of the Bodhisattva to the Buddha' (Chap. 22).

All hierarchies of gods then gather around the one who has awakened to the Buddha in order to pay their solemn respects. First the 'gods of the pure abode' appear (*śuddhāvāsakāyikā devaputrā*), then the 'ones glowing with light' (*ābhasvarā*), the Brahma-deities, the sons of Māra who turned towards the Bodhisattva during the fight, the *paranirmitavaśavartin* gods, the god Sunirmita with his following, the gods of the Tuṣita heaven, the *suyāma* gods, the 33 gods with Indra at their head, the four guardians of the world (*māhārāja*), accompanied by heavenly maidens (*apsaras*), and finally the deities of the air and the earth. All celebrate the Buddha with heavenly flowers, perfumes and garlands, with gifts of all kinds, and praise him with their songs (Chap. 23).

During the first seven days after the enlightenment, while the deities venerate him, the Buddha remains in the *bodhi* circle in the seat of meditation (*paryaṅka*), looking up to the *bodhi* tree and devoting himself to the bliss of contemplation. 'Like a king who remains in the place where he has received his coronation for seven days, the Awakened Ones remain in the circle of enlightenment for seven days.' And like a hero who overlooks the host of enemies he has overcome to the last man, the Awaken One in the *bodhi* circle looks at the sinful passions he has destroyed:

> Here I have cut off the thicket of passion on the tree of world existence with the axe of reflection and burnt it in the fire of realization, dried up is the stream of sensual desire (*tṛṣṇā*) by the sun of knowledge; here my eye of realization has opened in its purity and torn the fabric of illusion, all fetters of worldly existence have been opened by me. Here I have crossed the sea of the cycle of births (*saṃsāra*) on the ship of strong courage, here

> reached the memory of my past lives; I remember innumerable world eras like one who has woken up from sleep. I have drunk the nectar of immortality through the forces of love and compassion; the tip of sainthood has been attained, sin has been destroyed, defeated is Māra's army; I have awoken to the highest enlightenment, the suffering of birth, old age and death has been ended.

During the second week the Tathāgata (lit. 'the One who has gone thus', Buddha) roams vast spaces, during the third week he again looks up at the *bodhi* tree, during the fourth he undertakes a 'small journey' from the Eastern to the Western sea.* Then Māra, the tempter, approaches again, and suggests that he enter *parinirvāṇa*. But Buddha refuses him: he must not think of passing before his earthly task had been fulfilled to the last and until the ground has been prepared in the world for the Buddha, the norm and his community. Māra then knows that the Buddha has left his sphere and leaves with his head bent low. For their father's sake, his daughters, Rati (lust), Arati (longing) and Tṛṣṇā (desire) once again try their arts of seduction with the Buddha. He turns them into ugly old women. Filled with remorse they ask the Holy One for forgiveness. During the fifth week, the Buddha stays in the palace of the snake king, Mucilinda. During a severe storm, Mucilinda puts his coils around the Holy One seven times in order to shelter him from the cold winds. During the sixth week, the Buddha goes to another tree (*ajapālanyagrodha* 'the Nyagrodha tree of the goat herd'). During the seventh week he returns to the *bodhi* tree.

At this time, two brothers, Trapuṣa and Bhallika, young merchants, are trekking with a caravan of 500 draft animals from the South to the North. In the vicinity of the *bodhi* tree the caravan suddenly cannot move from the spot any more, held by invisible influences. Even two excellent oxen fail, Sujāta and Kīrti who accomplish more than all the others in the trek and who never need to be driven by the ox goad. Only when the forest deity has intervened in a helping and soothing way do they draw the chariot up to the place where the Buddha sits immersed in meditation, glowing like the sun, adorned with the 32 signs of a great being. The astonished merchants first take him for a divine being, but when he opens his robes, they know him as an ascetic, and since they see that he is in need of a gift of food, they ask him – bowing at the feet of the Holy One – to accept as alms a dish made from honey which they find in their supplies. Buddha receives the alms in a stone bowl given

---

* This, of course, has to be thought of as a meditation experience.

to him by the gods filled with heavenly flowers. The bowl from which the Buddha has taken his first meal is transposed by a deity to the Brahmā world where it is venerated as a holy object. After his meal, the Buddha blesses the two givers: 'Salvation be in your right hand, salvation in your left, salvation may rest in all your limbs like a wreath lain on your head. Peaceful may be the cardinal directions to you, may no evil meet you anywhere; return laden with profit, protected by all the gods. In whichever direction you may be travelling, may the stars of that cardinal direction protect you. Led by the gods, move on happily, see your relatives again and enter into immortal salvation (*amṛtaṃ śivam*).' Highly pleased the merchants take their refuge in the Buddha and in the norm and thus become the first followers of the Buddha as lay disciples (Chap. 24).

c) The proclamation of the doctrine

While the Buddha is still sitting in inner contemplation under the tree, the following concerns arise in him: 'Profound,' he says to himself,

> and subtle is the norm I have found; it is a holy norm, one that is difficult to realize, not accessible to mere rational thinking (*atarka avitarkāvacara*), only to be known by wise men, one that exceeds the realm of sensual perception (*ṣaḍviṣayasamatikrānta*); it is one where one loses all firm ground (*sarvālambanasamatikrānta*) and where the annihilation of all sensual passion—*nirvāṇa*—is the goal. If I now proclaim the norm to others, it might be that they do not understand it, and that would be oppressive and a reproach to me for having disclosed the doctrine in an improper place. Thus I will, unconcerned by anything further, remain in silence.

The gods, whose sphere has been aroused by the rays of light emanating from the meditation of the Holy One, seek in vain to move him to proclaim the norm by the vision that otherwise the world will be ruined. 'My path,' the Buddha replies to them, 'is difficult to see; it will not be realized by those blinded by passion. As slaves to sensual desire, people allow themselves to be carried away by the current, thus enough, I cannot reveal what I have found with such difficulty.' Saddened, the gods retreat.

As the Buddha closes his mind to the communication of the doctrine, people in the country of Magadha are seized by horrible sensations. They feel as if no winds would blow, no fires burn, as if the sky did no longer rain, the rivers slowed in their course, the seeds no longer germinate and as if birds did no longer fly through the air. Realizing the danger to mankind resulting from the Buddha's hesitation, the god Brahmā makes a final attempt to change the Tathāgata's mind. He appears in front of the bodhi tree in his divine radiance and implores the Holy One with the plea to reveal the pure doctrine, the immortal salvation, to mankind who were thirsting for it like the dried-up earth for rain. The Tathāgata then looks across the world with his Buddha eye and beholds three different kinds of beings. As three kinds of lotus can be found in a lotus pool—quite a few which are entirely immersed in the water, several that rise over the water's surface, and those which just reach the surface of the water—with the eye of realization the Buddha sees beings which are entirely immersed in perversity, so that they will under no circumstances understand the doctrine, those who appear destined to reach the realization of the truth, and finally those for whom everything depends on the revelation of the doctrine: if it is communicated to them, they will reach its realization, otherwise they will remain excluded from realization. Out of compassion with these the Buddha assents to Brahmā's plea. 'May the gate of immortal salvation be open to them, may those with ears to hear believe'—with these words he decides, 'to set in motion the wheel of the norm'. In all the worlds of the gods there is great rejoicing in the Buddha's decision which he has made 'out of compassion with the world, for the salvation of the gods and mankind'. The Buddha then reveals his intention to the deities of the *bodhi* tree who ask him about it, and he is asked to proclaim the doctrine in Benares, in the deer park of Ṛṣipatana, where the Buddhas of previous eras also set the wheel of the norm in motion (Chap. 25).

11. *Setting in motion the wheel of the norm* (*dharmacakrapravartana*). While the Buddha is considering to whom he should first tell the doctrine, his thought falls on his two teachers in Yoga. His intuition, however, imparts to him the knowledge that Rudraka has not been among the living for seven days, Ārāḍa Kālāpa for three days. He then thinks of the five disciples who had followed him then and who had left him when he turned away from asceticism. With the vision of his clairvoyant eye he finds them in the deer park Ṛṣipatana at Benares. There he now turns his steps. After revealing himself as the perfect Buddha to a wandering ascetic who admires his radiant appearance, he reaches the banks of the Gaṅgā whose waters have swelled up. The ferryman refuses to take him across, because the mendicant cannot pay the ferriage. The Holy One then transposes himself to the other shore

by his supernatural power (*ṛddhi*). The ferryman realizes too late to what an elevated person he has refused his services and falls to the ground in remorse. By a decree of king Bimbisāra, mendicant monks are freed from paying ferriage in the future.

Upon reaching Benares, the Buddha makes his way to the deer park after his first alms round. There, the five disciples see him approaching from afar. They think: the venerable ascetic Gautama is coming there, who has deviated from the path of serious effort; if he had not been able to reach superhuman clairvoyant realization by his asceticism he certainly will not reach it now that he is enjoying abundant food again and is living comfortably. This is why they do not find it necessary to meet him or to rise before him. But the closer the Holy One comes the more uncomfortable are the five on their seats, and in spite of themselves they are driven to rise before the Buddha. 'Like a bird in the cage, under which a fire has been lit, will soon try to fly to the top because of the heat, the five disciples felt uncomfortable on their seats when the Tathāgata came closer, and they had the desire to get up.' After they had greeted him reverently and had paid their respects to him, the Buddha sits down on the seat indicated to him by the disciples. His radiant face arouses the disciples' astonishment and they ask him whether any supernatural realizations have occurred to him. The Buddha replies that he had found immortal salvation (*amṛta*) and the path to immortal salvation; henceforth, they should not address him as 'venerable' (*āyuṣmat*) like a mendicant monk. He was now the Awakened One (*buddha*), the Knowing, Seeing One, the One Without Sin from whom the fire of passion had parted:

> I will proclaim to you the norm above all norms; listen to me, I will speak to you, I will teach you so that you, too, will find liberation of the heart (*cetovimukti*), the liberation of knowledge (*prajñāvimukti*), and that you will realize: birth has been destroyed, the holy way of life has been completed, the duty has been fulfilled, henceforth there is no return to being-in-the-world.

And with his clairvoyant vision he tells them those thoughts that had been passing through their souls when he was approaching. At that moment all that had still been clinging to them of their former delusion falls away and they are standing before the Buddha with the marks of the disciple (*bhikṣu*). They ask him for forgiveness for their arrogance and formally accept him as their teacher. And soon there appears on the spot where the Buddhas of previous world eras had put the wheel of the norm in motion, a throne made from the seven precious stones. The Buddha sits down on it in the sitting position of meditation (*paryaṅka*). He lets that ray of light emanate forth from his body again which illuminates everything and dispels the darkness of the worlds, and the earth shakes and roars without causing fear. Passion, hatred and all lower emotions are silent in the entire circuit of the Earth; all creatures are filled with friendliness and goodwill towards one another at this moment. From the ray of light the following heavenly words sound forth:

> The One who descended from his dwelling in Tuṣita into his mother's womb, who after having been born in the Lumbinī grove was taken into Indra's arms, who executed the seven steps like a lion, who renounced the world for the salvation of all creatures, who practised austerities, vanquished Māra and gained the enlightenment of a Buddha, he, having reached Benares, will now set the wheel of the norm in motion.

And all deities and the Bodhisattvas of all the heavenly regions and world spheres gather around the Buddha and ask him to set the wheel of the norm in motion 'for the salvation of many beings, for the happiness of many beings, from compassion with the world, for the wellbeing, the salvation, the happiness of the gods and mankind'. A Bodhisattva hands to the Buddha the wheel of the norm, decorated with wonders and signs of all kinds as it has already been set in motion by the Buddhas of former times. And gods and men set their eyes in silent excitement and meditation on the Buddha who will proclaim the doctrine to them.

During the first wake of the night Buddha shows his consent to the plea of the gods by his silence. During the second wake of the night he engages in light-hearted conversation. In the third wake of the night he then turns to the five disciples and says:

> Two paths, my disciples, are to be avoided by one who has entered the spiritual life: the path of the satisfaction of sensual desire (*kāma*) which is low, mean, unworthy of the noble and pointless, which does not lead to the holy life, to renunciation, to freedom from passion, to realization, to awakening, to *nirvāṇa;* and the path of self-torture which is painful and pointless, and which is followed by suffering in this visible as well as in the future life. Avoiding these two directions, the Tathāgata is proclaiming the *norm of the middle path* which is right vision, right thought, right speech, right action, right living, right effort, right awareness, right meditation. These, my disciples, are the four noble truths of suffering, of the origin of suffering, of the annihilation of suffering, of the path which

leads to the annihilation of suffering: birth is suffering, old age is suffering, illness is suffering, death is suffering, to be united with what one does not love or separated from loved ones is suffering, not obtaining one's wishes is suffering—in short, the five ways of grasping the sensual [sic] are suffering. The origin of suffering is sensual desire (*tṛṣṇā*, 'thirst'), which leads to rebirth, is accompanied by passion which lusts here and there. Overcoming suffering is the annihilation of sensual desire, the perfect freedom from passion. The path which leads to overcoming suffering is the noble eightfold path: right vision, right thoughts (decision), right speech, right action, right living, right effort, right awareness, right meditation. These, my disciples are the four noble truths. In realizing these, the spiritual eye, the knowledge, the realization, the insight, the truth about previously unknown, unheard-of norms dawned on me. As long as I, my disciples, had not realized those four noble truths from their foundations in my mind, I was unable to awaken to the highest Buddha enlightenment. But when the truth about the four noble truths had dawned on me, the liberation of the heart and the liberation of knowledge which is no longer to be shaken by anything was gained; at that moment, my disciples, I awakened to the highest Buddha enlightenment, thus I realized. The eye of realization was opened to me, destroyed is my birth, completed is the holy course of life, fulfilled is the duty, henceforth there will not be a return to being in the world.

d) Buddha's *Nirvaṇa* (according to the Mahāparinibbānasutta)

12. *The great Parinirvāṇa (mahāparinirvāṇa,* Pali *mahāparinibbāna).*[*] To the Buddha who was staying on the Gṛdhrakūṭa ('Vulture Peak') mountain near Rājagṛha has come an envoy of King Ajātaśatru of Magadha in order to ask him on behalf of the king for advice concerning a war planned by Ajātaśatru against the confederation of the Vṛjji (Pali *Vajji*). The Buddha advises peace: 'As long as the Vṛjji stick together in right harmony, as long as they preserve the pure doctrine,

[*] The 'great *parinirvāṇa,*' although mentioned (p. 29) as one of the 12 main events, is not told in the *Lalitavistara.* It forms the content of self-contained works among which the Mahāparinibbānasutta (abbrev. MPS) from the *Dīghanikāya* is the oldest and most famous. (See also about this work above, p. 33). The above description follows this account. (Page numbers refer to Childers' edition.) The language of the text is Pali. Thus many personal names had to be given in their Pali form in the following. It has to be noted that between the above-mentioned events and those related here the entire public activity of the Buddha lies, which spanned decades.

show respect to their elders and honour justice and custom everywhere by preserving tradition, so long the Vṛjji will prosper and not go downhill.' Continuing with the words spoken to the envoy, the Holy One then speaks to his disciples about the norms whose observation guarantees growth and prosperity: 'As long as you, my disciples, show respect to your elders, preserve the pure doctrine and keep to the norms which I have given you, so long you will prosper and not go downhill.' The Buddha's admonitions again and again culminate in three aspects: right moral conduct (*śīla*), spiritual meditation (*samādhi*), insight (*paññā*). 'Beneficial and fruitful is meditation if it is carried by right conduct, beneficial and fruitful is insight if it is based on right meditation, and pervaded by such an insight the soul becomes free from all delusion of sinful passion and illusion.'*

A large group of disciples accompanied the Buddha on his last journey which led him initially from Rājagṛha via Ambalaṭṭhika and Nālandā to Pāṭaligāma. Just then, servants of King Ajātaśatru are busy laying the foundations for the later town and fortress of Pāṭaliputra which is to be built as a bastion against the enemy. Seeing this, the Buddha has a vision which he communicates to his disciple, Ānanda. With his 'divine, clairvoyant, superhuman eye' he sees how hosts of divine beings hover around the place of the future Pāṭaliputra. He explains to Ānanda that in those places where powerful beings protect the ground, powerful rulers feel compelled to erect their abodes. The king of Magadha's undertaking thus appeared to have the gods' consent. And he foretells the future flourishing of the town of Pāṭaliputra and the causes for its ruin one day.

By supernatural powers the Buddha crosses the Gaṅgā which has just swollen immensely (Chap. 1) and reaches Koṭigāma. There, he reminds his disciples of the 'four noble truths', whose non-realization was the cause of the long journey they all had to travel in the cycle of births.

> But now, my disciples, the noble truth of suffering, of the cause of suffering, of the annihilation of suffering, of the path to the annihilation of suffering has been pervaded and realized; the desire to be in the world has been exterminated with its roots, annihilated has been that worldly desire which leads to existence; there is henceforth no return (*ucchinnā bhavataṇhā khīṇā bhavanetti n'atthidānipunabbhavo*).

---

*This formula, which is important for an understanding of Buddhism, returns verbatim in different speeches (MPS pp. 8, 10, 16, 18, 21, 38, 40 ed. Childers).

Via Nādikā the journey continues to Vaiśālī (Pali *Vesālī*) where the Buddha stays in the mango grove belonging to Ambapālī the dancer. Here, he admonishes the disciples to remain in calmness and wakeful awareness. When Ambapālī learns that the Holy One is staying in her mango grove, she drives there in a magnificent carriage. Delighted and strengthened by the Buddha with spiritual counsel, the dancer asks him to take his food with her the next day. The Buddha expresses his consent through his silence. Following this, the Licchavi appear in ostentatious attire to ask the Holy One to take his food with them on the same day. When Ambapālī informs them that the Buddha had already given his consent to her, they offer a large sum to the dancer should she be willing to leave the hospitality to them. But Ambapālī replies that she would not give up the honour of such a meal for the entire town of Vaiśālī with all its wealth. The noblemen then approach the Buddha himself with their plea. The Holy One however denies it to them, referring to the consent he had already given to the dancer. Disappointed, the Licchavi withdraw. After having finished his meal, the Buddha again delights the dancer by his spiritual conversation. Out of gratitude, Ambapālī makes the mango grove over as a gift to him and the community of disciples.

Following this, the Buddha goes to the village of Beluva in order to observe the monsoon there for himself in seclusion,[*] instructing the disciples to return to Vaiśālī for the same purpose. In Beluva, he is overcome for the first time by an intense pain of an illness which takes him to the brink of death. The Buddha bears the pain in steadfast composure, calmly and consciously. He does not think that the time has come to enter into *parinirvāṇa* before he has spoken to his disciples once again. He thus conquers his physical suffering by his will, supporting himself on the strength which maintains life in him.[†] His disciple, Ānanda, approaches him in deep worry, expressing the hope that the master would not enter *nirvāṇa* before having spoken to the disciples once more. The Buddha replies that he had communicated the norm as he was called to teach it in all its entirety, without holding back

[*] It used to be customary among Buddhist monks to spend the monsoon (the time of the most excessive natural experience and growth in India) in quiet seclusion in one particular place.

[†] *jīvitasaṇkhāra*. In Buddhism and in Yoga, the term *saṅkhāra*, Skt. *saṃskāra*, means those forces of the soul that work on the formation of the physical. The Buddha (just like the holy men of the Yoga school) masters these (otherwise subconscious) forces by his conscious will.

the best as other teachers might do. His 80-year-old body was now weak and frail from old age, and was carrying itself along laboriously and creakily like an old cart. It was now up to the disciples to be a light and refuge to each other, to make the norm their light and refuge and to persevere in wakeful mindfulness (Chap. 2).

Having returned from a begging round to Vaiśālī, Buddha directs the request to Ānanda to accompany him to the sacred place (*cetiya*) Cāpāla. When they are there, he praises the loveliness of the area in his conversation with the disciple. 'Charming, O Ānanda, is Vaiśālī, charming are its sacred places; whoever, O Ānanda, allows the four elements of supernatural perfection (*iddhi*, Skt. *ṛddhi*) to become strong in himself can, if he wants to, prolong his life until the end of the era. The Tathāgata however, O Ānanda, rules and masters the four elements of supernatural power and has attained the highest perfection in this; he could, if he wanted to, prolong his physical existence until the end of the era.' Not understanding the clear hint which has been given to him, Ānanda rests in silence because Māra has beguiled his heart. For a second and a third time, the Buddha speaks in the same words about the beauty of all earthly things and the possibility to prolong earthly existence by the power of the mind, but even now Ānanda does not have the intuition to ask his master to stay in existence. The Buddha then dismisses his disciple from his presence and Ānanda sits down under a tree to one side. Soon Māra, the tempter, approaches the Buddha and whispers to him the request to enter *parinirvāṇa* now. As on the earlier occasion, the Buddha invokes his earthly task which was his duty to fulfil to the last; as long as not all male and female disciples, all lay brothers and lay sisters had not attained firmness in all parts of the holy doctrine and the holy life, he could not think of departing from earthly existence. Then Māra asks him to consider how all this had been fulfilled in rich measures and that a lasting and safe place had been prepared for the holy doctrine and the holy life. The Holy One replies: 'Be unconcerned, you spiteful one, the Tathāgata's extinguishing will happen shortly; three months from today the Tathāgata will enter the great otherworldly *nirvāṇa*.' After he has given this promise to Māra, Buddha divests himself in mindful consciousness of the power of the soul (*jīvitasaṅkhāra*) which works in him as the cause of physical existence. Earthquakes and rolling thunder accompany this inner process. Upon these apparitions, astonishment arises in Ānanda. He approaches the Buddha again and asks him about the reason for earthquake and thunder. The Buddha replies to him that an earthquake, if it is not caused by processes in the water, air and ether layers of the interior of the earth and the behaviour of the beings working in the natural processes, happens with all those occurrences which are the main milestones in the biography of a Buddha: when the Bodhisattva, descending from heavenly heights, enters the mother's womb in mindful consciousness, when he is born on earth, when he awakens to the highest enlightenment of a Buddha, when he starts the wheel of the norm, when he divests himself of the power of the soul which works in him as the cause of physical existence, and finally when he, shedding all substrates of physicality, enters into the great *nirvāṇa*. And now he tells his disciple about Māra's request and how he had just now divested himself of the power of the soul working in himself as the cause of physical existence following the promise given to the tempter. Ānanda then asks his master: 'May the Holy One remain, may the Blessed One remain in existence until the end of the era, out of compassion for the world, for the wellbeing, for the salvation, for the happiness of gods and men.' But the Buddha reminds him how he had earlier—at Rājagṛha and more recently at Vaiśālī in different places and on different occasions, most recently here at the sacred place of Cāpāla—spoken to his disciple about the beauty of all things earthly and about the possibility of prolonging one's physical existence by the power of the mind, and how it had been wrong of him, Ānanda, to have failed to direct the request at the Tathāgata to remain in existence for longer in spite of having received a clear hint. Once he had divested himself of something he was unable to take it back. Now he had divested himself of the power of the soul working in himself as the cause of physical existence and had promised to Māra to enter the great otherworldly *nirvāṇa* within three months. It would violate the unalterable law of the order of the world if the Tathāgata took back his word for the sake of physical existence; this could never happen. And the Buddha warns his disciple to remember the doctrine which he had impressed upon him before, that everything born, everything that has become, everything created by the formative forces was by necessity subject to decay, and that one had to part with, say farewell to and avoid everything dear, everything on which one's heart was set. The Buddha then asks Ānanda to call all disciples to the assembly hall and again entrusts them to remain steady in the holy life for the wellbeing of all beings, from compassion for the world, for the salvation of gods and men. He reminds them of the supernatural powers of the Holy One and of the noble eightfold path and admonishes them to faithfully keep the doctrines given for the salvation of the world and of all beings.

> Well then, my disciples, I am saying to you: Everything created by the formative forces is subject to the law of passing, be steady in your striving efforts; the Tathāgata's extinguishing will happen shortly, three months from today the Tathāgata will enter into the great *nirvāṇa* (Chap. 3).

Having returned from his begging round, the Holy One casts a final noble parting glance upon the town of Vaiśālī. 'Now, O Ānanda, the Tathāgata beholds Vaiśālī for the last time.' At Bhaṇḍagāma, the next destination of their journey, he speaks to the disciples again:

> There are four noble norms, my disciples, whose non-realization has led to this our long journey through the cycle of births and rebirths: right conduct (*śīla*), meditation (*samādhi*), realisation (*paññā*) and liberation (*vimutti*). But now the norms of conduct, of meditation, realization and liberation have been penetrated, the desire for worldly existence has been destroyed, henceforth there is no return.

The journey leads via Haṭṭhigāma, Ambagāma, Jambugāma and Bhoganagara to Pāva. The Holy One stays there in the mango grove of Cunda, the goldsmith. Inspired by the Buddha and his spiritual encouragement, Cunda asks the Buddha and his disciples to take their meal with him. The Buddha expresses his consent by remaining silent. At the meal, a dish of wild pig (*sūkaramaddava*)* is served among other exquisite fare. Buddha gives the instruction to serve this dish to him alone and the other dishes to his disciples. After finishing his meal, he orders the leftovers to be buried in a pit as 'no being in all the worlds of

---

* *sūkara* means 'pig, wild pig', *maddava* 'softness, mildness'. This combination (which does not occur elsewhere in the entire literature) of the two words is usually explained as 'meat of a wild pig'. An alternative viewpoint which takes *sūkaramaddava* ('boar's mildness, boar's lust' or the like) as a provincial name of an edible species of mushroom has recently been presented by an expert (Andersen in the glossary of his Pāli-reader, p. 201 [Dinesh Andersen, *A Pali Reader with Notes and Glossary*, Copenhagen, 1907.]) as a possibility worth discussing. But even this hypothesis does not provide a safe solution [to the problem of the Buddha possibly consuming meat; *transl. note*].

the gods and men are able to digest this dish in the proper way except for the Tathāgata.'*

After pleasing Cunda, the goldsmith, with spiritual discourse, Buddha falls into heavy dysentery soon after the meal and strong pain appears, death's harbinger. Buddha bears the pain with composure, in mindful consciousness (*sato sampajāno*) and orders Ānanda to continue with him to Kuśinagara (Pali *Kusinārā*).

On the way, he is overcome by tiredness and thirst. Resting under a tree, he asks Ānanda for water. Ānanda thinks that the water nearby was muddy, since 500 passing chariots had just stirred up the ground, but there was a river with clear water not too far away; the Holy One should quench his thirst there. Buddha repeats his plea, Ānanda his concerns. Only upon his master's third request does the disciple do as bidden and lo! the water whose ground had just been stirred up by the wheels of the 500 vehicles flows pure and clear. Stricken with amazement, Ānanda praises the supernatural power of the Tathāgata. The Holy One then drinks the water.

After this, they meet Pukkusa, a noble man from the lineage of the Malla who is just on the way from Kusinārā to Pāvā and who is a former pupil of Ārāḍa Kālāpa (Pali *Āḷāro Kālāmo*). All that Pukkusa hears about the Buddha's strength in the concentration of the mind impresses him so strongly that he asks the Holy One to accept him as his pupil by taking his refuge in the Buddha, the norm and the community. To thank the master, he leaves him a pair of exquisite golden garments as a present. The Buddha orders that one of the garments should be put on him, the other on Ānanda. After Pukkusa has taken leave, Ānanda puts the second garment also on the Buddha and soon the Holy One's body shines as white as snow (literally: 'like white leprosy'). Full of astonishment and wonder, Ānanda beholds the luminous glow which outshines even the golden colour of the two garments. Buddha instructs his disciple that the body of the Perfected One would glow twice during his lifetime: first during that night where

* This instruction and its justification would indeed be somewhat strange if ordinary pork was mentioned here. But even the assumption that it was mushrooms among which there were several poisonous ones—Buddha had realized this and for that reason had denied their consumption to his disciples—would only explain this matter in a very external way, and it appears as if especially for this passage a deeper, spiritual interpretation has to be sought. Senart also expresses himself in this sense, *Légende du Buddha*, p. 332. [Beckh refers to Émile Senart, *Essai sur la Légende du Buddha*, E. Leroux, Paris, 2nd edition, 1882.]

he awakens to the enlightenment of a Buddha, and the second time during that night during which he, shedding the substrata of physicality, entered the great otherworldly *nirvāṇa*. Today, during the last wake of the night, the Tathāgata would enter the great *nirvāṇa* at Kusināra in the grove of the Malla between two Sala trees.

After a bath in the river Kakutthā the tired Buddha lies down in the adjacent mango grove for a rest. Before that, he instructs Ānanda to reassure Cunda, the goldsmith, in case the thought should weigh on him that upon enjoying the meal served by him the Holy One had departed this life. Two meals in the life of the Buddha were blessed and fruitful before all others: the dish he takes before awakening to the enlightenment of a Buddha, and then the meal which he enjoys before entering the great otherworldly *nirvāṇa*. Cunda had done a meritorious act to him which would become a blessing to him in this and in the other world.

By the river Hiranyavatī (Pali *Hiraññavatī*) near Kusināra the Buddha reaches the destination of his journey. In the Sala grove of the Mallas, between two twin trees, he has Ānanda prepare his last resting place for him, with the head towards the north. There he lies down in exhaustion, resting like a lion. Although it is not the season of their flowering, the two Sala trees are in full bloom and showers of blossoms rain down on the body of the dying Holy One. The Holy One then says to Ānanda:

> Covered all over with flowers, O Ānanda, although it is not the time of their flowering, are the two Sala trees, and they let a shower of flowers pour down on the body of the Tathāgata, heavenly flowers from the tree in Indra's paradise are falling from above in honour of the Tathāgata, heavenly sandal scents fill the air and descend on the body of the Tathāgata, and heavenly music from strings and heavenly singing resounds on high in honour and praise of the Tathāgata. But the Tathāgata is due another praise and higher honours. Disciples, men and woman, lay brothers and lay sisters, who are steadfast in the norm and keep to the right way, those pay the Tathāgata the true and right honours.

The disciple standing in front of him, fanning him, is now sent away by the Buddha, upon which Ānanda expresses his surprise to the master that he sends the disciple away now in the hour of parting after he had served him loyally for such a long time. But the Buddha enlightens him that just at this moment, flocks of deities from all world spheres have come in order to see the Tathāgata face to face for a last time. The tiniest space of the Sala grove and for miles around is now entirely occupied by exalted beings. And the deities are thinking: 'We have come from afar to see the Tathāgata, for it happens only rarely, over long periods of time, that a Tathāgata arises in the world, a holy, perfect Buddha. Today now, this very night, the Tathāgata enters the great *nirvāṇa*, but now this highly eminent *bhikṣu* is standing in front of the Holy One so that we cannot come closer in order to see the Tathāgata face to face for the last time.' And Buddha continues to speak about how deities of the air and the earth are now also possessed by the pain of parting and how the mournful thought moved them: 'Far too soon the Holy One will enter the great *nirvāṇa*, far too soon the Blessed One will be extinguished, far too soon the light of the world will set.'

The Buddha then speaks of those sacred places which after his passing will become the destination of pious pilgrimage.

> Four, O Ānanda, are the places that a pious son from a noble house shall behold and where his heart shall be moved: the place where the Tathāgata was born; the place where he awakened to the highest Buddha enlightenment; the place where he set the wheel of the norm in motion, and the place where he, shedding all substance of bodily existence, enters the highest *nirvāṇa*. And disciples male and female, lay brothers and sisters will visit these places and say to themselves with a pious heart: here the Tathāgata was born; here he awakened to the highest Buddha enlightenment; here he set the wheel of the norm, the incomparable, in motion; here he entered, into highest *nirvāṇa*, shedding all substance of bodily existence. And those on such a pilgrimage, having attained a calm heart, who pass from temporal existence, they will after the decay of the body, enter the blissfulness of the heavenly world.

Upon Ānanda's question what should be done with the physical remains of the Tathāgata, the Buddha admonishes him not to let himself be led away from the path of spiritual striving by worrying about these things. Noblemen and Brahmins who in their hearts are favourable to the Tathāgata, will care for the body which is to be burned with all those honours due to the body of a ruler of the world.

At this point, Ānanda is overcome by the pain of separation; he returns inside the hall and goes to a quiet place and there breaks out into tears and lamentations: 'I am still at the beginning of my apprenticeship, I still have to learn a lot, and my master, who had compassion with me, will now enter the great *nirvāṇa*.' The Buddha realizes his disciple's absence, has another disciple call Ānanda to him and says to him kindly:

> Enough, Ānanda, do not mourn, do not lament. Have I not taught you already that everything that is born, that has become, that has originated from formative forces, is by necessity subject to decay, and that one has to take leave from and miss everything dear, everything on which the heart hangs. But you, O Ānanda, you have been serving the Tathāgata for a long time with unlimited, unselfish, devoted love, with kindness in thought, word and deed, just stay firm in arduous effort and you will soon be free from all sinful passion.

Before the disciples the Buddha praises Ānanda's sensible feeling for what is proper which always teaches him to say the right thing in the right moment and to remain silent in the right moment.

One disciple worries that the small Kusināra was not a place worthy of the *parinirvāṇa* of the Holy One. The Buddha dispels this with a reference to the greatness and affluence of Kusinārā in times long past where it saw happy days as the capital of a powerful king. All this lies open to the Buddha's clairvoyance. He then orders Ānanda to give notice to the Mallas, the noblemen of Kusināra, of his imminent passing that very night, so that they should not be overcome afterwards by regret at the thought that they had missed seeing the Tathāgata face to face before his passing while he was still close by. The Mallas receive the news while occupied with a discussion of public affairs. In bewildered pain they fall to the ground and lament: 'Far too soon the Holy One will enter the great *nirvāṇa,* far too soon the Blessed One will be extinguished, far too soon the light of the world will set.' They then hurry with all their families to the Sala grove where they are introduced by Ānanda to the Buddha in family groups on account of the shortness of the time. Even an ascetic of another sect, Subhadda, appears in order to hear the doctrine from the master's own lips at the last hour, 'for only rarely, over the course of a long time, a Tathāgata appears in the world, a holy, perfected Buddha'. When Ānanda seeks to prevent him from entering in view of the master's tired state, the Buddha notices and orders the ascetic to be brought in. Ānanda communicates the master's wish to Subhadda: 'Come closer, venerable Subhadda, the Holy One is asking for you.' And the Buddha explains to Subhadda who had been confused by the maze of teachings and schools how the essence and epitome of all norms is the 'noble eightfold path', the true following of the path, and everything else is only empty school quarrelling and how outside of that path one cannot speak of any level of true discipleship. Subhadda's eye of realization is opened at this:

> It is wonderful, it is amazing. It is as if when one straightens out something that had been bent or opens something that was hidden, or when one shows the right way to one who was lost, or when one puts a light on in the dark so that whoever has eyes may see. In this way the Holy One has revealed to me the norm from many different points of view. I take my refuge to the Holy One, to the norm and to the community of disciples.

Thus Subhadda receives ordination through Ānanda as the last of the disciples accepted into the community by the Buddha himself. Within a short time, he reaches the level of *arhat* (saint).

Once again, the Buddha turns to Ānanda:

> The thought may occur to you, O Ānanda, that the doctrine was now orphaned, that you did not have a teacher anymore. You must not take it like that. But the norm and the instruction which I have shown you and in which I have taught you shall be your teacher after my passing.

After having given a few last orders regarding pending community affairs, the Buddha reminds all disciples that whoever had any doubts regarding the doctrine or the path may ask him now so that later on they should not be overcome by regret that they had failed to ask the teacher while he was still among them. Whoever from shyness did not want to ask him directly should open his soul to a friend. The disciples' general silence is taken by Ānanda to mean that none has any doubts and Ānanda's presupposition is elevated to certainty by the Buddha:

> You are speaking on faith, O Ananda, but for the Tathāgata it is known: there is not a single disciple in this entire assembly who has any doubts regarding the doctrine or the path, none who has not attained at least the first level of the path to *arhat*-hood and is not heading with a steadfast mind towards enlightenment.

And the Buddha addresses his disciples with his last words: 'Well then, my disciples, I am speaking to you: subject to impermanence is everything that originated from the formative forces, remain in striving effort.' Then the Holy One rises to the first and further up to the fourth level of meditation (*jhāna*, Skt. *dhyāna*), from there to the 'sphere of the infinity of the space ether' (*ākāsānañcāyatana*), from there to the 'sphere of the infinity of consciousness' (*viññāṇañcāyatana*), from there to the 'sphere of nothingness' (*ākiñcaññāyatana*, see above, p. 53); exiting again from the sphere of nothingness he reaches the 'sphere above the conscious and unconscious' (*nevasaññānāsaññāyatana*, see above, p. 54), from there to the extinguishing of the perception of consciousness (*saññāvedayita-nirodha*). Going through all these levels backwards, he again reaches the first level of meditation and after raising himself again to the fourth level, the Holy One enters the otherworldly *nirvāṇa* (*parinibbāna*) from there. And when the Buddha enters the great *nirvāṇa*, the earth trembles and thunder rolls, from heavenly heights the gods Indra and Brahmā speak the verse of the impermanence of everything created and of the bliss of liberation. Deeply moved Ānanda points out the significance of the event. Among the disciples some remain composed, others give themselves to passionate expressions of grief, and with them mourn the deities of the earth and the air and join in the lamentation: 'All too soon the Holy One has entered the great *nirvāṇa*, all too soon the Blessed One has been extinguished, all too soon the light of the world has set.' But the venerable Anuruddha admonishes them to compose themselves and reminds them of the words of the Perfected One that all that is born and become is subject to decay and that one has to bear separation and taking leave from everything that is dear.

The Mallas of Kusināra also give themselves to all expressions of pain when they hear the news about the Buddha's *nirvāṇa* from Ānanda. They lament that the Holy One was extinguished too soon, the light of the world had set too soon. Then they arrange a magnificent funeral reception, and when they have honoured the body of the Holy One with dancing, singing and performances, perfumes and garlands for six days, they prepare for the cremation of the body on the seventh day. Outside the Eastern towngate the Mallas, obeying the wish of the gods as communicated by Anuruddha, have erected the funeral pyre, and the Buddha's physical remains are made over to the flames with all the honours befitting the body of a ruler of the world. The gods themselves ignite the pyre and the body burns without leaving any traces of ash or soot. The bones are divided into eight parts as relics and are given to kings and noble families who had been close to the Holy One during his lifetime. Each of the recipients – among them also the Śākya of Kapilavastu – erects a grave monument (*stūpa*) for the keeping of the relics, so that all the people may worship them reverently, 'for it is indeed difficult to obtain a Buddha in hundreds of world ages'.

B. The historical Buddha

a) The course of his life

It is sufficiently clear from the narrative itself that the narrative of the Buddha's life as we tried to relate it on the previous pages according to the sources does not even want to constitute that which we call a historical report. This is especially true for the story of the Buddha's becoming in the *Lalitavistara,* but also everywhere in the Mahāparinibbānasutta the possibly historical has been interwoven with the legendary. In the attempt to 'decipher' the legend, scholarship has fallen into diverse fallacies. The most spirited of these fallacies was the solar hypothesis of the French scholar, Senart. The legend wants to illustrate spiritual events not atmospheric or astronomical ones (Senart himself speaks of *symbolisme atmosphérique,* see *Légende du Buddha,* p. 331); it narrates the inner spiritual course of development of Buddha in the same way the Buddhist seer views this course of development with his spiritual eye. But it should not be contradicted that these images in several respects touch the mythologies of the sun and other mythological and mystical concepts which go back to the depths of the Veda, yes, even to an older primal age. The mistake of those theories is their materialistic externalization of that which is to be grasped spiritually. If this mistake is eliminated, many valuable viewpoints and indications can be found in Senart's study.

Few serious scholars have doubted the fact that the Buddha was a historical person. Even Senart, the creator of the solar hypothesis, did not contest this (*Légende du Buddha,* p. 441 ff.). And if it has been said of the legend, especially of the story of the Buddha's becoming related in the *Lalitavistara,* that it illustrates inner spiritual events in the images of the myth and mysticism, this is not to dispute that memories of real external events may have also entered that narrative. With the gospel of the dying [of the Buddha] such an existence of historical elements is beyond doubt.

For example, the relic mount referred to in the end of that narrative which the Śākya of Kapilavastu are said to have erected over that part of the bones that fell to them, was found near Piprāva in 1898. In its inner chamber there was an urn marked by an inscription as the 'container of the relics of the holy Buddha from the race of the Śākya'. The authenticity of this find has so far not been challenged much. (Sceptical Franke, *Dīghanikāya,* p. 254).[1] All legendary texts, even those—like the *Lalitavistara*—that are much further from the sphere of the historical than the Mahāparinibbānasutta narrate the Buddha's affiliation to the Śākya race which is proven by this find. This alone shows that none of these texts contains merely phantasies or mere mysticism, but that they all relate to external facts, even where the narrators are concerned with the depiction of spiritual events in images. In detail however, the separation of the historical from the mystical-mythical-legendary is often difficult or impossible. Of that which remains after deducting that which is undoubtedly legendary, much may be historical, but no secure proof can be provided for any particular case. But to present that which is merely unproven as refuted is just as unscholarly as naïvely accepting the unproven. It is thus advisable to recur to the high-flying 'science has established' (in the positive as in the negative sense) as little as possible in those contexts where it is in the nature of things that only a weighing of probabilities is possible. If thus in the following the attempt is made to submit the life of the Buddha to a historical appreciation, it has to be clear from the beginning that the number of 'secure results' (in the general sense of the term) is not to be won from such an observation.

Regarding the time of the Buddha's birth no consensus has been reached; if—following dominant opinion—477 or 480 BCE is taken as the year of his death, the time of his birth would then, taking into account credible indications about the Buddha's life span, fall roughly into the middle of the sixth century BCE. The Buddha's affiliation to the Śākya race—thus the epithet *Śākyamuni,* the 'Holy One from the Śākya race'—is transmitted consistently by all the sources; after the above-mentioned find of the burial mount, it may be taken to be as historical with that probability which may at all be reached in these matters. We may also in agreement with Oldenberg (op. cit., p. 112 ff.)[2] take as historical the name of Buddha's hometown of Kapilavastu. The fact that the name of the town contains perhaps a reference to Kapila, the ancient *ṛṣi* and reputed founder of the Sāṃkhya-philosophy, cannot form an objection to this. For even if that assumption is true, one would have to say: not because similarities with the terminology of Sāṃkhya can be found in the Buddha's teaching has later invention named his hometown after Kapila, but because Sāṃkhya was current in Buddha's hometown—as the name Kapilavastu implies—the Buddha took some of the terminology of this system into his own teaching. The town was situated in the extreme north of India, close to the snow-capped mountains. Rhys Davids who visited the area[3] mentions that all year round one can see the snow-capped peaks of the Himalayas. From here, northerly winds carry a cool breeze from the glaciers (*Early Buddhism*, p. 28).[4] Most scholars believe the tradition regarding the name of the Buddha's father, Śuddhodana, but even this has received mythological interpretation.* His kingly status however is predominantly disputed by scholarship. It may already be deducted from the narrative of the *Lalitavistara* itself that he cannot have been a true king or autocrat, where in all important matters the elders of the Śākya are approached by Śuddhodana for a joint decision. According to this, his position would have been rather that of a *primus inter pares* in a feudal system of state than that of a true king. But even this latter status the latest scholarship wants to contest and allow him to have been only a 'noble landowner'. Unbiased observation however will hardly be able to reach the conclusion that the predicate *rājā* which is simply connected everywhere with the name of the Buddha's father is to be taken differently in its probability or improbability than the name Śuddhodana. One will have to just think of a wealthy ruler of a small area. (Windisch also, *Buddhas Geburt*, p. 1,[5] does not take it as absolutely necessary to deny Śuddhodana the predicate *rājā*.) The fact that the Jain tradition which in so many aspects follows the Buddhist has also branded the founder of their sect as a prince does not force us to consider the case of the Buddha as a mere fabrication, too. This question is among those where comprehensive certainty is not to be won with the means of philological research. Modern criticism brings less scepticism towards the name of the mother, queen Māyā, than towards the princely title of the Buddha's father. But maybe doubt is especially valid in this context. Where we cannot obtain certainty, we have to say: she may have been called Māyā, and it is possible that even in reality such revealing names occur in a suitable place, but the circumstance that Māyā is not otherwise known as a female name in India in con-

---

*The usual division of the name in *śuddha*, 'pure' and *odana*, 'rice dish' is linguistically indisputable and has given rise to a number of conclusions on the cultivation of rice in Buddha's home country. Senart (op. cit., p. 316) finds this explanation unsatisfying. From the point of view of his solar hypothesis, an interpretation appears plausible to him which in the final part of the name sees a contraction of *udayana* 'rise' (sunrise). The claim that the name can make on historical validity would be diminished by this interpretation.

nection with the metaphysical meaning of the term, which strongly suggests itself here, puts a lot of weight into the other side of the scales. It is far less important that *māyā* was not a technical term in the earliest Buddhism or in the Sāṃkhya system, for the term *māyā* as the divine power of illusion (also conceived of as a mystical female principle of creation)* is generally Indian, and the Buddha legend everywhere refers to a mysticism which is, as Senart already pointed out, far more comprehensive than the narrow early Buddhist teaching.

With the Buddha's birth in the grove at Lumbinī, related in such a fairytale-like manner in the *Lalitavistara* and the *Nidānakathā*, the indication of the place may correspond to an external fact. Near the village of Rummindēi (modern Indian for Lumbinī) a pillar has been found which was erected by King Aśoka in memory of the birth of the Buddha. It carries the inscription 'Here the Buddha was born, the Holy One from the Śākya race.' In the first instance, this only proves that 200 years after Buddha's death this was taken to be the place of his birth in agreement with the sacred tradition. However, this lends weight to the probability that in this case the memory of a true event has been preserved. Among the probable events of the legend is also the indication that the mother died soon after the birth of the child. The Buddhist generalization that the mother of every Buddha would die seven days after the birth and would be carried away to heavenly bliss is not in contradiction with this assumption. Quite obviously a true event has given rise to this dogma. From an earthly point of view, the birth of the Buddha thus appears to have not been as painless as the *Lalitavistara* depicts it from the point of view of the supernatural. With regard to the name of Buddha's step-mother, Mahāprajāpatī (*mahāprajāvatī*, 'great mother, [mother of many offspring]'), similar things hold true as for the name Māyā.

The story of the seer Asita, the Buddhist Simeon, leads to some problems of interest. It has already been pointed out (see also p. 230) that it is impossible at present to reach certain conclusions with the means of external research. The motif of a seer predicting the future fate of the newborn child is common in many (even Indian) fairytales and legends.

The story of the Buddha's youth has more legendary characteristics than any other. Yet it is not without deeper significance if the story-

---

* *māyāṃ tu prakṛtiṃ vidyān māyinaṃ tu maheśvaram* 'as māyā (magic, magical illusion) know nature and god as the magician' says the Śvetāśvatara Upaniṣad.

tellers insert supernatural experiences especially into those of the Buddha's childhood. The experience under the rose apple tree is not without significance for the appreciation of the Buddha's personality. Of course it is obvious that this story, as it is related to us in the *Lalitavistara* and other texts, does not contain events which some chronicler recorded. The child meditating in the seclusion of nature, the *ṛṣis* flying through the air and stopped by the power of the meditation, the voices of the gods etc. – all this refers to an entirely different area than that of the external events, namely the area of the supernatural, of meditation, Yoga. This area contains such an important key for the understanding of Buddhism. Inner psychological reasons – quite apart from all external historical considerations – support the fact that an inclination towards meditation which played such an important part in the Buddha's life already came through on a few occasions in the early years of childhood – and especially here, in the time before puberty. From this point of view this particular scene, so remote from the sphere of the external historical, contains an inner truth and shows us much more than others what the 'legend' actually is about and how it needs to be read and understood.

Most scholars take it as a fact that the Buddha was married before appearing in public as a spiritual teacher. Some have pointed out that, considering the entire position of Buddhism towards women and to the precept of chastity, fiction should have been more inclined to obscure an actual marriage of the master than to fabricate one that did not exist (Oldenberg, *Buddha*, p. 122). And certainly, this consideration is well founded, even if one may also say that the thought of 'renunciation' can be expressed more effectively if Buddha relinquishes a marital bliss already attained than if he had shunned it from the start. How far we are from actual historical certainty also in this context is shown by the vacillating of the texts regarding the name: in the *Lalitavistara*, the wife of the Buddha is called Gopā or Yaśovatī, the *Mahāvastu* calls her Yaśodharā, in some Pali texts the name Bhaddakaccānā occurs, the *Nidānakathā* only speaks of the 'mother of Rāhula'. This son Rāhula who, according to the *Nidānakathā*, is born just before the 'great parting', according to other texts is born only later, and the *Mahāvastu* relates in a meaningfully-poetic way the meeting between the master and his son when the former returns to his hometown as the Buddha after his enlightenment. In the *Lalitavistara*, Rāhula is not mentioned at all, and yet he appears to have been a historical person (a fact which would consequently also decide the question of the Buddha's marriage in the affirmative), and he is mentioned by the texts as a member of the community of disciples. The story of the contest before the wedding does not contain anything that could be taken with any certainty or even probability as an external event. Only that Buddha was a delicate, physically weak child who stayed away from the games of the companions of his own age appears to shimmer through the narrative like a memory of a fact. That the strength of a strong spiritual will enables him early on to achieve accomplishments that surprised those who took him for a weakling on account of his appearance, is, as such, not improbable. But the contest for the bride and the cocking and shooting of the bow which nobody can cock is a widespread fairytale motif. Furthermore, the story of the shooting of the bow in the *Lalitavistara* appears drenched in a plethora of symbolism through which the legend itself expresses that this is about other things than the reality of an external event. The entire story of the first meeting with Gopā and the ensuing contest is poetically one of the climaxes of the legend, but further removed from the sphere of the historical than other parts.

That a life in earthly happiness and overabundance preceded renunciation in the case of the Buddha creates the impression of a fact. If with the life in the women's quarters the legend speaks of 84,000 female dancers it is of course clear that this is not to be taken literally in the sense of an external fact; it can only mean that the Buddha was surrounded and crowded by all temptations of sensual desire, and it has an inner credibility that just this kind of experience had to inspire in him most strongly the longing for liberation from the sensuality that carries within itself the seed of death.

In the famous story of the four excursions this thought has found an especially moving poetical expression. Here again the 'historical' is very much in the background. Of course one can say that on some occasion the prince would have encountered the sights of old age, grave illness and death. One can also believe that his compassionate nature was moved by this sight. But the way the story is related in the legendary texts, especially in the *Lalitavistara* and the Mahāpadānasutta (in the latter in the context of Vipaśyin, a Buddha of previous eras) with that particular rhythmic sequence of encounters, clearly carries the stamp of poetry. What the 'argument from suffering' expresses in the abstraction of thought here seems to have been as it were unfolded into temporal events. One could say that it has been translated from the sphere of thinking into the imaginative, into a poetic-artistic form, and it is precisely this poetical and artistic of the legend which speaks so much more impressively to us today than the abstract thinking of Buddhist doctrinal sentences with their terminology which is often so foreign to us in its way of thought.

Whether the event of leaving the house, the 'great parting' then took place under such romantic circumstances as the legend relates has to remain a question. Much in the narrative—the voices from the air whispering to the prince, the visions in dreams and of gods—does not refer to external realities. The story of the horse Kaṇṭhaka, too (which was born in the same moment as the Buddha and which after 30 years still is the 'fiery horse'!) appears entirely spun into supernatural contingencies. We may remember how the Bodhisattva, when he parts from his horse after the nightly ride out, also sends away all the supernatural beings who until then have formed his retinue (*Lalitavistara*, p. 225 ed. Lefm.). If we discount the peripheral details and only focus on that which is essential in the narrative, the event of leaving home for religious reasons is not such an unusual step in the Indian context which at the time was taken by many and undoubtedly also by the Buddha.

With the story and its geographical details following these events some appear to be true to the facts. The encounter with Ārāḍa Kālāpa and Rudraka Rāmaputra especially has an inner credibility. Given the entire relationship between Buddhism and Yoga and the significance of the personality of a specific teacher in Indian Yoga, it is almost certain that the Buddha had a teacher in Yoga. The names of the two Yogis appear to correspond to actual persons, and most details of the narrative give the impression of truly mirroring the way such circles operated in India at the time. It equally makes sense that the spiritual level to which these two teachers were able to lead the Buddha did not satisfy him, as the Buddha precisely wanted to go beyond ordinary Yoga.

The execution of ascetic practices that are spoken of [in the legend] following the previous events is in full accordance with that which was normal in India among the circles of those striving in a spiritual way in the sense of the Buddha. That Buddha then realized as unsatisfactory any one-sided external asceticism and that he turned away from it is entirely in keeping with the doctrine he later stood for and which differs in this respect from other Indian schools of thought and that of the lower Yoga (Haṭhayoga).

With regard to the climax of the legend, the famous narrative of how the Bodhisattva awakens to the enlightenment of a Buddha (*bodhi*) under the sacred fig tree at *Urubilvā* (Pali *Uruvelā*, today, Urel near Gayā) in the Holy Night and turns from Bodhisattva to Buddha, Oldenberg (op. cit., p. 130ff.) already pointed out that even if it was impossible that this was a historically ascertained event there are inner reasons for assuming that this narrative has a factual basis. It may be taken as one of the most certain facts to which we may be led by a deeper study of the Buddhist sources that Yoga-experiences formed the point of departure for the Buddha's work as a spiritual teacher, and our entire understanding of Buddhism thus in a certain sense depends on our correct understanding of this important point of the 'legend'. We will thus not regard the story of the enlightenment as a mere empty fabrication, and even with regard to the more detailed circumstances of the narrative some—next to much which refers to an exclusively supernatural realm, a realm of spiritual experience—may be according to the external facts. For example, it is not improbable that just the meditation of one night brought about the trigger to a breakthrough in spiritual vision in the Buddha; that he sat under a tree is likewise a strong possibility if we consider the Indian custom of the forest life of the ascetics, and it is also quite possible that his tree of the meditation was a sacred fig tree (*aśvattha*), although in particular the *Lalitavistara* does not explicitly mention this.

But still it would not be correct to put the main emphasis on the possibly existing actuality of a single moment of the narrative. Like the fight with Māra, so grotesquely-horribly depictured in the *Lalitavistara*, everything that the legend tells us in this part, forming its climax, refers to supernatural, spiritual events. It puts before us in powerful symbolism the real mystery of Buddhism which cannot be expressed in external terms but only grasped in meditation. The *aśvattha* itself, the tree of realization, is for that mystery of Buddhism the symbol **κατ' ἐξοχήν**. The ancient songs of the Atharvaveda (V, 4; VI, 95; XIX, 39) already call the *aśvattha* the place of the vision of *amṛta*, the heavenly nectar of immortal salvation (there embodied in the *kuṣṭha* herb). The enlightenment won by the Buddha is also called *amṛta* in Buddhism. Here one can see again how the images of the legend are rooted in a mystic tradition which is far older than Buddhism. In Buddhist art, too, which often provides us with valuable indications for the understanding of the spiritual problems of Buddhism, this significance of the *aśvattha* has been grasped in a notable way. For example, there is a depiction of the *bodhi* in relief (printed in de la Vallée-Poussin, *Bouddhisme*, p. 224)[6] where the foliage of the sacred tree grows out of the head of the meditating Buddha like a crown (see plates).

To many an occidental judge of these things, the fact that the Buddha had to wrestle the decision to reveal his newly-found realization to the world from himself in painful struggles of the soul, will not appear very plausible, for how (thus such a judge will say to himself) should someone who had found some truth not feel the urge soon after to make it public in order to shine and win further advantages with it. But given the intimate nature of the 'Buddha realization'—which stands opposed to everything which to the realization through the senses, to our human everyday consciousness counts as truth and reality as something entirely heterogeneous and which regards as unsubstantial everything that [our everyday] point of view takes for the truth and that which the latter takes as trivial as substantial. However, it has to appear psychologically quite reasonable to everyone who has only a remote idea of those things we are concerned with here, that the will to be silent about the newly-found realization suggests itself more readily than the desire to profane it by communicating it to the public where it is exposed to the danger of being misunderstood and deformed. As legendary, even fantastical as the entire narrative of the appearance of the god Brahmā, who requests the Holy One to save the world from imminent ruin by revealing the sacred truth, may appear to the modern reader, there stands behind this narrative—which as such is of course only a legend—the actual spiritual experience to which we have already referred. There are only a few points in the entire Buddha legend which have the same measure of inner credibility for deeper contemplation.

How far the story of the five disciples, maybe already the episode of Trapuṣa and Bhallika, contains memories of actual events will have to remain open; equally, whether the first revelation of the newly-found truth happened under the very or similar circumstances as the legend (cf. also the report of the Mahāvagga in the *Vinayapiṭaka* which essentially corresponds to that in the *Lalitavistara*) relates. More important to us appears the much disputed question whether the revelation itself had already the same phrasing in the Buddha's own words in which it is transmitted to us now.

To either affirm or negate this question with full certainty will never be possible with all the resources of philological acumen. It is self-evident that over the course of centuries a great deal has been fabricated and added to that which the Buddha said, that much, very much, has also been lost, much has been augmented, changed, deformed, and that sources of error have crept into the tradition. This is equally true for the texts of the Pali canon (which, even if it is only to be the canon of a single sect, namely that of the Vibhajyavādin, after all appears to transmit the original teaching in the relatively most faithful way). But to regard everything that these texts ascribe to the Buddha himself as an invention of later monks appears quite impossible. Some researchers have gone too far in their scepticism here. Whoever works seriously and for a long time on Buddhist literature, especially on the texts of the Pali canon, and who unbiasedly allows these texts to take effect will not be able to close themselves to the impression that in that which has been transmitted to us undoubtedly much has coalesced from diverse sources, but that within all this diversity a *kernel*, a core stands out which clearly carries the stamp of a definite, unified, superior personality. It is not only and in general the greatness and nobility of the thoughts that waft through the texts like a breath of that superior personality, but a certain Something in these thoughts which comes to bear especially in the details of phrasing, especially that unique flow of rhythms on which rests in many ways the effect of the ancient Pali texts in particular. This is a fact many have bypassed, but which, once consciously realized, can no longer be over-looked. The only question that remains is: who has to be thought of as that personality whose breath we feel in the texts, especially in the old Pali texts? The thought might arise that it may have been this or that disciple or follower of the Buddha who has had this kind of inspiring effect on the tradition, and who consequently would have to be regarded as the true spiritual creator of everything which exists in the canon as Buddhist doctrine today. However, this assumption would be entirely arbitrary, lacking not only any proof but any probability. There have been many among the disciples and followers of the Buddha who have earned their merit regarding the collection and design of the texts, but no truly superior personality, no one we could take in the way already implied as the creator of that core in the sacred texts and thus for the inspirer of Buddhism in its entirety. Oldenberg is justified in saying that Buddhism has never had a St Paul.[7] We can thus hardly do anything but assume that the superior personality from which that inspiration emanated must have been the Buddha himself. In this context we have to consider that the Buddha's words left a deep and lasting impression on the listeners; given the reverence they felt for their teacher, the disciples' wish to keep faithfully what they heard was certainly true and serious, and the Indians' strength of memory which enabled them to retain faithfully what they heard was splendid—just consider the transmission of the Veda—and went far beyond our idea of memory today. Even if then over the course of time much has been added, amended, changed, deformed, for the reasons given it is still not unscholarly to believe that not only some, but much—especially in the Pali texts—in the form it has been transmitted to us *essentially* originates with the founder of the Buddhist norm, let us just say: the Buddha himself. It remains of course impossible to prove in detail that some particular word as it is available to us has been spoken by the Buddha himself. But through intimate immersion into the texts a sense for the probability of a particular case may certainly be acquired. And with regard to the phrasing of the sermon at Benares, with which we are presently concerned with here, the probability that it is close to that which the Buddha actually said himself can principally be affirmed.

That which in the above has been mentioned as an advantage of the Pali texts is especially clear in relation to the Buddhist gospel of death, the Mahāparinibbānasutta, whose main content was related above following the narrative of the Buddha legend according to the *Lalitavistara*. Here we no longer have a legendary text like the *Lalitavistara,* where the translation of thoughts into images, the mystical depiction of supernatural contexts forms the essence. The Mahāparinibbānasutta is one of those ancient texts which reverberates with the memory of words actually heard, events actually experienced, a text in which we feel more clearly than anywhere else that breath emanating from the personality of the master that we spoke of before. But of course this does not mean we can take everything in this text as history. The mystically-legendary element which recedes much further back here than with the *Lalitavistara* and other texts should not be overlooked even in the Mahāparinibbānasutta. Just consider the scene of Ānanda and Māra, followed by that of giving up the will to continue life, the meal of wild boar meat (see footnote p. 75), the purification of the turbid waters, the two garments and the radiance emanating from the Buddha's body, the sounds of heavenly music appearing to the Buddha as he lies dying in the Sala grove, the leave-taking of the deities, the events at the funeral pyre and many other incidents. It is not the case that these things have to be interpreted exclusively symbolically, some also allow a different interpretation. Especially with regard to the visions of gods of which we encounter several in the Mahāparinibbānasutta it can be said that Buddha was undoubtedly convinced himself that he was in communication with supernatural beings and that his contemporaries, too, especially his disciples, believed in this his ability, that they found nothing in it that they would not have been able to bring into congruence with their thinking, their world view. It is thus not correct to interpret, as it is still predominantly done today, everything mystic in the Buddhist texts as inventions of later centuries. Quite remarkable in this respect is a description of the Buddha's daily routine which the commentator Buddhagoṣa designs in the *Sumaṅgalavilāsinī*, the commentary on the *Dīghanikāya* (ed. P.T.S., p. 45 ff.).[8] In this description which otherwise is so sober and gives us the impression of lived reality, it is said that the Buddha, after finishing the day's work and the meal, retreats to a room scented by incense (*gandhakuṭi*) which serves his private affairs. In the first wake of the night, he receives visits from disciples there who ask him questions and request meditation practices (*kammaṭṭhana*) and other things from him. In the same room he holds conversations with supernatural beings (*devatā*, deities) who come from all realms of space in the second wake of the night. In contrast to the imaginative mysticism of the Mahāyāna texts, the visions of gods in the Mahāparinibbānasutta are similarly related with a certain realism; just remember the vision of Pāṭaligāma or the deities in the Sala grove who cannot manifest as long as the monk Upavāṇa is standing before the Buddha. It is clearly said that a sensory perception of some phantoms is not referred to here, but a spiritual vision of spiritual beings. The Mahāparinibbānasutta (p. 12, ed. Childers),[9] for example, says that the Buddha perceives the deities with the 'divine, clairvoyant, supernatural (lit.: 'superhuman') eye' (*dibbena cakkhunā visuddhena atikkantamānusakena*). This way of expressing clearly points to that realm which alone opens an understanding of these things, and a deeper understanding of Buddhism as such to us, namely to the realm of *meditation* (*dhyāna, samādhi*), of Yoga, as this is called in India later. The second part [of this book] will have to deal with their significance for Buddhism and their relationship with that which plays a role in Buddhism as the aspect of the supernatural. It will emerge more clearly what we have to conceive as the gods in Buddhism. These things are thus neither mere 'fabrications of later monks', nor external events, but simply experiences of the Buddha, experiences of the purely spiritual kind, which however did not have a lesser value of reality than the external events of the sensory world have for the ordinary person. We may thus also believe that the figure of Māra, the tempter, was real for him, and it is not necessary for us to declare the

Māra episode—which does not lack a certain transcendental momentum—from the Mahāparinibbānasutta a later interpolation.

Apart from the above-mentioned mystically tinged episodes of the Mahāparinibbānasutta, there are among the many aspects which among the remainder create the impression of bare external factuality first and foremost the geographical details: the numerous and exact information of places included in the narrative at this point indeed corresponds to actual circumstances. It is thus very likely that the Buddha's last journey, at least in its path, has been described to us in the same way it actually proceeded. The text also appears to us to provide a true image of the way the Buddha roamed the country during his long years of public ministry, surrounded by the flock of his disciples, teaching and preaching. We hear that he had certain favourite places where he would stay longer, and especially where he would, according to the custom of the order, spend the rainy season—for example the town Śrāvasti (Pali *Sāvatthī*), the capital of Kośala where a rich man, Anāthapiṇḍaka gave him a property, the Jetavana grove; Rājagṛha (Pali *Rājagaha*), at the time the capital of Magadha, where he gave many doctrinal lectures on the nearby Gṛdhrakūṭa (Pali *Gijjhakūṭa*) mount, and Vaiśālī (Pali *Vesālī*) which was especially dear to him because of the beauty of the natural surroundings, and where, according to the narrative of the Mahāparinibbānasutta, the dancer Ambapālī had given him a mango grove ... But it appears that he never suffered to stay too long in one place; the ministry which he had set himself as his life's task implied a perpetual wandering about, and even during his last weeks and days he felt driven from place to place. What the Mahāparinibbānasutta tells us about the place of his death acquires even more probability through the above-mentioned find of relics. We may thus believe that the Holy One died not far from the area where he came into this world, in the North of India, not far from the snow-capped mountains, at the age of about 80 years (according to latest calculations, 477 or 480 BCE). Different minor details substantiate just how close the narrative of the Mahāparinibbānasutta appears to be to the external truth. For example, among the last orders given by the Buddha on his deathbed a spiritual punishment (consisting in temporal ostracism) of an insubordinate monk is mentioned, further an irreverent expression of a monk, Subhadda, after the Holy One's death who expresses his satisfaction that they were now rid of the 'great ascetic' and free to do what they wanted. Those who allow these episodes to take effect in their context without bias will have to admit that if the narrators had wanted simply to fabricate, they would most certainly not have fabricated this just this way so that for the narrative in this context hardly any other motive besides the truth of that which is narrated can be assumed.

In the picture of the Buddha's life so far we have not considered all those events which fall into the years between the sermon at Benares and the last journey. Even if we may take some of what the texts here and there report about such events as true, it still does not have any significance for the actual problems of Buddhism and thus for the purpose of this description. From the moment when the Śākya prince becomes the Buddha and decides to appear as a spiritual teacher, that which we call experiences or events do not play any role in his life anymore. Externally, this life flows on evenly and uniformly, only dedicated to the service of the task of kindling the light of realization in other souls. We have already mentioned the success of his preaching, the power of the Buddha's word over his contemporaries. For the understanding of Buddhism not a selection of individual fates or events from this life of the Buddha is important, but rather the acquisition of a general impression of the Buddha's personality, the manner of his appearance and teaching, his relationship with his disciples and contemporaries in general. In order to penetrate into the true problems of Buddhism, of real, true, original Buddhism, we have to know especially who the Buddha was and what he wanted. In this context it is again particularly the texts of the Pali canon which offer us, as it were, overabundant material for the acquisition of such an impression. The breath of the great personality we referred to above is not only felt in many of the words ascribed to the Buddha, we also feel it in that which the texts convey to us about the entire manner of his appearance and teaching in such a lively and yet plain and thus characteristic way. In a purely theoretical way, far-reaching scepticism is possible even in this context. However, those who immerse themselves into these texts intimately in the way already hinted at and who allow them to take effect without bias will have to find much, very much, about which they will have to say to themselves: this is no fabrication, no picture of the imagination, this clearly bears the mark of reality, of the true memory of the personality of the master, of the way he taught and lived. It has also already been pointed out that often very precise and concrete aspects lead to such an irrefutable conclusion of such a congruence with reality. In spite of the uncertainty regarding all historical details in the life of the Buddha, the general image of his personality stands clearly and definitely before us. Indeed, there will be few historical personalities from such a remote past whose character has been drawn for us so clearly and vividly as that of the Buddha. In the following short description, mainly those traits will be emphasized that are of essential significance for a deeper understanding of Buddhism.

b) The Buddha as a human being and spiritual teacher

In Kern's *Buddhismus* (vol. I, p. 300),[1] we find the phrase that if we wanted to characterize the nature of the Buddha in a few words, this could best be done in the old high German '*Manno miltisto*'[2] ('of all beings the greatest [mildest]'). And certainly, the most outstanding characteristic of this unique man is formed by a mildness and friendliness paired with nobility. This mildness has been most movingly expressed artistically in the Buddha image at Kamakura in Japan (see plates).[3] The image appears to say to us that a hard, angry or unfriendly word has never flown from the lips of this man. Another essential characteristic of the Buddha is a certain cool self-restraint which in him has a characteristic tinge of the impersonal which is also characteristic of Buddhism in general. The warmth of the heart so central to all expressions of Christianity was, according to everything we know about him, foreign to the Indian founder of Buddhism. From the Buddha's personality the two above-mentioned characteristics then entered his teaching. The mildness is reflected in everything which makes Buddhism appear as a gospel of compassion and love, the cool self-restraint expresses itself in the general base note which reverberates through the Buddhist doctrine and which also finds expression in the language of the texts.

In his summarizing appreciation of the Buddha's personality (which ends his book *Leben und Lehre des Buddha* [Life and doctrines of the Buddha, p. 124])[4] Pischel says:

> In the old Buddhists texts the Buddha emerges as a man who exchanged a comfortable, opulent life for a life full of hardship and austerity, one who went from home into homelessness to seek the truth. During his long life he only wanted the Good and performed the Good.

Given all expressions of and about the Buddha which have come to us we have to indeed imagine him as a human being elevated entirely above all everyday concerns, all sensuality, all lowly personal fabrication and striving, who lived only in the spiritual. From this point of view we may already grasp that he appeared to his contemporaries as a miraculous being (*yakkho*), a 'phenomenon' as we would say. From this strong inner life that was only focused on spiritual matters, the power of the word flowed to him, that unique power which most certainly was not only ascribed to him by his followers, but which he must have possessed in reality, if we consider the entire success of his life's work. In the texts it is said of the preaching Buddha that he 'raises his lion voice', and we hear repeatedly about the 'miracle of instruction' and conversion which is effected by the Buddha's speech.

> It is wonderful, it is amazing. It is as if when one straightens out something that had been bent or opens something that was hidden, or when one shows the right way to one who was lost, or when one puts a light on in the dark so that whoever has eyes may see. In this way the Holy One has revealed to me the norm from many different points of view. I take my refuge to the Holy One, to the norm and to the community of disciples.

This is the standing formula of conversion in the texts through which the instructed person describes the impression he has received from the power of the master's words. The significance of this formula is instructive in several ways. On the one hand, it shows us that the Buddha was far from abusing any personal power in a kind of hypnosis, but that he merely wanted to kindle the light of realization in the instructed person and to work on him by means of *realization*. On the other hand, it becomes clear that this 'realization' is not ordinary, but a higher, intimate realization, a realization which is directly opposed to all ordinary thinking, which destroys all perceptions and prejudices of everyday consciousness, all delusions of personality. The Buddha was not bent on teaching some theory, some religious or philosophical dogma to the listener, but to effect a comprehensive ***μετανόησις***, a perfect transformation of his entire thinking and feeling. The transcendental power that his word had in this respect was felt to be like a miracle by his contemporaries. The truth that the Buddha had found – thus we are explicitly told – is a transcendental truth, one that ordinary thinking, ordinary logic, philosophy and speculation cannot touch (*atarka avitarkāvacara,* Pali *atakkāvacara*). He himself had found it through the inspiration of *bodhi,* the higher consciousness of enlightenment. This is an aspect which can be easily overlooked given the terminological-theoretical-logical form in which the Buddha coined his insights and theorems—for example the twelve-fold formula of conditioned arising. From this conceptual-abstract form one could easily conclude that Buddhism was merely a conceptual template, just one more addition to the already existing philosophical system. But all judgement of this kind would not strike home at the essence of the matter. The terminological form in which Buddhism has coined its 'truths' was a concession to the entire position of the development of the Indian consciousness at the time. Again and again the Buddha declares with the utmost clarity and decisiveness that these 'truths' were not something to be somehow grasped by the speculating, ruminating mind or by philosophical speculation. Especially in the way how in the instruction of individual persons according to the texts he always reveals the 'argument from suffering and deliverance' (the four 'noble truths') we can see how far the Buddha was removed from the teaching of dogmas or abstract terms and how much he was concerned with bringing about an inner transformation of the soul, a turning over of the entire thinking, feeling and wanting. In such passages (inter alia, *Vinayapiṭaka* I, pp. 15, 18, 19, 20; *Dīghanikāya* I, pp. 110, 148) it is said that the Buddha does not start the instruction with the argument from suffering, not with that which is the main thing, but that he starts by inwardly preparing the person to be instructed in an appropriate manner by talking about other subjects. Only when by such a talk the soul of the person to be instructed has been brought into a corresponding state does the Buddha open to him the essence of the doctrine: 'When'—such is the stereotypical phrase of such passages—

> the Holy One realized that the mind of the noble ... (here follows the name in question) was well prepared, compliant, free from hindrances (of obstructing thoughts of worldly passion), elevated and detached, he revealed to him that which is the most excellent doctrine of the Enlightened One: The truth of suffering, of the cause, of the overcoming, of the path.

It is very important that the Buddha reveals these things only when he has ensured and convinced himself that the instructed person is indeed in a position to give the communication the right welcome in his soul. It is then said of the effect of the instruction on the thus prepared: 'Like a clean garment from which all dark stains have been removed can take on the dye in the correct way, the pure, stainless spiritual eye opened for him at once, so that he realized how everything which is subject to the law of conditioned arising is also subject to the law of disintegration (of the reversion of the causes).' It is hardly possible to see in such passages anything but a memory of the way the Buddha actually taught. A certain esoteric moment in early Buddhism lies in the fact that even that which is openly communicated addresses a more subtle, more intimate spiritual understanding which has to be awakened through a particular kind of preparation.

Equally significant is the Buddha's behaviour when questioned. A question is not always answered in the same manner it was asked, but the person asking is entirely led away from the original intention of his question by *μετανόησις*, by an inner transformation of the soul through the Buddha's teaching. He learns to realize that all premises of thinking which led him to the question in the first place are rendered irrelevant, lose their meaning, dissolve into nothing, in the face of the higher realization caused in him by the Buddha's words. The Buddha's doctrine is averse to any application of ordinary thinking to metaphysical things; the Buddha does not answer questions asked on the basis of such thinking, but it is attempted to point the person asking to the mistake already contained in the question. For example, at the end of the Kevaddha-Sutta of the *Dīghanikāya* the question asked is presented as flawed and the person asking receives an indication of how he should have asked correctly. In the *Sumaṅgalavilāsinī* (the commentary on the *Dīghanikāya*) the commentator, Buddhagoṣa, who relates much that is of interest in this way, explicitly mentions that this is a general habit of the Buddha.

Nobody will want to claim that the Buddha gave all teachings word-for-word as they are related to us by the *sūtra* texts of the canon. But they still provide us with a true, illustrative and lively picture of the entire way of his teaching and preaching which we must not regard as a mere product of monastic fabrication. A Buddhist Sanskrit text, the 'lotus of the true norm' (Saddharmapuṇḍarīka),[5] distinguishes four ways in which the Buddha taught, namely through *sūtras* (doctrinal lectures, sermons), *gāthās* (poetic verses), legends and fairytales (so-called *jātakas* or stories of previous births). This corresponds to the general image of the Buddha's work in the canon. The doctrinal lectures, some longer, some shorter, as they are contained in particular in the two initial parts of the Suttapiṭaka,[*] the *Dīghanikāya* and *Majjhima-*

[*] The Pali canon (*Tripiṭaka*, 'three baskets') has three main parts: the *Vinayapiṭaka* (containing the discipline of the order), the *Suttapiṭaka* (the main source of doctrine), the *Abhidhammapiṭaka* (largely a more recent collection of terminological patterns from older parts of the canon). The *Vinaya* also contains important parts of doctrine and legend.

nikāya, often develop from questions or discussions. Their standing opening formula is: 'Thus I have heard (*evaṃ me sutaṃ*). At that time the Holy One stayed in such and such a place.' This is then followed by the communication of the discussion the Buddha started on that occasion, or the teaching which he gave. The above-mentioned 'sermon at Benares' and other texts sufficiently illustrate how far the terminologically abstract element played any part in these lectures. One might be tempted to conclude from some that these patterns of terminology contradicted the Buddha's lively way, and were only added to the texts by later authors. It appears more appropriate, however, to assume that it was the Buddha himself who emphasized this kind of—in the sense of the times—'scientific' phrasing of his 'truths'. He did not, by the way, invent the terminology used in this context himself, but took them from older philosophical systems which, as for example the Sāṃkhya system, were current among the followers of Yoga. The Buddha's appearance and ministry falls into an era where the earlier, more pictorial way of thinking and imagining, of which the Veda transmits much, gave way to the terminological, abstract, philosophical way of thinking. Accordingly, Buddhism itself demonstrates a striving to provide its 'truths' with an expression which corresponds to the new ways of thinking. But even though the Buddha incorporated this terminological element into his way of speaking, he never sought an empty intellectualism. In contrast with the manner of the Brahmins, he made an effort to give his words an ordinary turn of phrase, to speak to the general human understanding. The fact that he recurred to the language of the common people[*] in his sermons, that he gave orders that everyone should learn the Buddha word in his own language, and shunned its translation into Sanskrit (Cullavagga V, 33, 1)[6] is significant in this respect. The Buddha had to recur to a certain measure of technical, philosophical terms in order to meet any response from his Indian contemporaries. But beyond this we see how his effort was everywhere directed towards lively imaginativeness and a common touch. This is why he introduces the abstract, but he does not stop there. Beside this he seeks means of instruction which are quite different, concrete and which have a direct impact on human emotion. Thus we find the poetry of the *gāthas* (poetic verses) next to the prose

[*] In the area where the Buddha predominantly worked, this would probably have been the Māgadhī dialect. Close to this is Pali, the sacred language of the canon of the Southern Buddhists.

sūtras of the canon. Next to some that is later monastic poetry, there are certainly—especially in the *Dhammapada* and the *Udāna* of the *Khuddakanikāya*—quite a few verses which the Buddha already said himself (even though he might not have created them himself, but drawn from an earlier stock of proverbs and poetry). That he ended a doctrinal instruction with such a poetic verse as we encounter in the *Udāna* does not seem to have been merely ascribed to the Buddha by later authors, but to have corresponded to an actual habit. The poetic element with the Buddha, the effect of poetry and rhythm, must not be overlooked. It not only reveals itself in the occasional insertion of actual poetic verses, but in his entire way of speaking, in everything the Buddha said. We already (see p. 91) hinted at the effects of rhythm which have given especially the texts of the Pali canon their unique character. It is expressed in the broadly conceived periods of the longer doctrinal lectures, but equally in the detail, in single sentences and phrases, as for example '*ucchinnā bhavataṇhā khīnā bhavanetti, n'atthi dāni punabhavo*'[7] ('Uprooted is the longing for being, destroyed that which leads to being, there is henceforth no rebirth') and in numerous similar sayings. Characteristic for such phrases is the repetition of a thought or term already expressed with other expressions of the same meaning, a kind of *parallelismus membrorum* with the result that the thoughts are poured into the soul with a certain mild persuasion. The repetitions, so common especially in the Pali texts and met with so much offence in the Occident, have to be understood from the point of view of rhythm, and it is necessary to immerse oneself into the texts with a certain musical-rhythmical sensibility. An element related to poetry is also found in the *parables* which are used by the Buddha—as by other religious founders—in a frequent and unique way. 'By a parable', thus a word of the Buddha (*Dīgha*, p. 324), 'people with understanding may understand the meaning of what has been said.' Some, like the powerful sea-parable in the *Udāna*[8] (it is also found in the *Aṅguttaranikāya* and elsewhere)—which is as if sounded through by cosmic rhythms—in which the characteristics of the norm are compared to that of the ocean, are of remarkable poetic beauty, others are distinguished by profound meaning and richness of thought. This weighs double in the scales given the sparseness which to our [Western] perception often characterizes the Buddhist expression of thought. (We have already met with such parables in the context of the legend. Some, like the image of the Brahmin rubbing fire, used for the explanation of the meaning of the asceticism practiced by the Buddha, cannot be fully grasped by

Buddhist theory alone, but point to a deeper Yoga teaching for their understanding.) Especially that kind of understanding aimed at by the Buddha—an understanding of the soul of a higher order which transcends mere logical grasp—can be awakened intimately by parables. It is as if in the context of Buddhism, the parable has an inner, secret power to reach deeper connections no longer attainable with our usual, abstract terms. It thus had to appear in a way most natural to the higher consciousness, the Buddha realization, to speak in parables. The content of this realization often found a more profound expression in the parables than in the abstract doctrinal phrases. For example, that parable through which the Buddha sheds light onto the distinction between the higher realization taught by him and the teachings of the different speculative systems (*Udāna* VI 4, see also Oldenberg, *Buddha*, p. 236) is most remarkably telling. The followers of the different systems who argue about metaphysical questions that are portrayed by the Buddha as unattainable to speculative thinking, are compared to persons born blind who touch an elephant: each of the blind people touches a different part of the body and accordingly describes the elephant differently. The argument finally ends in a fight. Nowhere has the nature of Buddhism and its difference from all philosophy been named more clearly. One of the details is this: that we are told that each of the blind persons touches one part of the contested object and, in so far as he is able with his limited senses' abilities, describes it correctly. This means that according to Buddhism, not everything that philosophy and external knowledge about objects can express is outright false: all these external opinions correctly show us the truth *from one particular, low and limited point of view*, and the mistake their adherents make is only in the fact that they do not realize the limitations of this viewpoint and that they defend their opinion as if it already contained the entire truth. The Buddha, in contrast, wants to lead the soul to that higher level on which the 'seeing realization' opens up which is unattainable for that low thinking which is bound to sensuality. To that seeing realization all those who want to fathom the laws of the cosmos while clinging to sensual thinking then appear as those who are blind from birth. They are made to see only when the Buddha, as it were, pierces their cataracts by the transformation he effects through his word. There is much in such a parable which it would have been hardly possible to put into general, abstract forms of thought in the Buddha's time.

Even with regard to the relationship between the Buddha and

nature, many of the parables given by him—as for example the above-mentioned sea parable—are instructive. Even if it is true that no religion has turned so thoroughly away from nature and the earthly as Buddhism, it remains notable how what it has turned away from then acquires significance in a purely spiritual sense. Whenever the Buddha wants to make his disciples conscious of the nature of his norm which deeply renounces nature and everything earthly, he uses that parable which he takes from the nature of the sea, i.e., the very earthly realm above which his norm raises itself. With regard to a picture of the Buddha's character we can from the many parables taken from the life of nature gain the insight that he must have had a fine sensibility for nature, even though—or maybe precisely because—he entirely inhabited spiritual spheres. This sensibility was common in the ancient Indians. (The later Buddhist monastic poetry also emphasizes that one fares well in the loneliness of the woods and that in those places where someone of worldly outlook has no joys, they flower for the person who has conquered all passions.) To take the creator of the Buddhist doctrine as a mere derider of nature would not correspond to the facts at all. Rather, a love of nature seems to speak from some of the things that have been transmitted to us about the Buddha. We can remember here how in the Mahāparinibbānasutta the thought of staying longer in this earthly life comes before his soul in the face of the beauty of the earthly sphere (see above, p. 73), and how he casts a last look of parting on his beloved city of Vaiśālī before his *nirvāṇa*. And the legend tells us how the loveliness of the banks of the Nairañjanā brings the thought of meditating to attain the highest Buddha enlightenment there. According to this credible trait of the legend, nature thus was a source of spiritual inspiration to him, as to other spiritual seekers. Nowhere do we find a hint that the view of the highest snowy peaks of the earth which offered itself to him in his hometown during his childhood added to the planting of the seed of turning towards world-renouncing contemplation, towards transcendental heights of the spiritual in the boy. But perhaps we may in this connection draw attention to the fact that in one version of the Buddha legend (the *Nidānakathā*) the transcendental heights of consciousness, into which Queen Māyā is transposed during that night when the Bodhisattva enters her womb in a supernatural way, in the symbolism of her dream are imagined in the mountainous heights of the Himalayas (see above, p. 38). In the Buddha's parables, too, the Himalayas are mentioned several times.

With these images and parables an element of the concrete and pictorial enters the texts which forms an effective counterweight to the abstractness of the Buddhist series of concepts. And we may suppose that the Buddha's skill to speak in parables contributed to the impression his words evoked in his listeners. If the texts themselves point to the fact that the Buddha not only taught through doctrinal lectures, but also through poetic verses, legends and tales, we see how he seeks to meet all kinds of understanding: to the learned understanding of the Brahmins he offers a series of abstract metaphysical concepts, on the more naïve understanding he works with poetry and parable and by cladding the doctrine in legends and tales. It is self-evident that the wealth of fairytales which have come down to us in the form of the already mentioned so-called *jātakas* or stories of previous births have not been related like this or only in the smallest measure by the Buddha. But we are justified in assuming that the inclusion of such stories within the canon would not have happened if the Buddha had not occasionally included stories of this kind in his teachings. To the Buddha the memory of previous births—which in the Buddha's sense belongs to the higher abilities of the enlightened person and which has its theoretical basis in the Indian teaching of *karma*—was a fact which as an Indian he did not doubt; it is related how under the *bodhi* tree there was awakened in him the memory of numerous incarnations lived through in the past. We may thus also believe that he related stories where he remarked at the end that he himself had been this or that person of the story in a previous life. The *jātaka* stories of the Sanskrit text *Mahāvastu,*[9] which relate to the Buddha's wife, Yaśodharā, are especially remarkable. To the general Indian viewpoint, the love-at-first sight between the Bodhisattva and Yaśodharā must have had its karmic roots in the relationships of a previous life. Here the idea strongly suggests itself that the Buddha himself said something about this relationship in the sense of the Indian doctrine of reincarnation. This does not mean that we claim that he related the stories just as they appear in the *Mahāvastu*. (Nearly all tales and fables that existed in India were transformed into *jātaka* tales over time after the pattern of such narratives in an often rather superficial and schematic way.)

We thus find all kinds of instruction from the Buddha, from doctrinal lectures rising to the heights of metaphysical terminology down to simple folktales. However we may judge the narratives transmitted to us in the *jātaka* book, it remains a significant trait of Buddhism that it even gained a spiritual meaning from fairytales. In all the seriousness of his teaching the Buddha's speech has a lively pictorial quality paired throughout with simplicity and naturalness, and there is no dearth of episodes in the text that show that even a certain sense of humour was not at all foreign to him.

Those simple sentences or formulas which contain the essence of the doctrine in the most condensed, short form are also worth mentioning in connection with what can be said about the Buddha's way of speaking: 'The Tathāgata has realized the appearances (literally: 'laws') that arise due to a cause, and likewise their reversion, thus says the great ascetic.' (*ye dharmā hetuprabhavā hetuṃ teṣaṃ tathāgato hy'avadat teṣāṃ ca yo nirodha evaṃvādī mahāśramaṇaḥ*).[10] 'Avoiding all evil and practising the good and mindful watching the mind is the doctrine of the Buddha' (*sarvapāpasyākaraṇaṃ kuśalayopasaṃpadā svacittānurakṣaṇa etad buddhānuśāsanam*).[11] For those unable to remember much, these short sentences were nonetheless an inexhaustible object of repeated contemplation and meditation. Even if those formulas just mentioned do not come from the Buddha himself it remains credible that he emphasized summarizing his doctrine in short sentences and memorable phrases. In a way we can say that those two words *appamādena sampādetha*[12] ('continue in striving effort') of his last admonition to the disciples actually already contain the essence of Buddhism. They express in the most concise form that important thought of Buddhism that it is not important that the disciple acquires abstract terms, but that he makes an active, inner effort and strives for spiritual perfection in working untiringly on himself.

With regard to the Buddha's effect on his contemporaries, it would still be one-sided to only look at the power of his words. One does not know the Buddha as long as one judges him only according to what he said. But along with the power of speech there is with him another that is almost even more towering than the other, the power of *silence*. To grasp the significance of this silence correctly is of prime importance for the entire understanding of Buddhism. According to the Buddha, silence is among the best characteristics a human being can have or acquire, and Buddha himself was a master of this art.

'He never spoke clearly about many things in his environment, and all his life he knew how to be most exquisitely silent.' This phrase, coined by a more recent thinker (Friedrich Nietzsche in '*Jenseits von Gut und Böse*', Aphorismus 244) with regard to Goethe, can also be applied to the Buddha.

The Poṭṭhapādasutta of the *Dīghanikāya* illustrates how much the

Buddha loved being silent. At the approaching of the Buddha the ascetic Poṭṭhapāda here admonishes his disciples who were just engaged in discussions about all sorts of subject of worldly life: 'Be silent, do not make a noise. The ascetic Gautama is coming now who is no friend of noise and who praises being silent; if he sees that silence reigns in our congregation he will be inclined to come to us.'[13] And on another occasion (*Udāna*, p. 11) the Buddha forbids his disciples the kind of discussion in which he had just found them: 'It is not proper, my disciples, you noble ones, who have left your homes and gone into homelessness, to lead such discussions, but two things are proper for the disciples when they are congregated: the discussion of the sacred doctrine or *noble silence* (*ariyo tuṇhībhāvo*).' For the Buddha, silence is thus something noble, exquisite. But it is something more than a mere external habit. In everyday life often perceived as something negative, silence has a certain positive significance with the Buddha. Initially it is something entirely secondary, external when the texts mention again and again how the Holy One gives his consent to an invitation for a meal by remaining silent (*adhivāsesi bhagavā tuṇhībhāvena*, see above, pp. 69, 72). Here, silence expresses affirmation. And yet in this small trait—the fact that silence expresses affirmation—there is something very characteristic which we find again in larger contexts if we penetrate more deeply into Buddhism, and which can provide us with an important hint for the understanding of the Buddha and his teaching. In its terminology and technical expressions, Buddhism is largely congruent with other Indian systems, especially with Sāṃkhya and Yoga. That which distinguishes it from these systems in many ways is rather that about which the Buddha remained silent than that about which he speaks. The Buddha does not want to meet any theoretical needs, no curiosity nor thirst for knowledge with what he says. Rather, he wants to bring about that inner transformation mentioned above, or initially the active decision in the soul so that it may enter the path of inner effort which will lead to that transformation and with it the true seeing realization and the highest spiritual aim which still lies beyond it. The Buddha's entire striving culminates in this practical aim; abstract terms and realizations are only communicated in so far as this appears conducive to the realization of this practical aim. The theoretical for its own sake has no meaning in Buddhism. In the *Saṃyuttanikāya* (V, p. 437), that maxim of the Buddha's silence is illustrated symbolically in a typical way. While staying in the Siṃsapā forest, the Holy One takes a few *siṃsapā* [Dalbergia sissoo *(transl. note)*] leaves into his hand and tells the disciples: few like the leaves in his hand in comparison with the many in the Siṃsapā forest, is that small extent to which he has revealed to them the doctrine in comparison with the large amount he has realized but not revealed.

> And why have I not revealed it to you? Because it would not be for your benefit, because it does not have anything to do with the foundations of the sacred way of life, because it does not lead to renunciation (*nibbidā*), not to freedom from passion (*virāga*), not to destruction of causes (*nirodha*), not to calmness of mind (*upasama*), not to clairvoyant realization (*abhiññā*), not to awakening (*sambodha*), not to *nirvāṇa* (*nibbāna*).

It is justified that Oldenberg, who first drew attention to this passage (*Buddha*, 5th ed., p. 240), adds the comment:

> ... we can scarcely help forming the impression that it was not a mere idle statement which the sacred texts preserve to us, that the Perfected One knew much more which he thought inadvisable to say, than what he esteemed it profitable to his disciples to unfold. For that which is declared points for its explanation and completion to something else, which is passed over in silence ... but of which we can scarcely help believing that it was really present in the minds of Buddha [and those disciples to whom we owe the compilation of the sacred texts.]

That what is expressed here is entirely correct will emerge in detail in the second part in the context of our observations of the doctrine. Here we only recall what has already been said above in the context of the legend regarding the Buddha's initial hesitation to communicate the realization he had found to the world (see above, p. 66). All this would be impossible to understand if we were to presuppose the motivations of a modern occidental disciple of knowledge in the Buddha. But in order to understand the Buddha correctly, we have no choice but to raise ourselves to the thought that those motivations, so familiar to us, did not guide him, and that the knowledge found by him was something entirely different from all that we understand as 'knowledge' and 'realization' today. The Buddha taught his 'doctrine' in order to fulfil a task towards humanity which he felt laid upon him from spiritual worlds like a transcendental duty, not in order to win followers for a system. But with regard to what he had to reveal and how he had to reveal it, only this one purpose, this one task was acceptable, not some personal need or personal ambition. He only measured it according to the needs of his times and his listeners' capacity to understand. (This is among the reasons why it has to appear wrong to propagate Buddhism in the West today. For it is self-evident that Buddha communicated his realizations in just that form which was appropriate for the epoch and its culture.)

The Buddha's silence, his reservation, is especially characteristic in those contexts where questions on transcendental problems, such as eternity or non-eternity, infinity or finiteness of the world, or questions about the relationship between body and soul (life, *jīva*) and life after death—so close to the religious needs of all times—were put to him. The Buddha always denies both the affirming and the negative answer, equally an affirmation of both alternatives at the same time—which might possibly be conceived—as also their negation:

> The world is eternal—is not eternal—is eternal and not eternal at the same time—is neither eternal nor not eternal—I have not taught any of this. The Tathāgata lives on after his death—he does not live on—he lives and he does not live—he neither lives nor does not live—I do not teach any of this.

At times, all four alternatives are directly negated. The way of expression here is so unique that we want to count it absolutely among that which goes back to the Buddha himself. In this context it is not sufficient to conclude, like some more recent scholars, that the refutation of those questions indicates that the Buddha was merely not interested in metaphysical problems, or to suppose that such problems for him did not exist. In a famous parable, the Buddha expresses clearly at what he was aiming. We read in the *Majjhimanikāya* (in the Cūḷa-mālunkyasutta, P.T.S., vol. 1., p. 426ff.) that once a monk called Māluṅkyaputta came to the Buddha. He felt dissatisfied with the fact that the Holy One did not provide any information on whether the world was eternal or not eternal, whether the soul was different from the body, whether there was any continuation of life after death. He urges the Buddha to answer these questions for him in either the affirmative or negative, or with an 'I do not know.' Only then would he be willing to remain the Buddha's disciple, otherwise he would turn to the worldly life again. But the Buddha answers him with a parable: 'A man,' he says to him,

> has been struck by a poisoned arrow, his friends call the doctor. If he now said: I will not have the arrow removed before I know exactly who the man is by whom I have been struck, what his name is, to which lineage, which caste he belongs, what he looks like, whether he is tall or small, dark or blond, where he lives, and before I know exactly what calibre the

> bow was with which he has shot me and the arrow itself which pierces me (again, the most minute details are listed in the text) – the man would die before he could be healed. It would be just the same if someone would only become a disciple on the condition that those questions were answered. He would die before the Tathāgata could give him the answer to his questions.

This parable, too, is more profound than many abstract teachings of Buddhism. The story tells us that the Buddha knows the answer to these question, but that it is impossible to give them in the simple way imagined by the person asking. He would die and lose healing and salvation before he had heard the answer. The thinking behind it is that Buddha did not come in order to answer theoretical, philosophical questions, but to help oppressed humanity. The situation of a person caught in worldly life, still subject to earthly passion and longing for being, is like that of the man struck by the poisoned arrow. First and foremost, the arrow has to be pulled out before anything else can be contemplated, much less the answer to questions greedy for knowledge. Only the practical deed, the pulling out of the arrow and the healing of the wound, is important, not searching for the making or origin of the arrow or for name, kind and origin of the person who shot it. In the same way the wound from which the worldly person is suffering – according to Buddhism – has to be healed first, the arrow of sinful passion and a thinking bound in sensuality has to be pulled out before true realization of metaphysical problems is possible. For that purpose the Buddha came into the world, not in order to satisfy an empty thirst for knowledge which would only threaten the realization of the true goal.

And there is more that remains unexpressed between the lines in such parables. Indeed, it is not a mere absence of interest on the part of the Buddha in metaphysical concerns – in his innermost nature he had an inclination towards metaphysics. From a philosophical point of view there is behind that refutation of all logically possible alternatives, which is so characteristic, more wisdom than may initially appear to superficial observation. Let us remain with the first of those questions – whether the world is infinite or finite, eternal or not eternal. Those who have read Kant know that we are faced here with 'antinomies' (*Critique of Pure Reason*). In detail, some aspects may have been differently phrased, differently justified than with Kant: the antinomy as such, however, can and must be experienced inwardly in each person in their own contemplation of these things. For on the one hand the true, concrete concept of an eternity of space and time cannot be formed by our finite thinking which is bound to the brain. On the other hand the end of space (a point of space beyond which there is no more space) and equally a beginning and end of time is impossible to conceive for this brain-thinking. Conceptual thinking thus finds itself in a predicament from which it cannot find a way out by itself. An important distinction between Kant and Buddha now is—among many others—that for Kant it was a matter of self-evidence to remain within that thinking bound to the brain. In certain lesser known works he has discussed other points of view, but declined them. In contrast, the Buddha sets the task of exceeding, of leaving behind our ordinary, empirical thinking (which is bound to the brain, as we would say—the term 'brain' however does not play any role with the Indians). Thus the refutation of all speculation, thus the explanation that the highest mysteries of the world and of humankind are unattainable for abstract, philosophical thinking. Not logical thinking, but only *higher consciousness* (*bodhi*) resolves the contradictions in which the lower thinking that is bound to sensuality becomes enmeshed.

In this sense the Buddha speaks about all metaphysical teachings and opinions, of all viewpoints such as: the world eternal or not eternal etc. as a thicket, a wild jungle (*kāntāra*), a comedy (*visūkaṃ*), a distorted cramp (*vipphanditaṃ*), a fetter full of suffering and pain (*Majjhimanikāya* I, p. 485, already quoted by Oldenberg, op. cit., p. 236). On the path that leads to the annihilation of that kind of thinking which is the prerequisite of all those questions, the Buddha wants to free the soul from this painful thicket. Instead he wants to lead to seeing, to clairvoyance, to higher consciousness. It will emerge from the detailed discussions in the second part what these are in the sense of Buddhism. An important passage from the Poṭṭhapādasutta (*Dīghanikāya* I, p. 195) must be mentioned here, where different levels of the consciousness-self (*ātman*, Pali *attā*) are taught, of which the one bound to the physical body (*olāriko attā*), is the lowest. Each of the levels is surpassed by the next higher one and consequently appears insubstantial. Thus all realization in Buddhism is relative, only available to a certain level of consciousness. The all-encompassing consciousness in which all contradictions dissolve is the *bodhi*, the true mystery of Buddhism which is symbolized by the sacred fig tree. But the Buddha does not even want to construct a theory about higher consciousness, but show the path which leads to it. Kant shows on a theoretical level where the limits of realization are within the given consciousness. The Buddha teaches the practice, the path with which that given consciousness can be surpassed. While Kant thus proves how within that thinking bound to sensuality—'pure reason'—the realization of that which is real in a higher sense is unattainable, the Buddha wants to rise to higher realization by leaving behind that thinking bound to sensuality. He thus had to reply to those questions that came to him from that thinking with the answer which in truth is silence and which only shows how none of the wrong paths of thinking touches the great world problems.

After all this, the silence of the Buddha appears as something almost self-evident, something no longer surprising in the context where we would usually pose the question of 'god' or some highest principle however formed or called. Buddhism speaks quite sufficiently of divine or spiritual, supernatural beings to whom the Holy One relates in meditation. Undoubtedly, the Buddha himself has talked about such beings and such relationships (see above, p. 93f), but that which suggests itself so strongly to religious need as well as to the speculating mind to conceive as the highest unity above and within all earthly beings, and which especially suggests itself in India, he shrouds in silence. Once, in a discussion with Brahmins (*Dīghanikāya* I, p. 249), he does indeed mention that he knows *brahman* and the *brahman* world and the path which leads to the *brahman* world, but with that he does not refer to the highest *brahman* (*parabrahman*) of the Vedānta, the world-soul of ancient Indian metaphysics that mystically weaves through space, but only to god Brahmā, originally identical with the Indian creator of the world, who in Buddhism is a god among gods, and who is often mentioned along with Indra, the highest of the 33 gods (*sakko devānaṃ indo*). The history of religions clearly shows where all talk of a highest principle most often led: under the best circumstances to a 'belief', a dogma, a theology, i.e., to a standstill in that very form of consciousness and thinking which the Buddha wants to leave behind. Even before the Buddha, much, too much had been said in India about *brahman*, the supernatural, macrocosmic world being, and *ātman*, the highest self which reveals itself on the path into the innermost realms of the soul, and the mystical union of the two. In reading some of the learned Brahminical texts it is impossible not to feel that in spite of all original profound thinking, in the end only empty terminological schemata remained in all that talk of *ātman* and *brahman* which exhausts itself in the perpetual repetition of the same thought. The Buddha realized the danger for his people and his era which lay in getting caught in mere terminological schemes. He was opposed to all theological quarrelling, to all speculation; he wanted to lead the soul out of the painful 'thicket of dogmas, the jungle of dogmas, the cramp of dogmas, the comedy of dogmas', and lead it towards the path of true meditative inner experience, of the overcoming of lower consciousness and all forms of cognitive thinking. He wanted to provide it only with as many terms and abstractly phrased 'truths' as appeared conducive towards the attainment of his practical, pedagogical aim. To speak about *ātman* and *brahman* in that way which was then common in India did not appear conducive to him. Even where he recurred to the terminology of Indian systems in phrasing his truths he left those terms out of the scheme in question that named such a highest divine or spiritual principle. Consequently, an initial member of a series of concepts which logic demands may appear to be lacking in a given sequence of terms, and the known problems of the logical understanding of Buddhism result that appear hopeless to some scholars. The Buddha, as it were, puts a simple blank line where other systems put those positive highest terms. That blank line which is founded in the deepest nature of Buddhism has given rise to many misunderstandings. That view which sees an 'atheist' in the Buddha is still widely accepted. Dahlmann's criticism of Buddhism[14] from this point of view is especially misled. With a personality so inclined towards the spiritual-supernatural as the Buddha we cannot speak of an atheist in our modern sense. As we have seen, it is mentioned all the time that the Buddha related to gods as spiritual beings with whom meditation opens an opportunity of personal interaction. But neither did he refute a highest divine or spiritual principle; to refute it was as far from him as to positively speak about it. The *highest divine-spiritual principle* of which other religions speak in different ways *for the Buddha was – silence,* a silence which can reveal much to us, which is not purely negative, but also had – as Buddha's silence often did – a positive aspect. And even with him we sometimes hear in dark words, but in a positive sense, of a highest supernatural principle in which the appearances of the sensual world originate, and into whose womb they can return:

> There is, my disciples, something which is not born, not become, not created, not produced from the formative forces; if this which is not born, not become, not created, not produced from the formative forces did not exist, for all that is born, become, created, produced from the formative forces no way out could be seen. (*Udâna,* p. 81).

The impact of such expressions lies especially also in their simplicity and rarity which is in remarkable contrast to the infinite repetitions of *ātman* and *brahman* in the Brahminical texts. In this silence, with regard to the highest things, a certain purity of Buddhism may be found; it may be felt as a silence of awe towards that which cannot be expressed in words, 'not grasped by thinking' (this expression is the one the Buddha preferably uses), which even retreats from meditation—for which the 'gods' in the Buddha's sense are something quite attainable in reality—by disappearing further into the distance and into higher heights, into deeper depths the further this meditation penetrates into spiritual spheres. To other people, the Buddha only wanted to speak of those things which they could actually grasp, with which they could enter into a relationship and which were meaningful for their spiritual education and development. Thus the Buddha taught raising oneself to the supernatural without having spoken about 'god' in a way known to us. Precisely from his silence on some things that many regard as essential for the idea of 'religion' there is something we can learn. In his turning towards supernatural realization and towards the 'holy life', Buddhism clearly exhibits the character and mood of a religion. Each word of the Buddha is infused with this religious mood, this religious breath. It is not about approaching Buddhism with a pre-formed idea of 'religion', but about considering Buddhism when forming an idea of 'religion'. For this reason we were able to say (cf. above, p. 21) that for a deepening of our idea of religion we can learn a lot especially from a study of Buddhism.

The Buddha was not a philosopher, but the *teacher of a path.* He already emerges clearly as such from the picture sketched up to here. Rarely one of the spiritual leaders of humanity has taken such a negative stance towards all philosophical speculation as the Buddha.

Given the deeply rooted inclination of the ancient Indians (and humanity in general) towards theory we must not be surprised if a 'Buddhist philosophy' has nevertheless developed over the course of time although it is so very much opposed to the original intentions of the Buddha. The history of any religion shows how from that which was given to humanity or the people something develops which is far from the original intention of the founder. For someone familiar with Indian circumstances it is easy to understand that from the Buddha's words, among many other things, a philosophy, indeed a whole range of philosophical systems and schools, also emerged. In the present description it is impossible to go into detail here. But it is of interest to hint at the fact how precisely the most important and famous of those systems, the Mādhyamika-philosophy which aligns itself with the

Mahāyāna, departs from the above-mentioned (p. 108) habit of the Buddha when answering certain metaphysical questions, of refuting or negating all kinds of opposite alternatives at once in a way that from the point of view of logic appears contradictory. If we observe it as a 'philosophy of contradiction' which has followed with a certain necessity from the Buddha's original anti-philosophical way of instruction, a new light is cast on that strange 'philosophy' which, if we approach it on our terms, may appear to us as the most meaningless and abstruse that has ever been offered to humanity as a 'philosophy'. (Thanks are due to Max Walleser[15] whose works have made this philosophy accessible: *Die mittlerer Lehre des Nāgārjuna,* Heidelberg 1911, 1912, reviewed by the author of the present work in *Theologische Literaturzeitung,* vol. 38., Nr. 13).[16]

In later years, 'Yoga' was coined in India as a name for that meditative spiritual direction—as opposed to theoretical philosophy—to which the Buddha adhered as a teacher of a path directed towards the liberation from the fetters of sensualities. Here the intention is not to equate Buddhism with systems which especially carry the name 'Yoga'. Only the context in which we have to conceive the entire ministry and appearance of the Buddha should be noted here. According to more recent studies the Yoga-system of Patañjali belongs to a considerably later period. However, Yoga had a long history in India as the effort of raising oneself to higher states of consciousness, and the supernatural powers thought to be associated with them, through spiritual methods of concentration and meditation. To this end served those practices of asceticism (*tapas*) which—according to the legend—the Buddha followed for some time until he discarded them as unfruitful as they did not lead to the highest goal. There are indeed parts of the Yoga system (the so-called Haṭha-Yoga) where they are emphasized in a certain way, but this kind of preference for external asceticism is entirely alien to the more spiritual school later codified in the systems of Patañjali. Here it only counts as a supplementary aid to the spiritual methods. These spiritual methods of concentration and meditation are really the essential aspect of Yoga, and in the present context the word is only used in this sense. In the older Pali-texts the terms *yoga* (in the technical sense), and *yogī* (i.e., practitioner of Yoga) are still rare; in later Buddhist texts, namely Sanskrit texts, they are met with frequently, and there it is quite normal that the Buddha is called a *yogī.* A Sanskrit text that has been preserved in Tibetan, the *Śrīvajra-maṇḍālaṃkāra,* calls the Buddha the 'greatest of all Yogis' (*saṅs · rgyas ·*

kun · gyi · rnal · hbyor · che, vol. 94, leaf 116 of the Berlin ed. of the Kanjur).[17] As can be concluded from what has been said so far, this corresponds in a certain way to the texts, but it has to be taken with a number of reservations. It has already been pointed out that the Buddha did not at all relate to the behaviour of the ordinary Indian *yogīs* who only sought their own spiritual development and who shut themselves off from the outside world with a certain egoism. His intention was enlivened by true love for mankind in an entirely different way; he wanted—as much as this could be reconciled with the nature of realization—to make this realization and the methods that lead to it available to the widest audiences. This is why his personality is much more powerful than that of an ordinary Indian *yogī*. But in so far as Yoga designates practical effort, a method of spiritual concentration and meditation aimed at supernatural goals, in contrast to speculative philosophy, we do indeed have the right to bring the spiritual approach followed by the Buddha under the viewpoint of Yoga. He himself went the path of spiritual concentration and meditation in order to become a Buddha, and the norm which he left as his inheritance to his disciples also culminates in spiritual concentration and meditation. His approach to all that which points towards the realm of the supernatural was essentially the same as in Yoga. This entire aspect of his personality—which had to be mentioned often in the present description—can only be understood from a familiarity with the Indian Yoga. Even the oldest Pali texts often designate the Buddha as *mahesi*, i.e., the great *ṛṣi*. The Sanskrit word *ṛṣi* in the sense of the Indians, however, means the seer and singer of prehistory 'who sees with supersensory eyes' (*atīndriyadraṣṭar*), that is, the one who had those abilities in the old days which the *yogī* wants to acquire with his methods in later eras. With the Buddha, too, this supernatural vision is mentioned, for example in the context of those visions of gods already discussed, where the text says that he saw the deities with the 'divine, clairvoyant, supernatural (literally: superhuman) eye' (*dibbena cakkhunā visuddhena atikkantamānusakena*).[18] Right into the details, this corresponds to the terminology of Yoga. How the Buddha and his doctrine positioned themselves in detail towards these questions will emerge from the deliberations of the second part, and then the relationships of Buddhism to Yoga will be more clearly illuminated. Here we are first and foremost concerned only with acquiring an image of the personality of the Buddha, and for this image we cannot disregard those characteristics that fall into the realm of the supernatural, Yoga. He speaks himself about his strange vision, about his ability to penetrate the thoughts of others, of controlling body, health and vitality through willpower, of remembering previous incarnations, and of other things. Here, these things are presented as achievements of spiritual discipleship (for even the striving disciple, thus teaches the Buddha, can attain them), but not as abilities which should be sought for their own sake. The true aim of the path is a higher one which lies beyond these abilities; by the Buddha they are, just as in Yoga (*Yogasūtra* III, 36) only viewed as concomitant appearances of meditation which occur before the attainment of the true aim. We would create a wrong image of the Buddha's pesonality in ourselves if we were to assume that he wanted to somehow boast of higher abilities or display them in the manner of a quack. On the contrary, he appears to have been very reserved in these things and only occasionally does he appear to have given proof to one familiar disciple or another—for whom this kind of intimation could be of any value—of that which to that era appeared as a special psychic ability. However, the Buddha never put any decisive emphasis on the psychic, but always on the ethical which in every way forms the basis of the 'path'. The Buddha was entirely adverse to everything that ordinarily belongs to base occultism or ordinary superstition, and he warns his disciples imploringly not to concern themselves with such practices. Thus in the Brahmajālasutta (21ff.), in the Sāmaññaphalasutta and elsewhere, in a passage which is of some interest for the history of culture, all manners of soothsaying are enumerated which in the Buddha's day were practiced for money in the circles of Brahmins and ascetics. The Buddha calls such things 'base arts' (*tiracchānavijjā*) which the truly striving disciples does not want to know. They did not correspond to the nature of a path which the Buddha did not designate as the 'noble' (*ariyo*) for nothing.

The Buddha's inclination towards silence is also to be understood from Yoga. Yoga taught (*Haṭhayogapradīpikā* I, 11) that practice acquires strength through silence, while any relinquishing of 'knowledge' works in the opposite sense. If the Buddha had perceived his 'knowledge' as a philosopher or scholar in our sense, it would be difficult to understand why it cost him inner strife to reveal this knowledge. But if we look at it as a supernatural realization won through Yoga, i.e., meditation, then Buddha's worries appear directly comprehensible. What is remarkable about his behaviour, what then distinguishes him from the ordinary *yogī*, is precisely the fact that he went so far in the communication of what he had realized. But from the point of view of

Yoga it remains characteristic how he keeps to a particular limit here: he reveals that which appears to be conducive to bringing his contemporaries inwardly further in the direction of the spiritual aim sought by him, and shrouds everything else in silence; no request, however motivated, may wrestle from him the relinquishing of his knowledge.

One relationship that is particularly illuminated by the viewpoint of Yoga is the Buddha's relationship with his *disciples*. The texts allow us to form a concrete and lively picture of this relationship, of the entire interaction between the master and his disciples. Even if we can only consider the smallest part of the rich material of the sources in such a short description, we would like to point to the exceedingly lively description in the Upakkilesasutta of the *Majjhimanikāya* (vol. III, p. 155, partially transl. by Pischel in *'Leben und Lehre des Buddha'*, p. 81). We hear how Buddha calls on Anuruddha and two other disciples in their hermitage at Pācīnavaṃsadāya, how the disciples welcome him respectfully, how the master inquires after all the details of their wellbeing and daily life, how he especially asks them if they always lived together in peace and friendship and look at each other with loving eyes, how Anuruddha affirms all this and explains to the master that he counted himself lucky to have such companions in the spiritual discipleship, and that he felt of one heart and mind with them even if their bodies were separate. The Buddha then further asks his disciples about the state of their spiritual life, if they were successful in their practices and what progress they were making in meditation. Anuruddha answers him faithfully what he was able to do in his practices, what he could not yet do, how he already had certain supernatural appearances, but that he could not yet hold on to them, and the Buddha gives him different advice and hints in which he extensively refers to his own practice of meditation and certain experiences from before his enlightenment. The passage (not translated by Pischel) contains numerous details which are interesting from the point of view of Yoga, and it shows how deeply the entire spiritual life of the circle of those around the Buddha was steeped in the atmosphere of Yoga. The Buddha's preceding inquiries into the loving and harmonious life of the disciples have to be viewed from this angle. This is not only an edifying episode, but something which is inwardly connected with the nature of meditation. One important rule of Yoga was that where more than one practitioner of meditation lived together, a spiritual atmosphere of peace and friendship had to reign as the first basic condition of success. In giving meditation practices (*kammaṭṭhāna*) to his disciples and serving them as adviser in this respect, the Buddha entirely takes the place of the 'teacher' (*guru*) in the sense of Yoga towards them. In this context we have to refer again to the above-mentioned description of Buddha's daily life by Buddhagoṣa. There he mentions that the Buddha gives each one those kinds of practices that are appropriate to their individual need and progress in discipleship (*cariyānurūpaṃ kammaṭṭhānaṃ deti*). Only from this point of view can his relationship to his disciples be understood correctly, and we can now gauge what a turning point the Buddha's death signified for the entire life of the community, for the organization prepared for all contingencies. Now the 'norm', the doctrine, took the place of the personal teacher who had hitherto watched over the spiritual development of each individual: 'The norm which I have revealed to you may be your teacher when I have passed on' (see above, p. 80). From the word of the teacher developed a religion, from the circle of disciples gathered around the person of the revered teacher and united in spiritual discipleship, an ecclesiastical community.

The story of the Buddha's life already showed us how that circle of disciples which had gathered around the Buddha accompanied him on his journeys, how the Holy One addresses words of instruction and edification to his disciples time and time again, and how the interaction between master and disciples took place. We can see how some are especially close to the master, how they enjoy the preference of living in direct proximity of the Holy One and of serving him personally. In the Mahāparinibbānasutta, Ānanda particularly emerges as one of these intimate disciples. He was the Buddha's favourite disciple who distinguishes himself among all the others by his dedicated reverence for the master, by the warmth of his heart and a certain impulsive nature and sanguine temperament. We often see the Buddha meet his disciple's over-eagerness in this characteristic, measured way. In front of the disciples, the Buddha praises Ānanda's sense of tact, his ability to speak or be silent at the right moment, and to find the right way of regulating the interaction between him and the outer world (see p. 79). This last task was a particularly important and difficult one, given that many naturally sought the opportunity to speak to the master in person, and that the danger that the Buddha was encroached upon too much by persons from outside was always close at hand. Ānanda appears to have carefully ensured that nobody who was not entitled could come close to the master. The gospel of dying tells us how shortly

Bodhi tree emerging from the head of Buddha

The Tibetan Wheel of Life

The Buddha at Kamakura, Japan

before his *nirvāṇa* the Buddha personally grants Subbhada the ascetic who had already been sent away by Ānanda the sought-after audience. At the Buddha's passing, Ānanda is that disciple who appears most painfully moved of all and who is most lovingly comforted by the Holy One. While Ānanda represents more the soul element among the Buddha's disciples, two others represent the spiritual more: Śāriputra (Pali *Sāriputta*) and Maudgalyāyana (Pali *Moggallāna*), who are also called the 'blessed pair' (*bhaddayugaṃ*) and who in many respects count as the main disciples of the Buddha (see Mahāpadānasutta I, 9). Regarding this passage, the commentator Buddhagoṣa remarks that every Buddha has such a main pair of disciples and that one of them is the greatest in knowledge (*paññā*), the other the greatest in meditation (*samādhi*). Another disciple, the above-mentioned Anuruddha, appears as the most talented in clairvoyance (thus, for example, Mahāparinibbānasutta, p. 63, 67 and others). For some, the psychic abilities pointing to the Yoga appear to have proven dangerous rocks, especially for Devadatta, the Buddha's hostile cousin, who already in the legend in the narrative of the contest enters the arena against the Bodhisattva as the opponent 'inflated by Śākya-pride' and who is later said to have continually created difficulties for the later Buddha in the leading of the community. One *sūtra* from the northern canon tells us how he urges the Buddha in vain to tell him the elements of supernatural spiritual power (*ṛddhipāda*), and given the circumstances at the time it appears quite credible that his hatred towards the Buddha was caused in part by such incidents. Devadatta always appears as the representative of wrong ambitious striving. In opposition to the 'middle path' preached by the Buddha in rejection of one-sided asceticism, Devadatta tries to establish a more strictly ascetic movement within the community of disciples and to bring the leadership of the community into his own hands. He is said to have taken his enmity so far as to set a wild elephant on the Buddha. But the Buddha calmed the elephant by suffusing it with thoughts of love (*Vinaya* II, p. 195). For love, the feeling of friendship with all beings, is the strongest of all magical powers in Buddhism. All other assaults by Devadatta failed likewise.

Apart from this, the Buddha appears to have been largely spared from external assaults. Even the Brahmins probably never met him with open enmity. He never saw his task in fighting anything traditional. He only emphasized the true spiritual content, the true inner experience, true moral cleansing as opposed to the external form. Even the Indian caste system is accepted by the Buddha without contradiction as something rooted in the entire order and development of the world (the Aggaññasutta especially speaks about the relationship between the caste system and the development of the world [see footnote p. 35]). But caste loses its meaning for those who become partakers of a higher sphere of life by entering into the community, by entering the 'path'. 'Just as streams lose their previous names when they enter the sea,' the Buddha teaches, 'and are only called sea from then on, the members of a caste lose the name of their caste by renouncing the worldly life and henceforth are only called disciples of the Buddha.' (*Udāna*, p. 55). Above the Brahminhood of external caste, which as such is not fought against, Buddha places the ideal of the 'true Brahmin' who wins the name through his purity in thoughts, words and deeds, through compassion and realization (cf. Dhammapada 26). In this sense, the perfect disciple of the Buddha is also called a Brahmin. The 'sacred life' of the disciples of the path is also always called *brahmacarya* (Pali *brahmacariya*), i.e., *brahman* life. In this way, the Buddha almost always connects with the traditional in the external terminology. But it should not be overlooked that he fills the old terms with new content and new life.

The Buddha and his disciples also appear to have lived in relative harmony with ascetics (*samaṇa*) and followers of other schools. The texts often show us the Buddha in discussion with such people. Even here, all utterances of the Buddha reveal his unique mildness and patience. He seeks to convince his opponent by giving reasons and effecting inner transformation in him. But he never once budged from that which he had once represented as correct—Buddhagoṣa's dictum 'there is no doubt for a Buddha' (*'buddhānaṃ saṃsayo nāma n'atthi'*, *Sumaṅgavilāsinī* I, p. 265 of the Burmese edition)[19] appears to correspond to a real character trait of the Buddha—and in refuting that which appeared to him a wrong doctrine he did not hesitate to speak a harsh or even just a strict word occasionally. His most decisive opposition was against Makkhali Gosāla, the founder of a sect (see above, p. 17) which denied the freedom of the will, the self-determination of actions through one's own power and moral self-determination (Sāmaññaphalasutta 20).

Much could still be said about the interaction between the Buddha and those striving spiritually from different schools, with lay followers and outsiders from all castes and classes of society, with kings and Brahmins and members of the lower classes which cannot be listed within the scope of the present description. Only his attitude to women, which is important, after all, for the entire understanding of Buddhism, should be mentioned in passing here. The well-known position of Buddhism towards this – according to its own view – most dangerous of all temptations finds a characteristic expression in the following discussion given to us in the Mahāparinibbānasutta (p. 51, ed. Childers). Ānanda asks the master how one should behave towards women. The Buddha laconically answers: '*adassanaṃ*' ('don't look'). 'But if we do see them?' asks Ānanda. '*anālāpo*' ('don't speak to them') is the Buddha's answer. 'But if we do enter into talk with them?' Ānanda asks. '*sati upaṭṭhā-petabbā*,' says the Buddha, i.e., 'then you have to take refuge in wakeful mindfulness.' As everywhere with the Buddha, it is right inner attitude, not external behaviour which is the decisive point. Other than that, it is of prime importance to consider that the problem in question here is one of those which cannot be decided in the same way for all times and all people, but that changes of general cultural conditions and inner life – as they occur in the course of the development of humanity – are of far-reaching significance here. There cannot be any doubt that the Buddha decided the problem of women in the way necessary for the conditions of the times and the conditions of his people. But just as conditions in the West are generally different, much has changed here especially through [the influence of] Christianity – not Christianity as a representation of doctrines, but as a force actually working on the external ground of history. In the judgement of women the differences between Christianity and Buddhism emerge particularly tangibly. But as much as we may feel particularly in this context the position of Christianity as the superior one, this is not to say that the Buddha was not correct in the position he assumed with regard to his times. From a certain point of view the Buddha in particular could be taken as a first announcer of that which was later realized in a more superior and perfect way in Christianity. In the acceptance of spiritual sisters he opened access to the spiritual life to women [In orthodox Indian thinking (largely equivalent to Hindu here, including the earlier forms of Brahmanism and the religion of the Vedas), only men can attain spiritual salvation – trans. note] and thus put the two sexes in this decisive and most important aspect on an equal footing. The *Therīgāthās* which belong to the *Khuddakanikāya* of the *Suttapiṭaka* have preserved for us remarkable poetic offerings of this spiritual life of the female disciples. In the Cullavagga (X 1) of the *Vinayapiṭaka* we are told how the Buddha affirms a question posed by Ānanda, whether women also had the opportunity to take the path from the home into homelessness and to attain the highest spiritual aim, *arhat*-hood or holiness, on the path indicated by the norm through all preliminary stages. Thus the Buddha's earlier reservations regarding the acceptance of the female sex into the religious order are dropped. However, he is said to have mentioned that the norm which otherwise would have lasted a millennium would now only last 500 years. The truth of this narrative may be allowed to rest. It was not otherwise the Buddha's way to allow others to influence his decisions of will and the carrying out of his life's mission. A trait which we do find elsewhere is that he does not immediately grant a wish he has inwardly decided to grant in order to test the seriousness of the desire (cf. Mahāparinibbānasutta, Chap. 3). He certainly would not have accepted sisters if he had not realized this as a necessity demanded by the development of the times. The hindrances in the nature of women regarding the spiritual life—thus we may somehow grasp the Buddha's position on this problem—are greater than those in male nature, but the path to victory over these hindrances is no less open to women than to men. If he ordered the sisters to largely submit to the male disciples in all external matters of discipline this was only congruent with the above. Such patronizing was founded in the entire cultural and judicial circumstances of the India of that time, and as we have seen, the Buddha nowhere turned against the external conditions. In the context of the spiritual life, and this is the most decisive factor, the difference was suspended. Although he may have spoken many a harsh word about the nature of women, the Buddha granted the spiritual needs and wishes of women as far as possible. To take some expression ascribed to him and conclude that his character contained an attitude of misogyny would be entirely wrong. The fact of his marriage already speaks against this. If in those few passages of the Buddha legend that describe the relationship between the prince and his beloved and later wife a certain gentleness and knightly grace of deportment emerges, this is of course first and foremost merely 'legend'. But even the texts of the Pali canon which are closer to historic credibility do not know anything of a true misogyny of the Buddha. We see him dine at the table of women, even courtesans—his acceptance of an invitation to a meal by Ambapālī is upheld even when a princely invitation follows (see above, p. 72)—and he pleases his hostesses with friendly talk and spiritual encouragement. As a credible characteristic there sounds forth through all these narratives the particular, devoted veneration the Buddha received especially from women. Whatever the weaknesses or at least difficulties of a spiritual way of life founded in female nature might have meant according to the Buddha, that ability of devoted veneration which has always been part of the nature of women forms a condition which must make it easier for women to find access to that spiritual life, indeed it makes them appear especially preordained for it. This inner transformation at which the Buddha always aimed is more easily aroused in devoted natures than in those that are more intellectual-critical. Maybe here is the chief reason why he decided to accept spiritual sisters in spite of certain practical difficulties seen by him.

The devotion which the Buddha received from all sides—from male and female disciples, male and female lay followers, from outsiders of all kinds, from kings and Brahmins, high and low—thus not only forms part of the general picture of his personality which can be gained from the texts, but it also contains an aspect which is significant for the general understanding of Buddhism. It is most vividly depicted in the Sāmaññaphalasutta how even the violent King Ajātaśatru who killed his own father from motives of imperiousness, approaches the Holy One with a certain anxious respect. The simplicity of the description already—among many other aspects—renders it unlikely that we have to take this veneration as a mere fabrication of the Buddhist writers of the text. On the contrary, we may believe that an impression of the holiness and exaltedness of the Buddha's appearance actually effected this veneration in many. It was (and still is) true to Indian nature to show a kind of superhuman awe to everyone who walks the path of spiritual striving detached from the world. In the Sāmaññaphalasutta (I, 36-38), this respect towards not only the disciples of the Buddha, but towards all kinds of religious people is most vividly and drastically depicted: the king himself rises before someone who had formerly been a despised slave, used for lowly services, if this slave 'has gone from the home into homelessness' and has put on the yellow robes. Spiritual concentration, contemplation and Yoga always counted as something sacred in India, and everyone was respected as a holy person who appeared to have reached a perfection beyond the ordinary human measure in these abilities. For the one who sought to acquire sacred knowledge and spiritual abilities of the kind mentioned, the deepest venerating devotion to his spiritual teacher (*guru*) counted as the first prerequisite. In the ancient Vedic times any passing of knowledge from teacher to disciple rested entirely on this devotion—the idea of instruction was entirely different from that familiar to us today—and what we are told about the measure of devotion demanded from the disciple in the old *Brāhmaṇa* texts and Upanishads (as also in the epic texts like the *Mahābhārata*), even if sometimes in a legendary manner, surpasses everything a contemporary person in the West can imagine today. The Buddha stands on the border between two eras, between the ancient Vedic or *Brāhmaṇa* era and a later era in which the faculties of reason had already been called to play a bigger role. He did not want to tie his disciples at all to his own person as this was the case in the old Vedic education. He rather wanted to educate them to a certain independence by giving them a 'norm' which was later to substitute the personal teacher for them. But under the circumstances in India it was natural that he to a large extent also received that kind of veneration which was paid to the *guru*, and the more so as certainly there had occurred no spiritual teacher in India for a very long time whose personality appeared to demand veneration so much as that of the Wise One from the Śākya race. The idea that there is in the veneration of the teacher who is perceived to possess sacred knowledge a strength which increases in the disciple the receptiveness for the knowledge to be absorbed, is quite justified in the context of the Buddhist conditions. In a certain way this veneration has also found its dogmatic expression in the first part of the formula to be spoken by the disciple upon his acceptance into the community: 'I take refuge in the Buddha.' Now we can understand quite well how after the Buddha's death from this former veneration of the master who personally dwelt among the disciples, there emerged, over time, within certain schools of Buddhism, the veneration of those above-mentioned transcendental spiritual beings of the Buddha as 'original Buddha' (Ādibuddha) or 'Buddha of meditation' (Dhyāni-buddha). This, too, has a parallel in Yoga, where the personal teacher (*guru*) is a reference to Īśvara, the 'divine lord' as the primal *guru* (*Yogasūtra* I, 26).

The veneration paid to the Buddha by his followers is also expressed in the various epithets and by-names they used to designate their master. The most important of these names and epithets are compiled in a formula which is often repeated in the texts (e.g., Sāmaññaphala-sutta I, 40): *'idha tathāgato loke upajjati arahaṃ sammāsambuddho vijjā-caraṇa-sampanno sugato lokavidū annuttaro purisadammmasārathi satthā devamanussānaṃ buddho bhagavā'* — 'here emerges a Tathāgata (someone 'gone-thus', i.e., someone who has truly followed the Buddha path) in the world, an *arhat* (Buddhist saint), a perfect Buddha ('perfectly awakened'), who possesses the knowledge and the path, who has gone the good way (*sugata*), one who knows the world, an incomparable teacher of mankind (lit. 'one who reins in the human yoke-cattle'), a teacher of gods and men, an Awakened One (or 'enlightened one', *buddha*), a blessed one (or 'Holy One', *bhagavā*, from *bhaga*, salvation, blessing. The general, but not literal, translation of this most frequent of all epithets of the Buddha is 'the noble one'). Remarkable and important with respect to what has been said above, appears namely the designation of the Buddha as a teacher of mankind. It expresses in succinct brevity how even his own followers did not venerate him as a philosophical theoretician, but as a teacher of a path directed at the realization of practical aims of salvation who was effective through the power of his personality. The entire norm taught by the Buddha culminates in this 'path' which shall be discussed in detail in the second part of this account.

Part II

THE TEACHING

A. General viewpoints

The truth of suffering and the Path

In Part I we have come to know the Buddha as the *teacher of a path*, one of practical knowledge and of salvation. In his final teaching which he imparts to the ascetic Subhadda shortly before he enters *nirvāṇa*, he emphatically places the path as the quintessence of all the norms. He emphasizes how none of the steps to true discipleship can be found outside this Path. Even that principle which is always celebrated as 'the most exquisite teaching of the Awakened One' (*buddhābaṃ sāmukkaṃsikā dhammadesanā*), this fourfold sentence about the nature of suffering etc. (see p. 69f.), culminates in the 'noble Eightfold Path' (*ariyo aṭṭhaṅgiko maggo*). In the Sermon of Benares, in which for the first time the basic principles of the 'norm' taught by Buddha are clearly outlined, this 'Path' is placed there as the essential element of the norm. Only when linked to the formulation of the Eightfold Path, of the 'correct way of the middle', does the fourfold principle of the argument from suffering become proclaimed in its final part. Western descriptions of the Buddha's teaching usually start with this 'argument from suffering'. As we have already seen (p. 98), Buddha himself in his personal teachings did not place it at the beginning but at the end of his instruction. Only the listener who has been correspondingly prepared in his soul seemed to him to be capable of receiving into his soul this highest 'truth' of Buddhism.

In order to reach a deeper understanding of Buddha's teaching, one has at first to bear in mind that this 'argument from suffering' plays a double role; to a certain extent it has a twofold function in Buddhism, that of a belief and of a realization. It is important to separate them. For someone who has not yet become an *arhat*, or who has not yet followed the Path, 'the argument from suffering' can be a matter of faith, an inwardly felt truth. In order to walk the Path in the right way as Buddha meant it, this person must actually take his start from the 'right belief' (*sammādiṭṭhi*), whose essential content forms the argument from suffering. But this principle can only become inner *recognized* truth, an insight in the sense of Buddhism, by travelling on this Path itself. Indeed, it is only the final and highest step on the Path, in which this truth is revealed to the spiritual eye of the disciple (clearly discussed in

Sāmaññaphalasutta 98, and elsewhere). Only through the Path, according to the Buddha's teaching, not through logical thought or philosophical speculation, can the truth of suffering be attained as a true realization.

Indeed through the impression of the Buddha's personal teaching the goal of the Path can be attained in a single moment. In the canon [of his teaching] such cases of spontaneous enlightenment are quite frequently cited. And so it emerges from this in the way we describe Buddhism that a mere theoretical study of the argument from suffering cannot lead to a deeper grasp of the Buddha's teaching. Only from a description of the Path can such an understanding be gained. The 'Path' includes the 'argument from suffering'; in this proposition there stands in a certain manner at the beginning of the Path a belief (*diṭṭhi*), as the end of the Path, a realization (*paññā*).

After we may assume the phrasing of the 'argument from suffering' is known from the account of the 'Sermon of Benares' as provided here, the following account will draw appropriate attention to the argument at that point where it occurs in the course of the progressive development of the disciple as a 'realization' won on the Path. It will then be shown that this realization what suffering is, has originated not in any pessimistic mood of Buddhism, as it is very often assumed, but from a very different soul-experience.

As we already showed in Part 1, the Path taught by the Buddha is a Path of meditation. This clearly emerges already in the formula containing the 'argument from suffering, etc.' of the 'noble Eightfold Path' that culminates in 'right meditation' (*sammāsamādhi*) for which the other seven stages are only preliminary steps (see *Aṅguttaranikāya* IV p. 40, V p. 236). These sources teaching us in detail about the essence and content of the Buddhist path of salvation describe it as a path of meditation. This shows the connection of Buddhism to the spiritual stream of Yoga in India (Yoga as 'yoking, harnessing, exertion').* This is

*This observation deserves a comparison with the *Aṅguttaranikāya* (III, p. 28), where, as in the Kāṭhaka-Upaniṣad, which contains so many connections with Buddhism, the reining-in of the spirit in meditation (*sammāsamādhi*) is compared to the reining-in of horses and draught-animals through a skilful charioteer/driver. What is remarkable in this comparison is the designation of the charioteer as *yogācariyo* (which means 'master of the harnessing'; another justifiable reading: *yogācariyo*, meaning 'master of the draught-animals/beasts of burden'), because *yogācārya* (the Skr. form of the word) later meant for the followers of the mystical direction of Buddhism, the *yogī*.

true in so far as Yoga—this has to be emphasized always—is not a particular single system, but is to be understood as a general way of gaining supersensible knowledge and capacities as well as methodically practised spiritual concentration and meditation, leading to the goals of salvation. It is of the greatest importance for Buddhism that one quite clearly sees the difference of this spiritual direction from a theoretical philosophy or a philosophical theory.

We can explain this difference as follows:

—philosophy (*tarka*) remains at a standstill in the prevailing form of consciousness; we can gain knowledge from this consciousness with our usual logical thinking and with this it intends to answer existential questions, whereas
—Yoga, the meditative direction for spiritual life, sees consciousness as changing in its scope. It seeks to go beyond the given forms of consciousness by rejecting, even suppressing, the thinking that is only rational, in order to rise to higher levels of knowing and the highest spiritual goals lying beyond all knowledge.

In his lectures on psychology, Kant speaks of a 'treasure lying in the field of dark mental images that make up the deepest abyss of human knowledge, but one we cannot reach.'[1] To raise up this hidden treasure is very much the aim of those who strive, including the ones who take up the Buddha's intentions, for whom the word Yoga has been coined in India. Philosophy remains in a set form of consciousness; Yoga has to do with surpassing this and seeking higher states of consciousness. Buddhism acknowledges a whole range of such states of consciousness; in the sacred texts these are repeatedly mentioned (especially in the Poṭṭhapādasutta of the *Dīghanikāya*).

As we saw earlier, the main purpose of the whole of the Buddha's teaching is to lead the listener from his everyday consciousness by awakening a transformation of his soul. For this reason there is a rejection of metaphysical issues, such as the finite and infinite worlds, or eternity and non-eternity, or the soul's existence beyond death (see p. 108). The people who ask such questions remain fixed in their normal consciousness, wanting to construct an answer using their habitual thinking, whereas the Buddha's whole striving is directed at transcending such fixed states (in the sense of Yoga). The Buddha consequently teaches the 'argument from suffering' because it is meant to free the soul on the Path from the fetters of the sense-world. A theoretical answer to those metaphysical questions, even if it were possible, in his opinion would produce the effect of keeping the questioner captive in his own view of the world. He has to free himself from this view in order to participate in true realization and salvation. From this the Buddha derives his robust rejection of all merely logical thinking, philosophizing, speculating and thought-spinning.

If we grasp the difference of these two directions, the theoretical-philosophical on the one hand and the meditative direction of Yoga on the other, then we cannot only speak of a connection of Buddhism to Yoga, but we have every right to say: the whole of Buddhism is through and through nothing but Yoga. How this statement can be justified in detail will emerge from the following considerations. It is important that there is no confusion between Yoga, meaning practical Yoga and the (theoretical) 'yogic system', the 'philosophy of Yoga'.

In order to come to know better the cultural foundations and the spiritual roots of Buddhism and its relationship to the development of Indian spiritual life, we have to investigate, even if briefly, the history of those spiritual endeavours known as Yoga in India. The term Yoga is itself relatively recent; it seems to have been little used in the time of Buddha. The word Yoga in the technical sense of methodic practice of spiritual concentration and meditation appears very often in the later writings of the Sanskrit canon. In the Pali canon it only occurs very rarely and only in the more recent texts.* The actual spiritual stream connected with these endeavours known later as Yoga is very old in India, even if the methods have not always been the same everywhere and at all times. We have heard from Buddha himself how the goals of those who were his Yoga teachers left him feeling dissatisfied. He turned away from the methods that were current in those days.

In ancient India the leading belief was in a prehistoric power of seership that gave rise to the inspiration flowing into the words, the sacred words, or sacred knowledge, of the Veda, which became the basis of the whole religious and spiritual development of India. The ones who carried these inspirations were called *ṛṣi* (approximately pronounced: rishi), a word which was interpreted by the Indians as *atīndriyadraṣṭar* 'seer of the supersensible', or the ones 'who saw beyond the sense-world'. (It is remarkable that even Buddha is frequently

* E.g. *Theragāthā*, p. 61, ed. P.T.S., where it is said of the disciple: *viriyasātaccasampanno yuttayogo sadā siyā*, 'devoted with energy and persistence may he always be given to spiritual concentration'. Cf. the parable of *Aṅguttaranikāya* told in the footnote on p. 130.

called 'the great *ṛṣi*, see above, p. 115.) An ability to see into the higher worlds, a conversing with beings and forces of the supersensible world was attributed to those seers of very much earlier times.

> These indeed were the ones who sat with the gods at table (*devānāṃ sadhamādas*), the preservers of a sacred world-order, these enlightened seers (*kavayas*) of an earlier epoch.
> These Fathers found the hidden light.
> With truly magic words (*satyamantrās*) they revealed this dawn.

So sings one of the verses of the Rig-Veda, the most ancient of all literary memorials of Aryan humanity. Those who belonged to a later age, who saw themselves cut off from this higher form of seeing, from this dialogue and this dining with supersensible beings, sought to regain these capacities by all those methods that have the purpose of subjugating the physical senses and allowing the spirit to gain a mastery over their bodily nature.

In older ages these were more methods of external chastisement. Later on there were in addition more spiritual methods by means of which it was attempted to raise consciousness to a higher level. The external form of asceticism was called *tapas* ('burning, glowing') by the Indians. It was the enkindling of a mystical, inner fire. (One may recall the similes in the *Lalitavistara*, where the kind of activity in Buddha's ascetic efforts is pictured as a friction to ignite fire, see p. 54.) In an ancient Upanishad (*Muṇḍaka*) it says *tapasā cīyate brahma*,[2] 'through *tapas brahman* is built up'. (The *brahman* originally was that which the human being offers to the gods in feelings of sacred, mystical veneration. At the same time it is that which is strength and nourishment for the gods. Later it is seen as the divine presence in the universe and in man, the flowing supersensible element in the world that is incorporated in the sacred word and in its carrier the Brahmin caste.)

Besides the physical chastisement which is part of the concept of *tapas*, there is a spiritual aspect which is not to be overlooked. And so it is that the world-creative power of the musings of the primordial spirit that enkindles world-warmth is also called *tapas*. With this concept of *tapas* another concept was linked, *brahmacarya*, which means the holy life. The sacred, divine life, whose most essential characteristic is chastity, became in the sense of this spiritual stream the human being able to draw to himself supersensible powers through chastity. However, when the opposite happens he is cut off from such powers. In *Brāhmaṇa* and *Upaniṣad* texts there is mention of finding the supersensible *brahman* world through *tapas* and *brahmacarya* (e.g., *Chāndogya-Upaniṣad* 8, 5, 3). It is worth noting that we meet this linking of *tapas* and *brahmacarya* (Pali *brahmacariya*) also in Buddhist texts (e.g., *Theragāthā*, p. 64). The 'holy life' of the Buddhist pupil is normally called *brahmacarya* or *brahmacariya*. The word *amṛta* ('immortality' or also 'water of life') is used for the supersensible salvation achieved through *brahmacarya*, as shown in the Brāhmaṇa texts, both in Buddhism and in the Veda. This *amṛta* (Pali *amata*) relates to the sacred fig free, the Aśvattha (see p. 89). In the great Indian epic, the *Mahābhārata*, the concept of Yoga plays an important role beside *tapas* and *brahmacarya*; Yoga as a practical endeavour, as methodical practice of concentration and meditation is contrasted with *sāṃkhya*, theoretical philosophy. The technique of meditation appears in the *Mahābārata* already developed in detail. During the course of time it becomes fixed in the teaching manuals in a more scientific manner and placed on a basis which lies close to the theoretical Sāṃkhya which is philosophically affiliated to it.

It should not be forgotten that many of the Sāṃkhya-teachings, in fact most of what appears in India as philosophy, has its true origin in practical mysticism—in other words, in what later is called Yoga. In this later theory of Yoga *tapas* and *brahmacarya* no longer signify a comprehensive concept as was the case in the earlier phase of Yoga, but rather certain aspects of Yoga schooling. Especially *brahmacarya* is no longer the 'holy life' in general, but chastity as an especially essential side of the sacred life. The most well known and important teaching manuals of Yoga, the *Yogasūtras* of Patañjali, earlier regarded as originating in the second century BC, according to the latest research by Jacobi,[3] is now placed to a much later century AD. The wide agreement of the technical terms of these *sūtras* with Buddhist terminology was already noted by É. Senart (*Revue de l'histoire des religions*, p. 345, *Bouddhisme et Yoga*, Paris, 1900). This should be obvious to any reader of the *sūtra* who is versed in Buddhism.

To draw the conclusion that the author of the *Yogasūtras* has drawn his wisdom from Buddhism would be inappropriate despite the chronological connections. For as we have already stressed, with reference to the technical expressions, Buddha appears to have been minimally creative with the outer concepts that clothe his teaching. We meet these expressions in question elsewhere, above all in the *Mahābhārata*. We can consequently assume that even though the copy of the *Yogasūtra* which we now possess in its available form belongs to a later time, the assimilated material comes from a much earlier time, as is often the case with Indian literary works. The Buddha and the author of the *Yogasūtra* have drawn their means of expression from similar sources standing in close proximity to one another. This suggests itself when studying the inner connection between Buddhism and Yoga.

Far-reaching conclusions should not be drawn from the outer correspondence in the terminology of Buddhism and the Yoga-system. It should also not be overlooked that especially in the Buddhist texts we find a much greater array of technical Yoga details than in the *Yogasūtras*. The real theoretical basis of the *Yogasūtra*, the dualism of spirit and matter taken from the Sāṃkhya-system, is remote from Buddhism. Despite all the individual correspondences there can be no question of any direct link between Buddhism and the Yoga-system. However, the existing correspondences can be explained by the above-mentioned links between both of them: Buddhism with the (theoretical) Yoga-system, and (practical) Yoga. A study of the Buddhist path of knowledge and the path of salvation in its individual parts shows that by drawing comparisons with the *Yogasūtra* one gains much in understanding Buddhism. It is the case that, for example, the essential elements of the 'argument from suffering' can be found in the *Yogasūtras* and through commentators we know that the terminology that is used there ('suffering—the origin of suffering—the destruction of suffering—the path to destroy suffering') derives from an old way of expression in medical handbooks. One can see from this that one should not automatically draw the conclusion from the uniformity or similarity of the teachings, or the technical expressions of the two systems, that one has borrowed from the other. The common origin of both is to be sought in a third, much earlier source.

Together with the foregoing remarks concerning the importance of the Yoga system to understand Buddhism it seems appropriate to offer some indications about the basic thoughts of this system. We can enter into details when discussing the Buddhist path.

The *Yogasūtra* speaks of a seed slumbering in every soul which has the capacity for a higher knowing and a higher consciousness—which is very similar to the Buddha's higher knowledge in Buddhism. This is delineated as *sarvajñatvam* (universal knowledge). This supersensible knowledge is to a certain extent only concealed due to the illusion of sinful passions (*kleśa*, which is in reality 'torment, worries, hardship', something with which the human being weighs himself down). This fetters the soul to the visible world of fallen matter and sensuality. The common source of all 'hardships' is *avidyā* (not knowing, error), which in the Yoga system is the confusing of the eternal, pure, non-suffering with the non-eternal, impure, full of suffering; of the true self (*ātman*) with that which is not the true self. The clouding of the soul, the illusionary ideas of sinful passion (*kleśa*) are present in consciousness as actual thoughts (*vṛtti*), in the unconscious potentially present as what is called *saṃskāra*. These potential thoughts are the unconscious memories and with it at the same time the unconscious formative forces (this is the actual literal meaning of the word *saṃskāra*); as such they give rise to rebirth and destiny, and the whole sum of pleasure and suffering that the soul has to endure in its subsequent incarnation as a consequence of its earlier deed (*karma*).

From the standpoint of higher knowledge all these karmic effects are painful (II, 15, the parallel of the Buddhist saying of the 'argument from suffering'). To overcome this suffering the soul goes through a process of purification (*aśuddhikṣaya*) which destroys error (*avidyā*) that is the root of the illusion of sinful passion (*kleśa*). It frees the spiritual essence (*puruṣa*) from its entanglements in the world of the senses. This process of purification is the Eightfold Path of Yoga. This is the essential thing about the Yoga system, namely that the destruction of error is achieved not by mere operations in the thinking life, but by going through a formal process of purifying the soul.

In the first *sūtra*, Yoga is defined as the mastery or suppression (*nirodha*, one of Buddhism's most central concepts) of thoughts, mental pictures, in the field of consciousness (*cittavṛtti*, actually 'expressions of the thought-element', conceived both materially and etherically in the sense of the Sāṃkhya-teaching). In this way the various steps of the inner mystical contemplation are reached (*samādhi*) whose technical name we also meet in Buddhist texts. These inner contemplations, it is true, lead the soul to a true higher realization (*ṛtaṃbharā prajñā*) and spiritual power (*vibhūti*, corresponding to the *ṛddhi* of Buddhism), but the highest aim enabling the spirit to be freed (*puruṣa*) is achieved when concentration reaches right into the unconscious, achieving the destruction (*nirodha*) of *saṃskāra*. The inner contemplation is then called *nirbīja*, which means no longer containing any seed of rebirth. In this way the purifying of the soul (*sattva*) is completed. In relation to purity, it stands as equal in its archetypal spiritual form (*puruṣa*); it has now found liberation from the visible world, the 'isolation' (*kaivalyam*) (Y. S. III, 54). This destruction of the *saṃskāra* (Pali *saṅkhāra*) is the definite goal of Buddhism, too; without knowledge of the Yoga system it is not possible to comprehend Buddhism properly.

The capacities of clairvoyance and higher spiritual powers which already appeared at an earlier stage are not to be achieved for their own sake and have to be dropped if the highest goal is to be achieved (III 36. 49); here, too, there is agreement between Buddhism and the Yoga system). One must emphasize that in Yoga and all its achievements it is not a question of gaining or creating something new and strange, but of removing hindrances, so that certain latent slumbering capacities in the soul can unfold. This process can be illustrated with the parable of the farmer who by removing the dams allows the waters to irrigate his fields (Y. S. IV, 2. 3). The path of Yoga serving the purpose of purifying the soul divides into eight stages, as explained in Chapter two.

– The first stage (*yama*) contains the ethical basis of the whole of Yoga development,
– the second (*niyama*) involves the attitude of the mind and the feelings (*Gemüt*) and other things,
– the third (*āsana*) the attitude of the body,
– the fourth (*prāṇāyāma*) concerns the breathing,
– the fifth (*pratyāhāra*) the sense-organs.

These five are preliminary stages (*bahiraṅga*) of the real spiritual concentration and meditation that proceeds in three steps (*dhāraṇā, dhyāna* and *samādhi*), which in actual fact also exist in Buddhism, only that in Buddhism *dhyāna* (Pali *jhāna*) and *samādhi* are not distinguished from each other in the same way. These three steps are another preliminary stage for the above-mentioned *nirbīja-samādhi*. On the one hand, in the number of stages as well as in the essence and naming of the final stage (*samādhi*) the path of Yoga agrees with the 'Noble Eightfold Path' of Buddhism. On the other hand, the first seven sections of the Buddhist formulation are not identical with the first seven steps on the Yoga path. As we shall see in the further description, the fact is that these steps within the path of Yoga are essentially also present in Buddhism. There are many Buddhist texts which quite clearly reveal this continuous and marked correspondence on this very point. Consequently, it seems necessary to gain clarity about the relationship of the eightfold formula to these texts.

Those who study the argument of the 'Noble Eightfold Path' with real penetration will have to say to themselves that the question about the actual content of the aim of the Path has not been answered at all.

When it says 'right viewpoint, right thought (or decision), right word, right deed, right living, right striving' and so on, one has to ask above all: what is right viewpoint, what *does* right thought comprise, and right word, right deed, right living, right striving, and so on? In the wording, the whole teaching and the complete ethics of Buddhism are presumed, without the wording telling us in what this teaching and this ethics consist. If one only bears in mind the fourfold 'argument from suffering' then it can appear as if just at this decisive point regarding the Path, the Buddha has left an empty scheme for his followers.

In reality this is not the case. Rather, the Buddha has definitely left clear answers to the questions about what is right thought, right deed, right striving, and so on, just as the content of other stages on the Path have with certainty been defined by him. The wording of the Eightfold Path is consequently not superfluous or without significance, but it has to be placed beside those other expressions of the Buddha, if this one is to attain full comprehension. In its imprecision as a blanket coverage, the wording takes on a certain general meaning and adaptability. It leaves open that which is correct in its content. It only instructs one to accept this correct thing into one's belief, then to express it in thoughts, words and deeds, in one's whole life and striving, and to keep it continuously in one's memory (*sammāsati*). Finally, it works into the soul in such a way that it becomes inner contemplation and meditation.

Buddhist explanations of the wording can be found in many places in the canon, for example, in the Mahāsatipaṭṭhānasutta of the *Dīghanikāya*. That the first seven stages of the Eightfold Path are only aids (*parikkhārā*) and preliminary steps for the eighth stage, for spiritual contemplation and meditation (*samādhi*), is important for understanding Buddhism and is emphasized in many places (e.g., *Aṅg*. IV, p. 236). In the wording of the Eightfold Path it is not expressed how *samādhi* is, once again, itself the preliminary step and requirement. It only says concerning this Path in general that it is 'the way to end suffering'. The 'meditation' which concludes the Eightfold wording is not the final goal, but only a means to achieve it.

There is no lack of sayings in the canon that extend the line of development beyond *samādhi*. We can point to the passage already mentioned (*Aṅguttaranikāya* IV, p. 236 and the following extracts up to p. 240), where everywhere *sammāsamādhi* is followed by *sammāñāṇaṃ*—'right realization,' followed then by *sammāvimutti*—'right liberation.' In saying this we have shown the most important basic thought of Buddhism in its most precise form. The goal of the striving is designated in the general Indian manner of expression as 'liberation'. It is attained through realization and this through contemplation or meditation. Also in Yoga teaching, realization (here in the sense of the Yoga-system as 'discriminating realization' – *vivekakhyāti*) is the preliminary stage of the goal of redemption (*kaivalyam*); the way to this realization goes through the purification process of Yoga, the Eightfold Path of meditation (*Yogasūtra* II, 25. 26. 28).

Looking from below upwards, it becomes clear in Buddhism that the real first step of the Path – already called the first step in the Eightfold formula – is the 'right view' of belief. The further steps on the Path preceding meditation can be summarized as the *norm of right behaviour* in thought, word and deed, wherein the seventh stage, *sammāsati*, already stands closely linked to meditation. Just as right meditation emerges from right ethical behaviour, so out of meditation emerges right realization, liberation out of realization. We recall the last sermons of the Buddha to his disciples in the Mahāparinibbānasutta, where he repeatedly points to the significance of the main parts of the aim:

– *sīla* (right behaviour),
– *samādhi* (meditation),
– *paññā* (realization), followed by
– *vimutti* (liberation) as the fourth stage:

> rich in blessings and fruit is meditation when it is borne by the right behaviour, full of blessings and fruit is realization when it rests on meditation and is permeated by such realization; then the soul is freed of all illusion regarding worldly pleasures, being in the world and of error.

This formulation reappears at eight places in the Mahāparinibbānasutta; in other places one can frequently meet this arrangement of *sīla, samādhi, paññā,* and *vimutti*. However, it is important that the Pali canon produces texts that describe the Path, not only in an external and schematic way, as does the formula of the Eightfold Path, but its detailed description reveals its full content in all its different steps. All these texts are based on the four main sections: *sīla, samādhi, paññā,* and *vimutti*. Strictly speaking, it is a matter of only one segment that shows the aim of the Path, returning in the same formula in all the more important teaching texts of the *Dīghanikāya* (not in the texts concerning the legends). We can see the Sāmaññaphalasutta as the most significant of these texts, where the section in question, beginning at paragraph 40, continues to the end of the *sūtra* (*Dīghanikāya*, Vol. I, 62–86, P. T. S.). It returns in the same wording in the Ambaṭṭhasutta (p. 100), in the

Soṇadaṇḍasutta (p. 124), the Kūṭadantasutta (p. 147), the Mahālisutta (p. 157), the Jāliyasutta (p. 159), the Kassapa-Sīhanādasutta (p. 172), the Poṭṭhapādasutta (p. 181), the Subhasutta (p. 206), the Kevaddhasutta (p. 214), the Lohiccasutta (p. 232) and according to some readings also in the Tevijjasutta (p. 249, Note 8).

The Brahmajālasutta is also similar in many respects, in some passages with similar wording (pp. 4–17). The *Dīghanikāya* is that part of the Pali canon that represents the norm in larger interconnected pieces; it is one of the main sources for the teaching of Buddha.

The above-mentioned section, often appearing with the same wording in all the important teaching texts in this collection, holds a special significance within the canon. That is also true of how the main viewpoint is divided into *sīla, samādhi, paññā,* and *vimutti,* which the Subhasutta (p. 206) also emphasizes in passages in the 'section on ethical behaviour' (*sīlakkhandho*), the 'section on meditation' (*samādhikkhandho*) and the 'section on knowing' (*paññākhandho*). Not merely external reasons, but above all inner and objective reasons reveal to us here a Buddhist aim/norm before all other valuable viewpoints. We are justified in saying that in this division of the main four sections, of ethics (*sīla*), of meditation (*samādhi*), of realization (*paññā*) and of liberation (*vimutti*), the entire Buddhist objective is contained in a nutshell. It appears inwardly credible when it is related that on his final walk, wherever he went Buddha pointed with special emphasis to these four main elements. Even in later Buddhist literature the above-mentioned viewpoint is used, and also in the *Visuddhimagga* of Buddhaghoṣa.

The section of the *Dīghanikāya* should first and foremost serve as an external indication for the following description of the norm of Buddhism; other textual sources will be included where it is of significance. In describing the Path as it is contained in each section, very noticeable parallels to Yoga teaching will stand out, especially to the *Yogasūtra* of Patañjali. Further light will be shed on the links between the true essence of Buddhism and Yoga, on which we have touched many times. Thereby, as we have seen, a division of four main parts follows: ethics (*sīla*), meditation (*samādhi*), realization (*paññā*), and liberation (*vimutti*). The most important text of that section seems from several points of view to be contained in the Sāmaññaphalasutta (the relevant section in its full wording is printed in the Pali Text Society edition). For this reason it was natural to consider the Sāmaññaphalasutta above all in the following quotations.

B. The individual stages of the path

a) Faith (*saddhā*) as a prerequisite of the path

Before the Sāmaññaphalasutta and its parallel texts enter into a description of the individual steps of the path and their accomplishments, it is pointed out that the decision to tread the path is brought about in such a way that the words of the Tathāgata (Buddha) give rise to that impression in the listener which is called faith (*saddhā*). This implies an emotional grasping of the Buddhist truth of salvation, especially of the truth of suffering, which occurs before the actual *knowing* or realization which is not attained until a much later stage of the path. Here, too, it is not about something theoretical, but about a lively emotion which effects that transformation in the soul of the listener that has been described above (p. 97). An essential characteristic of this Buddhist 'faith' is the desire to give up one's previous life entirely in order to exchange it for the 'sacred way of life' (*brahmacariya*), 'to go from home into homelessness' (SPhS 41). The disciple is so moved by the truth of the suffering of all earthly things and the bliss of salvation communicated by the Tathāgata that he feels his continued sojourn in his familiar environment, all earthly belongings and all relationships with relatives and friends to be a burden. He feels the urge to free himself from them. A similar shade of the term 'faith' (*śraddhā*) is also encountered in the *Kāṭhaka-Upaniṣad* which contains various connections with Buddhism.

The description in the *Dīghanikāya* corresponds to the formula of the Eightfold Path in such a way that there, too, *sammādiṭṭhi*, right view in faith, is named as the first step on which all further steps of the path are built. It is clearly said in the sacred texts that the mood in which the Buddhist believer allows the 'truth of suffering' to work on himself is not one that is somehow tainted by a weariness of the world. The mood of the true disciple is rather an inner tranquillity and uplift which increases to the highest bliss on the higher stages of the path. After showing how in the sense of the twelvefold formula of emerging suffering eventually follows from birth, the *Saṃyuttanikāya* (vol. II, p. 31f.) continues in a notable passage in a very remarkable way: from suffering follows faith (*saddhā*), from faith inspiration (*pāmojjaṃ*), from inspiration joy (*pīti*), from joy tranquillity (*passaddhi*), from tranquillity blissful pleasure (*sukha*), from bliss contemplation (*samādhi*), from contemplation the right-sighted realization (*yathābhūtaññaṇadassanaṃ*), from realization freedom from passion (*virāga*), from freedom from passion liberation (*vimutti*). According to this, in the sequence of conditional arising, suffering only means the point of passage to bliss, realization and liberation for the disciple of the path.

The actual first stage of the path (according to the *Dīghanikāya*) is 'right ethical behaviour,' moral discipline (*sīla*). But according to the Buddhist viewpoint, this practical behaviour again has faith as its basis which at the same time is the actual driving force for the decision to tread the path in the first place. In the *Aṅguttaranikāya* (vol. IV, p. 314),[1] too, it is emphasized that faith (*saddhā*) along with right behaviour (*sīla*) is necessary, that initially it all comes down to faith, and how only then one may speak about right behaviour and knowledge. And in another passage in the same collection (vol. III, p. 236) it is said in a beautiful parable that in the same way that sunrise is preceded by dawn, everything else which is won by the disciple in terms of virtues and accomplishments on the path has to be preceded by faith. By leading to knowledge, the path is a 'path of realization', and in the sense of this parable, faith can, as it were, be regarded as the dawn of realization. Faith, or 'right view', is thus that which is of first and foremost importance for everyone. The right treading of the path of discipleship has as its indispensable prerequisite this 'faith', and even those who have not yet entered this path profess themselves true followers of the Buddha through 'faith'; indeed, if they have truly grasped the doctrine of the Buddha in the right faith and with the right earnestness they have, in the sense of the eightfold formula, already taken the first step on the path. The steps that follow may then, if one cannot or does not want to take them now—we have to take the Buddha's teaching in this way—be taken in a later existence. This applies to many who avow themselves to Buddhism without entering the path of discipleship. They are called lay disciples (*upāsaka*, lit. 'devotees'; fem. *upāsikā*) in Buddhism. By their faithful, devoted acceptance of the truth proclaimed by the Buddha they have, however, according to the Buddhist view, laid the foundations for the path to be trod in a later life which will then lead them to realization, to salvation, to liberation. The others, however, the true disciples, do not remain with mere faith in their present existence, but they tread the path which leads them to that point where they are able to see the truth of the revelation of salvation for themselves, the pious acceptance of which leads them to the treading of the path. 'There is a path, there is an entry (*atthi maggo atthi paṭipadā*) through which a person can realize by himself (*sāma*) that the ascetic Gautama (Buddha) proclaims the norm in accordance with the times, appropriately and truthfully.' (Kassapasīhanādasutta 13).[2] In the following, the details of this path will be discussed.

b) First Stage of the Path: Right Conduct (*sīla*)

In the formula of the eightfold path ethical behaviour (*sīla*)—which, according to the *Dīghanikāya*, forms the first stage of the path—includes the second to the seventh of its limbs, i.e., right decision (or thoughts), right word, right action, right livelihood, right effort, right contemplation (these last two already turn towards the next stage of the path, meditation, and they are occasionally already counted with it in the texts [*Majjh.* I, p. 301]).[1] The answer to the question: what is right thought, right speech, right action etc.? is not found in the eightfold formula, but very clearly in the paragraph about the path as it occurs in the Sāmaññaphalasutta and the other texts of the *Dīghanikāya* mentioned above. It is important that we see and appreciate the nature and significance of these Buddhist ethics and their relationship to the 'path' correctly. Many Western descriptions of Buddhism make it appear as if the Buddha had given certain moral doctrines in the same way that he revealed the 'truth of suffering' and other doctrines of salvation, some only for his disciples, others also for outsiders, but it is not emphasized clearly enough how these ethics are positioned within the whole of Buddhism, how a certain ethical behaviour not only belongs to the path, to the 'cessation of suffering' in general, but how it forms a very particular prerequisite for the next step of the path—right spiritual concentration and meditation (*samādhi*). It is often said that the whole of Buddhism was actually mere ethics. There is thus far a kernel of truth in this, that in the context of the 'path' which forms, as we know, the essence of the norm, it is *initially* indeed just about moral discipline, right ethical behaviour. This practical ethical behaviour is the only thing Buddhism expects of the disciple in the first stage of development. 'Avoidance of evil, doing good and watchful guarding of the mind is the (entire) admonition of the Awakened One (Buddha),' thus an old Buddhist saying. In this we should not overlook that [on the one hand] this treading of the path which initially involves only a practical following of ethical commandments has to be after all preceded by hearing and faithfully accepting the truths of salvation, especially of the truth of suffering, and that on the other hand this path does not remain permanently confined to the sphere of the ethical, but that this outer discipline forms the passage to other stages which lie beyond the ethical. Even in the above-mentioned formula which sets the ethical in the foreground so very much, the 'watchful guarding of the mind' is also referred to alongside the doing of good and the avoidance of evil, i.e., that spiritual concentration, so important in Buddhism for which everything ethical is only a preliminary stage and which is itself again the necessary prerequisite of all realization and all those goals of salvation, still lying beyond.

In Yoga just as in Buddhism, the first stage of the path includes right behaviour. The idea certainly is that the kind of concentration and meditation central to Yoga cannot come about in the right way if not all its preliminary stages, first and foremost ethical behaviour, have been practised in the right way first. Those ethical demands are not made in order to burden the Yoga-aspirant with something which does not have any direct bearing on his efforts, but because they are thought to have an immediate connection with everything which is striven for as supernatural achievements in the practice of Yoga.

That first stage of the path which corresponds to the Buddhist *sīla* (Skt. *śīla*) carries the name *yama* in Yoga. It includes five individual precepts which are essentially in accord with those of the Buddhist *sīla*. The first of these precepts is the sparing of life (in Yoga: *ahiṃsā*), the compassion that shows itself in not harming living beings (YS II, 30; SPhS 43: *pāṇatipātā paṭivrato hoti*). In Yoga (YS II, 34) as in Buddhism (note the formula: right thought, right word, right action etc.) it holds true of all precepts that they have to be fulfilled not only in the outer action, with the 'physical' (*kāya*) as Buddhism puts it, but also in the inner spiritual attitude of thoughts and emotions (*mano*) and in speech (*vācā*), i.e., in thoughts, words and deeds. In this sense, any hostile feeling towards any living being and any hard, unfriendly or hurtful speech already constitutes a violation of the first precept. This is why the Buddhist texts (SPhS 44) explicitly mention the avoidance of hard, unfriendly speech (*pharusavācā*) in this connection. The corresponding spiritual attitude is the sentiment of compassion towards all beings of which Buddhism always speaks (see also ibid. 43). That this compassion is not only an abstract 'cardinal virtue' of Buddhism, but that even in this context the connection with meditation exists which is to be urgently emphasized everywhere. This follows quite clearly from what is said (e.g., Tevijjasutta 75ff[2]) about the suffusion of meditation with the feeling of love (or 'friendliness', *mettā*), of compassion (*karuṇā*), of shared joy (*muditā*) and equanimity towards the impure and evil (*upekkhā*). These four emotions correspond directly to the fourfold terms *maitrī* (Pali *mettā*), *karuṇā, muditā, upekṣā* (Pali *upekkhā*) which in the *Yogasūtra* (I, 33) are recommended to the meditating Yogi to gain a detached soul. In Buddhism, these are called the four 'immeasurables' (*appamaññā*), i.e., the sensations which expand into infinity in meditation: the Tevijjasutta (76ff) describes how the meditating person penetrates all four cardinal directions with the rays of his love, compassion, shared joy and equanimity. And just as according to the Yogasūtra (II, 35) the perfected applied practice of compassion magically calms the hostility of all beings, the Buddhist saint, too, has an irresistible magical power in that 'feeling of friendship' with all beings which can calm even the anger of the wildest animals (cf. p. 119). Buddhism (as Indian Yoga in general) here converges with the mysticism of St Francis of Assisi. Both share especially the practical extension of compassionate charity to include the animal kingdom.

The precept of not harming life is also known in the older Brahminical religion, but Buddhism is different from it in the practical consequences it has drawn from that precept—initially with regard to the [animal] sacrifice. In extent, expression and metaphysical justification very different from Buddhism (but therefore from a historical point of view not without interest) we find the precept of sparing life in an old Upanishad (*Bṛhadāraṇyaka* 1, 5, 14) which speaks about the mystical unity of the moon year with Prajāpati, the creator of the world who with a sixteenth of his being (represented by the individual phases of the moon) enters everything that lives. 'That is why,' it is said, 'one should not take the life of any living beings, even if it were only a lizard, out of respect for that deity.' Buddhism has stripped the precept of all metaphysical justification and has thereby extended its practical field of application in accordance with Yoga.

The second of the main Buddhist precepts is the precept to not take what is not offered. This corresponds to the third of the *yama* precepts of the *Yogasūtra* (II, 30) *asteya* (cf. SPhS 1, *athenena ... attanā viharati*), the 'non-stealing' which includes, as any precept also extends to thoughts, words and deeds, not only theft in our sense, but any attachment of any desire to foreign property. The *Yogasūtra* mentions that all treasures will flow to someone perfected in this characteristic. (And have not precisely the most liberal gifts for the service of his cause flowed from kings and the wealthy to the Buddha, who was himself more liberated from egoistic striving for earthly things than any other being?) While the second precept has a more negative aspect for the true disciples of the path, for those followers of the norm who have not yet entered the path themselves, generosity as the positive side of this precept, as it were, is especially important, its blessing is everywhere praised very highly in Buddhism. Among the subjects preparing the communication of the 'truth of suffering' the 'discussion of giving' (*dānakathā*), instruction on generosity, always appears first (e.g., *Mahāvagga*[3] p. 19 and in many similar passages), even before the instruction on the general indications of duty (*sīla*). Even more significant is the third precept of chastity which, in unison with general Indian terminology, in Buddhism as in the Yoga system (YS II, 30) is called *brahmacarya* (Pali *brahmacariya*), i.e., Brahminical conduct, sacred life. (In the *Yogasūtra*, *brahmacarya* is the fourth of the *yama* precepts.) The significance of this precept is also expressed in the fact that not only this single aspect of discipleship, but the whole of discipleship, the entire practical striving focused on the path, is called *brahmacariya* in Buddhism. (In this way, e.g., in the recurring formula in SPhS 40.) It is in this sense that the liberating realization, too, is called 'completion of the sacred course' (*brahmacariyapariyosāna*). In the older Brahminical mysticism the significance of the word was similarly comprehensive (above p. 133); only the later Yoga teaching takes the word as a technical term for a particular part of the entire Yoga education in another, narrower sense. In Buddhism, the narrower and the more extended meaning of the word are used alongside each other. It is important that with the third precept we meet with a difference between the disciples of the path and the outsiders (lay people) for the first time. For the latter, only the avoidance of adultery and unchastity (in the usual sense) has been made a duty, while of the disciple of the path the full abstinence and purity of body, speech and thought is expected. It is founded in human nature that this precept is only fulfilled by a few. Others only reach the first stage of the path (in the sense of the Buddhist opinion), the further stages are attainable for them only in later lives. It is in this point that it becomes especially obvious that the Buddhist precepts are anything but a 'quotidian morality', but something especially leading entirely out of the sphere of daily life. With the third precept it is again particularly important to note the connection with meditation: those who cannot fulfil this precept are in this present life barred from 'right meditation' (in the Buddha's sense) without which there is no path to realization and liberation in Buddhism. The concentration of the mind as Buddhism and Yoga demand it in the sense of these teachings is connected with the concentration, the contraction of certain other forces which is to be effected precisely through *brahmacarya.* It is said in the *Yogasūtra* (II, 38) that *brahmacarya* is the true source of strength for those seeking spiritual concentration (Yogis). The old Brahminical texts already talk about the finding of the (supernatural) world of *brahman* through *brahmacarya,* even the word *brahmacarya* basically expresses the thought which is central here: those who free themselves of the grip of those powers which want to put them in the service of sensuality and the lower life, open access to those worlds which lie beyond the sphere of the sensual; supernatural beings bow to the saint who has overcome the lower nature within himself. Thus the third precept names the critical point where for many the possibility of attaining higher stages of the path and thus the realization of the Buddhist goal of salvation already in this present life, is ruined. (It has to be emphasized strictly that all of this is only said in the context of Buddhism and not presented as a truth valid for all eras).

Here again there is an important difference between the teaching of the Buddha and the views of Brahmanism as they are laid out in the Laws of Manu.[4] This Brahmanism, too, knows Yoga as the striving to attain union with *brahman* through spiritual concentration and in this striving attributes the same importance to chastity as Patañjali and Buddha, but this path is only open to the Brahmin in a later stage of life after fulfilling his duty of establishing a household and fathering male offspring. Those who wander the path of asceticism evading this duty are in Manu's view guilty of a sin through which they enter the downward path.

The fourth precept, *truthfulness* (*satya,* Pali *sacca*) Buddhism also shares with the *Yogasūtra* (II, 30 where it takes second position among the *yama* precepts). It is in the nature of this precept that it applies particularly to speech. With a certain worldly wisdom the Buddha demands being particularly mindful of one's speech. For those who seek spiritual concentration create a hindrance for their striving through each untruthful or thoughtless word: in the *Udānavarga* (VIII, 2) it is said that in the mouth of a human being an axe develops already at birth through which those who indulge in foolish and evil speech injure themselves. According to the Buddha (and the doctrine of Yoga) those not inspired by the purest striving for truth cannot be disciples of the path whose aim is, as we know, the liberation from all delusion (*avidyā*). It is characteristic for Buddhism that it demands friendliness in speech along with truthfulness. Hard, unfriendly speech is to be avoided by the disciple (see above, p. 144); he should say whatever 'is harmless, pleasant to hear, lovely, moving ('going to the heart', *hadayaṃgama*), dignified (*pora*, lit. 'urban') and beneficial to mankind' (SPhS 44). He should take particular care to avoid idle chat (*samphappalāpa*), he should only speak where appropriate, where it has meaning and serves the benefit of others. (On the value of 'noble silence' see above, p. 105.) 'Never' a beautiful *sūtra* (Abhayarājakumārasutta) of the *Majjhimanikāya*[5] states,

> does the Tathāgata speak words which are untrue, not for the benefit of others or unpleasant to them, just as little as words that are true, but not for the benefit of others or unpleasant to them, or words which are pleasant to hear, but untrue and not beneficial, equally not words which are true and pleasant to others, but not beneficial; in contrast he speaks words which are true and beneficial, even if the other does not like to hear them, and he prefers to speak words which are true and beneficial and pleasant to the listener,

because the Tathāgata—it is added—is compassionate towards all beings. In Buddhism, even in the oldest texts, it is always stressed that the true disciple not only keeps the right behaviour because it serves his own development, but because it is for the well-being of the world, for the welfare of all beings (cf. *Itivuttaka* 84).[6]

The fifth precept which concerns the avoidance of intoxicating drinks is not mentioned in the Sāmaññaphalasutta (or the passage on the path to salvation of the *Dīghanikāya*; but it is mentioned elsewhere, e.g., Soṇadaṇḍasutta 20, Kūṭadantasutta 26).[7] The reason for this prohibition is probably not only—as some have thought (Pischel, p. 89)[8]—consideration for the Indian climate, but the idea that to consume such drinks is a hindrance to the right concentration, i.e., that concentration carried by right prudence and clear self-consciousness. Thus the point of view of Yoga here also provides the key to understanding. This precept however—like the previous ones (excepting the qualifications with the third precept) also applies to outsiders. In the *Yogasūtra* (II, 30), the fifth of the *yama* precepts is *aparigraha*, i.e., complete unconcern for earthly possessions and all business and worries of external life. (This is why, according to the teaching of Yoga, perfection in this quality grants memories of that which lies beyond the present existence, YS II, 39.) Inasmuch as the disciple of the path may be considered, this precept is not only in substance found in Buddhism in its entirety, but even the Yoga expression *aparigraha* (Pali *apariggaha*) is found, e.g. in Tevijjasutta 80. In the passages on the path to salvation in the *Dīghanikāya* (SPhS 45ff.) a series of details is enumerated instead which are observed by the disciple. Apart from the sparing of all seedlings and plants which appears like an extension of the first main precept, the respective prescriptions largely contain nothing but a paraphrase of the Yoga term *aparigraha*. In the first instance, this is all that which is ordinarily taken as the five special monastic precepts (rather: precepts of the disciples) that are added to those five which are binding also for lay people, namely: to take only one meal a day and no longer enjoy food in the evening, not to visit performances of dancing, singing, music and theatre, to abstain from the use of wreaths, perfumes, ointments and jewellery, not to rest on a high or lavish bed, not to accept gold and silver. But the term *aparigraha*, the abstinence from all busy-ness, distraction and hunger for profit, is here described in a much more extensive manner: the disciple of the path avoids all participation in mercantile business, in untruthful behaviour in trade and conduct, in all kinds of folk diversions and games etc.; finally also the practice of all kinds of lowly arts for the sake of earning money (this passage which is of interest from the point of view of history of culture has been mentioned above p. 115f.). It is impossible to enter into all the details here.

With the above, the passage on *sīla* in the Sāmaññaphalasutta (and the parallel texts in the *Dīghanikāya*) is complete. Up to here, it corresponds quite exactly to the *yama* of the Yogasūtra (II, 30), only the term *aparigraha* is circumscribed in concrete details. The question is: do we also find the other stages of Yoga in the passage on the path to salvation of the *Dīghanikāya*? The second stage of the path of Yoga, *niyama*, includes outer and inner purity, contentment, *tapas*, recitation of sacred texts or formulas (*svādhyāya*) and worship of Īśvara (YS II, 32). With regards to Īśvara, the divine lord and master, the initial *guru* of Yoga, the human-superhuman teacher, the Buddha has taken his place in Buddhism (Īśvara's qualities as pointed out in YS I, 24. 25 – that he is free from sinful passion and the consequences of *karma*, and that the seed of all-knowing which is present in everyone has come to full fruition in him – in the sense of the Buddhist opinion, also apply to the Buddha). The significance which in Buddhism is assigned to the veneration of the master has already been discussed. In the Sāmaññaphalasutta this veneration is presumed as a fact (cf. the formula in § 40), not mentioned as a precept. In the same way nothing is explicitly said of the recitation of sacred texts; the role this has actually played in Buddhism already follows sufficiently from the existence and extent of these texts, from the entire devoted care which has been applied to the preservation and transmission of the Buddha's word. The extent of these texts, their peculiar rhythm (on this, see p. 101), the many repetitions and some other aspects can only be understood if we see that they did not serve a mere theoretical need of the kind we perhaps conceive of in Western terms, but that they first and foremost in the Indian manner served the purpose of recitation and meditation. It is always repeated that the short 'argument from suffering' contains *everything* for the needs of knowledge and faith. With regard to *tapas* which in the Yoga system is counted among *niyama* we have seen that it is precisely characteristic of Buddhism that this *tapas*, this external asceticism, plays no role in it. The legend (see p. 55ff) tells us that the Buddha before his enlightenment tastes all stages of ascetic self-mortification to the very end, but then turns away from it because he realizes that this does not lead to the highest spiritual goal. In the Sermon of Benares he then constructs the doctrine of the *middle* path which keeps an equal distance to the excesses of sensual desire and those of asceticism. The Buddha only opposed these excesses, not all asceticism in general. ('If through *tapas* practised by a Brahmin his good qualities diminish, the bad increase, such *tapas* is refuted by me; but if the good qualities increase and the bad diminish, such *tapas* is accepted by me,' *Aṅguttaranikāya* V, p. 191). It is only said of asceticism itself that it is not the decisive factor, not that which is essential. (The subject is discussed in the Kassapasīhanāda-sutta of the *Dīghanikāya*.) In Buddhism, the entire emphasis is on the spiritual; the struggle which the Buddha imposes as a duty on his disciples is a spiritual struggle. To a certain degree, even the Buddhist disciple may have used asceticism as a subordinate means, and in the texts the word *tapo* (Skt. *tapas*) is occasionally also used in the sense of a normal striving for salvation (e.g., *Theragāthā* 631).[9] It has to be remembered that there was also a higher, more spiritual understanding of *tapas* in India: the acceptance of the suffering imposed on a person by life, i.e. by *karma* in the sense of the Indian doctrine, as a means of purification (cf. *Bṛhadāraṇyaka-Upaniṣad* V, 11). Perhaps the *Yogasūtra* is already based on a similar interpretation. Apart from that it has to be noted that particularly in the *Yogasūtra*, *tapas* is only mentioned in passing and does not play an essential role, so that even on this point the *Yogasūtra* corresponds to Buddhism rather than differing from it. With respect to the two remaining parts of *niyama*, purity (*śauca*) and contentment (*santoṣa*) it has to be said that the Buddha put inner above outer purity (here also, details can be found in the Kassapasīhanādasutta); the demand of contentment with everything outer life brings corresponds to the *Yogasūtra*. In Buddhism the necessity of cheerful equanimity for the disciple of the path is always stressed. The respective paragraph (66) of the Sāmaññaphalasutta (*kathañca ... bhikkhu santuṭṭho hoti*) in this description of the path takes, as it were, even outwardly the place of *niyama* in the *Yogasūtra* as the second stage of the path. The fact that particularly this part of the path of Yoga which relates more to outer aspects retreats on the Buddhist path corresponds to the entire nature of Buddhism, and in the interest of the correct understanding of Buddhist ethics we may here be reminded of that passage (27) of the *Itivuttaka* which says that all actions of outward merit are not worth even a sixteenth of love (*mettā*, see above, p. 145). The Buddha also points out to the ascetic Kassapa, who discusses such matters with him, the fact that not the observance of any outward practices, but perfection in moral conduct, in spiritual self-discipline and in knowledge brings the disciple closer to his goal. Liberation only beckons a loving heart which has overcome all hatred and hostility *within itself*. Kassapa thoughtfully expresses how difficult it was to tread the path of asceticism and Brahmanism (here in the sense of the true Buddha-striving; Kassapasīhanādasutta 15).

This passage of the Sāmaññaphalasutta which can—with the above-mentioned limitations—be put alongside the *niyama* of the *Yogasūtra* is preceded by another which speaks about that quality which before all else gives the attitude of the Buddhist disciple its characteristic imprint, the *mindful consciousness* or wakeful mindfulness (*satisampajañña*) which the Buddha does not tire to commend to his disciples. Just as the Buddha appears always 'mindful and conscious' (*sato sampajāno*) in all situations of life—this has already been pointed out in the context of the consideration of the legend—it is also emphasized in the respective passage of the Sāmaññaphalasutta (65) that the disciple accompanies every glance, every move, every action, every performance of the body with this mindful consciousness; how in all situations of life, in walking, standing and sitting, in talking and being silent, in waking and even in sleeping he should keep this mindful consciousness in himself. In the *Majjhimanikāya* (III, p. 252) *sammāsati*, the seventh stage of the Eightfold Path, is similarly explained. This precept of penetrating with consciousness, as it were, all expressions of life happening in the realms of the physical and the psychological, to raise them to the sphere of consciousness, is of deep significance in Buddhism. We have already seen several times, and it will be repeatedly submitted in further examination, that the aim of the spiritual task to be fulfilled on the Buddhist 'path' is the mastery of *saṃskāra,* i.e., that which in the usual condition of body and mind is the subconscious, which forms the formative forces effective in the subconscious. As we know according to the Indian opinion it is in this *saṃskāra* that eventually the seed for rebirth is found which the disciple wants to destroy. Thus his effort has to focus on bringing up everything from his subconscious as it were and to raise it into the sphere of consciousness. It is thus important for him to accompany everything he does by wakeful consciousness. Of the utmost importance is finally the maintenance of mindful consciousness in the various stages of spiritual concentration and meditation. Those, it is said, who reveal themselves as weak in this quality fall more easily into Māra's snares than all others (cf. *Majjh.* III, p. 94). In the eightfold formula *sammāsati,* 'right mindfulness' thus immediately precedes 'right contemplation' or meditation (*sammāsamādhi*). As a preparation for meditation it already stands in closest connection with that area to whose consideration the following passage is devoted. (In the noteworthy concordance *Majjh.* I, p. 301, right effort and right contemplation are put in relationship to meditation in the passage on *samādhi,* just as right word, right action, right livelihood to *sīla.*)

c) Second stage of the path: meditation (*samādhi*)

The eightfold formula which puts meditation or contemplation (*samādhi*) as the highest stage of the path for which everything else is only a pre-stage already lets the 'path' appear as a path of meditation and thus clearly expresses the significance of meditation within the Buddhist norm. In Buddhism the path to realization leads through meditation, it is the key to higher consciousness, the actual means through which the disciple wrestles salvation from the fetters of sensual existence. For a correct understanding of this, the relationship of this meditation to the ethics described in the previous section has to be kept in mind: the Buddha teaches that only if it is 'carried and filled by right conduct, meditation can be fruitful and full of blessings'. The aims which Buddhism present as a prospect can thus not be surreptitiously obtained by meditation that is practised in opposition to that moral discipline. Those who want to seek meditation without the right inner preparation and without knowing the right paths are—thus the Buddha explains in a remarkable parable (*Aṅguttara* IV, p. 418)—similar to the clumsy mountain cow (*gāvī pabbateyyā*) which in its youthful immaturity, without knowledge of the place or experience in treading rough mountain paths, driven by the desire to seek out new and unknown areas, eats unfamiliar herbs and refreshes herself at foreign waters, did not apprehend to go step by step as appropriate. It would neither reach the coveted herbs and waters, nor find its way safely back to its shieling, or meadow, from which her curiosity and urge had driven her far away. 'And why, my disciples? Because she is just a youthful, immature mountain cow who does not know the place and who does not know how to tread on rough mountain paths.' The disciple who wants to raise himself to the four stages of meditation without knowing the right path would fare exactly like this clumsy shieling cow, says the Buddha. He would not only not attain the spiritual heights he seeks, but be seriously harmed and not return safely to his starting place (i.e., the state of his former consciousness). Thus he would, in the Buddha's expressions, stand like one who 'has lost any chance in both directions (i.e. both for the ordinary worldly life as also for the higher spiritual life)' (*ubhato parihīno*). Behind the sobriety and seeming triviality of such parables by the Buddha remarkable depths are often hidden, for example here the comparison between aspiring for spiritual heights and the treading of rough mountain paths, as well as some other aspects which may have been intentionally obscured for the superficial listener by choosing a grotesque way of expressing the thought. Only those who stand entirely steadfast in ethical behaviour, in moral conduct, and who know and follow the predetermined path exactly, have—according to the Buddha—the opportunity to reach that which is called 'right meditation' in this present existence. It has already been emphasized that the Buddhist path of meditation in its relationship with ethics corresponds to the path of the Yoga.

Between the stages of *yama* and *niyama* already discussed (of which the first is also entirely, the second to a limited extent, contained in the Buddhist path) and true meditation the Yoga system sets out three preliminary stages: *āsana, prāṇāyama* and *pratyāhāra,* the first of which relates to physical posture, the second to the mastery of the breath, the third to the mastery of the senses. In essence they also exist in Buddhism, but in the path to salvation of the *Dīghanikāya* only the first and the third of these preliminary stages are mentioned, and in reverse order. The teaching of the posture in meditation, of the so-called 'seat' (*āsana*), has been developed by the Indians with great artificiality and has found a fitting, unique elaboration suitable only for the Indian circumstances, namely in the teaching manuals of the Haṭhayoga. The Yoga system of Patañjali distances itself from these artificialities, it only demands the strength and comfort of the position as it is suggested especially by the imagination of eternity (II, 46. 47). Buddhism—loyal to its principle of only ascribing decisive value to the spiritual—cannot place any importance on an artificiality of physical posture and thus corresponds to the Yoga system in this regard, and just like this system, the scheme of the path of salvation of the *Dīghanikāya* (SPhS 67) also, at least, mentions the 'seat' (*pallaṅka*) as a prerequisite for meditation. The custom of sitting with crossed legs (*paryaṅka,* Pali *pallaṅka*) was a very widespread one among the Indian Buddhists. The Buddha himself is depicted in this seat in innumerable pictures and sculptures. The legends tell us that even as a child meditating under the rose-apple tree, he involuntarily assumed the posture of the *paryaṅka*-seat, and the Bodhisattva, when chastening himself by the Nairañjanā and when awakening to the Buddha under the *bodhi* tree is quite imagined in that position of sitting crossed-legged. If the *paryaṅka*-seat is also mentioned in the respective passage of the *Dīghanikāya* (SPhS 67), this is because the entire context speaks about Indian circumstances. That here, too, Buddhism in its universal tendency does not give any importance to holding fast to that which is specifically Indian, is best illuminated by the fact that Maitreya, the Buddha of the future, is depicted sitting in the European manner. Of a more general importance in the *Dīghanikāya* is the rule of a straight physical posture (*uju-kāya*). The entire passage is of interest as a parallel to the *Yogasūtra*. *Prāṇāyāma,* the mastery of the breath or restraint of the breath in Yoga is not mentioned in that passage. But it emerges from other passages of the canon that the Buddha, too, gave attention to the physical breath and advised others to do the same. It seems to be a general Indian Yoga experience that there is a connection between the concentration of the mind and the mastery of the breath (cf. YS II, 53). This is already expressed in the Upanishads (*Chāndogya-Upaniṣad* 6, 8, 2: *prāṇabandhanaṃ manaḥ* 'the mind [*manas*] is connected with the breath [*prāṇa*]'). Here we cannot go into the details of this teaching, but it should be pointed out that in Buddhism, the breath is designated as a *kāyasaṅkhāra,* a *saṃskāra* of the body (*Majjh.* I, p. 301). In this expression lies the Indian-Buddhist (and Yoga) view that the formative forces (*saṃskāra*) for the conscious intellect dwell in the subconscious while in the breath are the formative forces or *saṃskāras* for the formation of the physical. To work into all these *sāṃskāras*, these formative forces, and to master them, is the aim of both Buddhism and Yoga. In Buddhism the *saṃskāra* is well-nigh presented as the master builder (cf. *Dhammapada* 154) which has built the house of physical existence. In order to attain liberation, he has to be conquered first and foremost. This explains that even in Buddhism the mastery of the breath, because it has something to do with the *saṃskāra*, is ascribed with a certain significance which can only be grasped from the depth of Yoga teaching. However, Buddhism does not really speak about artificial retention of the breath (as in Yoga). (It only plays a role in the asceticism the Buddha practises for some time before his enlightenment [see p. 55].) It is only mentioned that the practitioner should accompany the individual breaths with his/her consciousness. (Thus already *Vinaya* III, p. 70, similarly *Saṃy*. V, p. 323, *Aṅg*. V, p. 311. In the *Saṃyuttanikāya* a longer chapter, the Ānāpāna-saṃyutta 'the section on breathing in and out', is devoted entirely to this subject; p. 315 speaks about the beneficial influence of breathing exercises on the calmness of the body.) Thus this is about a special application of 'mindful consciousness' (*satisampajañña*), discussed above, to the realm of breathing. The disciple wins mastery over the subconscious which works within himself as a formative force (*saṃskāra*) as he 'sees' it, i.e., brings it to consciousness. Buddha's admonition to 'mindful consciousness' is nothing subordinate or peripheral, but something which is in immediate relationship with the actual principal idea of the entire striving for salvation. Conscious mastery of the appearances of the breath is thus the first goal the Buddhist disciple strives for, the complete retention or suppression of the breath (parallel to the *prāṇāyāma* of Yoga, YS II, 49) according to the Buddhist doctrine then follows spontaneously when the fourth stage of meditation (the fourth *dhyāna*) is reached (*Aṅg*. IV, p. 409).

The fifth stage of the Yoga path, *pratyāhāra*, mastery of the senses or withdrawal of the sense organs from the sense objects (YS II, 54. 55) is a general Indian striving which is not to be separated from the entire development of Yoga. Certain passages of the *Mahābhārata*, for example, talk about it on almost every page (the *Yogasūtra* of course is only a certain way of determining doctrines which have existed for a long time, and it is only from this point of view that the comparison with this text is always made here). We will thus not be surprised to meet with the 'mastery of the sense organs' also in the scheme of the path of salvation in the *Dīghanikāya*. In imaginative pictures it is there (SPhS 64) called the 'guarding of the gates of the senses' (or, in the verbal expression: *bhikkhu indriyesu guttadvāro hoti*) and mentioned even prior to 'mindful consciousness,' contentment and physical posture (*pallaṅka*), that means in a slightly different position than in the *Yogasūtra*. Just as in Yoga, the striving in Buddhism is directed at the complete shutting off of all impressions of vision, hearing, smell etc., and in the *Mahāparinibbānasutta* (ed. Childers, p. 44f., see above, p. 76f.) it is said that the Buddha had attained mastery in this art of shutting the gates of the senses, so that once in his meditation he did not hear or see anything when during a strong thunderstorm lightning strikes in his immediate vicinity, killing two farmers and four oxen. Hereby the immediate preliminary stage of that spiritual concentration has been attained; the following passages (SPhS 75ff.) are devoted to this discussion.

In Yoga, the stages discussed so far are designated as the preliminary stage, the forecourt (*bahiraṅga*, cf. YS III, 7), so that the actual meditation (or its highest stage, the *nirbīja-samādhi*, III, 8) in the sense of those doctrines, has to be regarded as the *sanctum sanctorum*, as the inner space (*antaraṅga*) of Yoga. Thus the disciple in Buddhism is also admonished to approach this realm only in a state of complete internal purification, and the passage on meditation in the *Dīghanikāya* here (SPhS 68) names five further fetters or impeding emotional affects from which the disciple has to free himself entirely prior to entering the meditation: any (possibly still hidden in him) worldly desire (*abhijjhā loke*), any wishes to harm other beings and any hatred (*vyāpāda-padosa*), sloth and sleepiness (*thīna-middha*, cf. *styāna* and *ālasya* in YS I, 30), vanity and contempt (*uddhaccakukkucca*, others possibly understand it more correctly: 'fearfulness and restlessness'), and finally any doubts (*vicikicchā*) regarding the right path. (In the Buddha legend the hostile forces mentioned here appear as the hosts of Māra whom the Bodhisattva drives away before rising to the first stage of contemplation under the *bodhi* tree.) The disciple drives away his internal enemies by purifying his soul with thoughts of compassion with all beings, 'conscious of the light' (*ālokasaññī*), in mindful consciousness and with a tranquil mind. When he has freed himself through such (as it were preparative) contemplations from all impeding motions of the mind, he feels—this is described in a series of parables—like one who has removed an oppressing debt, or has been healed from a painful illness draining the forces of the body, or been released from prison or bondage, or has happily found the way back to the security of his home village from the desolate, dangerous forest wilderness (SPhS 69–74). Thus from the consciousness of having overcome those hindrances there grows first a feeling of satisfaction (*pāmujjaṃ*), from satisfaction joy (*pīti*), from joy the tranquillity of the body, from tranquillity well-being (*sukham*). And while the mind is thus filled with bliss, it reaches concentration (*samādhiyati* as a verb from *samādhi*). In this state of concentration it then rises from the first to the fourth stage of introspection, of 'contemplation' (*dhyāna*, Pali *jhāna*). The description of the four stages of meditation is, as in that main passage of the *Dīghanikāya* and thus in many other passages of the canon, given in a stereotypical formula (e.g., Aṅg. III, p. 25ff., IV, p. 410; 419ff). The northern Sanskrit texts, too, are in accord; in the *Lalitavistara*, for example, in the context of the meditation of the young Bodhisattva under the rose-apple tree as also the meditation of the Bodhisattva awakening to the Buddha, the four stages are essentially described in the same words as in the Pali canon. In the first stage, it is said, separation from all base desires is achieved, but a concept of objects is still present, and the entire body is filled with a feeling of joyful well-being (*pītisukha*) which springs from seclusion (*viveka*) and which is compared with the foam artificially created by a bather. In the second stage, the person meditating does not form any concepts of objects any more, and the mind is concentrated on unity in complete tranquillity (*ekodibhāva*). Here, too, the body is filled with a blissful well-being which springs from concentration (*samādhi*). It is compared with a cool stream which has its origins inside a lake which is not fed by external tributaries. In the third stage that feeling of blissful well-being vanishes; the person meditating remains in equanimity and mindful consciousness (*sato sampajāno*), and the body is filled with 'bliss which is higher than joy'. The state is compared with the lotus flowers which are entirely surrounded by cool water without reaching the surface of the water. In the fourth stage the person meditating finally leaves all feelings of joy and pain behind, he remains in the purity of mindful consciousness, the entire body is filled with the rays of spiritual brightness and purity. In this state, a parable says, the disciple is as if clad with a white garment which envelopes him from head to toe so that not even the smallest part of his body is not covered by white.

The *Yogasūtra* III, 1 ff. which has here been used repeatedly as a reference for comparison with the Buddhist doctrine, initially distinguishes three stages of concentration: *dhāraṇā* 'concentration' (*sensu stricto*), the focusing of the mind on a *single* point; *dhyāna* 'contemplation', the remaining in this state, the meditation *sensu stricto; samādhi* 'immersion', 'contemplation', 'reverence', the highest stage. The expression 'contemplation' (*dhyāna,* Pali *jhāna*) which Buddhism uses for all four main stages of meditation is thus used in the *Yogasūtra* in a certain narrower sense. *Samādhi* in the *Yogasūtra* is only the designation of the highest stage of meditation, the true 'immersion'; in Buddhism it is equally a general designation for the entire field of spiritual concentration and meditation in the widest sense, essentially having the same meaning as *dhyāna* or *jhāna*. It is thus explained in the Pañcaṅgikavagga of the *Aṅgūttaranikāya* (Vol. III, p. 25f.) that *sammāsamādhi,* 'right contemplation', includes all four stages of *jhāna* which are described using the same terms and parables of the canon as the *Dīghanikāya*. This description of meditation which recurs in so many passages of the canon with the same phrasing is among the subjects most frequently touched on in all Buddhists texts. From the non-adherence to the differentiation between *dhyāna* and *samādhi* made in the Yoga it should not be concluded that the doctrine of meditation was less developed in Buddhism than in the true Yoga system. Rather, especially in this chapter Buddhism shows a greater wealth of technical Yoga details than for example the *Yogasūtra* of Patañjali. The expressions *savitarka* and *savicāra* used in Buddhism for the characteristics of the first stage of meditation also belong to the Yoga system. Here, *savitarka* means: 'while a concept of sensual objects is still present', while *vicāra,* at least in the *Yogasūtra,* refers to the concept of supernatural-etheric[1] (*sūkṣma*) objects (YS I, 44, 45). Meditation—this is true for Buddhism as well as for Yoga in the sense of the Yoga system—starts from a particular object at which one's spiritual concentration is to be directed. Earlier (see p. 118) we have spoken about how in this regard the Buddha gives different concentration exercises or tasks (*kammaṭṭhāna*) to his disciples. On the higher levels of meditation these clues are then dropped until finally the state of pure spiritual contemplation results which is entirely withdrawn from any external sense impressions. Occasionally, three stages of *samādhi* are distinguished in Buddhism in a terminology which connects even more closely with the *Yogasūtra* than the main passage: a first stage which is still connected with the concept of sensual and supernatural objects (*savitakko savicāro samādhi),* a second stage where only the concept of supernatural-etherical objects are present (*avitakko avicāro samādhi*) and which thus would include everything which in the sense of that other terminology lies above the first *jhāna*. Buddhism (e.g., *Aṅg.* III, p. 25) also speaks of the 'five-membered' (*pañcaṅgika*) *samādhi*. The five 'members' are the four stages of *jhāna* to which is added as the fifth 'the sign of contemplation' (*paccavekkhanānimitta*). In the Buddhist doctrine of meditation 'sign' means a certain supernatural apparition which ensues as the immediate consequence of meditation and which confirms the success of practising to the person meditating. In the context of the useless meditation attempts of the disciple who is compared with an inexperienced alpine cow who does not know the place, and who does not know the proper paths of meditations, the non-appearance of the 'sign' is spoken of as a characteristic circumstance (*Aṅg.* IV, p. 418). When once the Buddha visits Anuruddha and other disciples in their hermitage (see p. 117) and inquires about the success of their practices, Anuruddha complains that they were not coping well with understanding *nimittaṃ*; in part they had the apparitions in question, but were unable to maintain them. The Buddha then tells them that before his enlightenment he was struggling with similar difficulties and had only attained the correct results when he had step-by-step overcome within himself by tenacious wrestling all hindrances and impediments to right meditation—doubt, inattention, sloth and sleepiness, rigid stupor (*chambhitattaṃ*), lacking spiritual harmony, inertia, excessive energy, lack of energy, absentmindedness, excessive self-preoccupation (*Majjh.* III, p. 157ff.). Some of the enemies of the soul mentioned here are illustrated by the Buddha in vivid parables. 'Rigid stupor' for example resembles the paralyzing shock of the wanderer who is attacked by two murderers, one from the right and one from the left, on a lonely road; with 'excessive energy' it is the same as when someone grasps a quail all too strongly so that it is squashed dead; with 'lack of energy' as if the quail is not held strongly enough so that it can fly from the hands again. Lacking spiritual harmony is compared to the all too joyful excitement of someone who is looking for treasure and finds five at the same time. To grasp this understanding of 'inner harmony' correctly is important for the understanding of Buddhist meditation. This meditation in the Buddha's sense is not about some dampening down of normal consciousness, i.e., not about 'ecstatic' or 'pathological' states, but about a light-filled and strong reinforcement and concentration of the spiritual forces resting on inner purification and inner detachment.

Above the three stages of concentration, meditation and contemplation there is in the Yoga system *nirbīja-samādhi,* which also targets the subconscious formative forces (*saṃskāra*) and which thereby destroys the seed of repeated existence. The technical expression for the destruction of *saṃskāra* is *nirodha.* The Buddhist path strives for the same goal. In Buddhism, however, the path towards the attainment of this goal leads through an entire stepladder of states of consciousness (*viññāṇaṭṭhitiyo, Aṅg.* IV, p. 39) which are beyond the fourth stage of meditation. These states are the ones already mentioned in the Mahāparinibbānasutta (see p. 80) through which the Buddha passes successively before entering *parinirvāṇa.* They are not described in the passage on meditation in the Sāmaññaphalasutta, but mentioned and described elsewhere in numerous passages of the canon. The fourth *dhyāna* is first followed by raising oneself to the 'sphere of the limitlessness of the space ether' (*ākāsānañcāyatana*), then raising oneself to the 'sphere of the limitlessness of spiritual consciousness' (*viññāṇañcāyatana*), this is followed by raising oneself to the 'sphere beyond conscious and unconscious' (*nevasaññāṇāsaññāyatana*). The following, last stage which leads the disciple to the attainment of the highest goal attainable in an earthly body is called *saññāvedayitanirodha,* 'the dissolution (effected by the will) of cognitive consciousness (*saññā*) and emotion' or simply 'dissolution' (*nirodha*). The person meditating thus raises himself stage-by-stage to ever higher states of consciousness and in the Poṭṭhapādasutta of the *Dīghanikāya* (paragraphs 16 and 17) it is said that this development of higher and ever higher states of consciousness (cf. in 17: *tato amutra tato amutra anupubbena saññaggaṃ phusati*) can be attained by way of methodological training by extinguishing the previous state of consciousness. In *Aṅg.* IV, p. 410ff. the four stages of *dhyāna* and the following four stages of *āyatana* (up to *nirodha*) are described as the nine states of 'abiding in turn [in one state after another]' (*anupubbavihārasamāpatti*). The expression *samāpatti* (lit. 'attainment, acquiring a perfection') in the sense of a stage of meditation is also known in the *Yogasūtra* (I, 41–44). What has been presented above (see p. 131) as an essential characteristic of Yoga – that in contrast to philosophy and all other human striving for realization it does not want to remain within the given state of consciousness and rise to realizations with the help of experiences and rational deductions possible within this state, but that it precisely seeks to go beyond the given state of consciousness – also applies entirely to Buddhism, to the striving for realization and salvation which expresses itself in the Buddhist 'path'; as follows from everything said so far, and in the description of the states of consciousness Buddhism goes into even more detail than the *Yogasūtra*. The Buddhist texts, or, we may say this, the instructions of the Buddha, dwell with particular exhaustiveness on the problem of consciousness.

Because the attainment of each higher stage of consciousness requires overcoming the preceding one in such a way that everything that formed the content of that earlier stage of consciousness is felt to be no longer present, as devoid of essence (cf. *Majjh.* III, p. 104; *Aṅg.* IV, p. 410f.), the individual stages are also designated as stages of resolution or breaking away (*vimokha*). As such they are also met with in the Mahāparinibbānasutta (p. 30, ed. Childers). Here, the raising to the 'sphere of the limitlessness of space ether' is preceded by three stages, with which a vision of the appearances of form (or colour) is still present; on the third stage the person meditating is devoted entirely to the observance of the beauty of these appearances (*subhaṃ adhimutto*). While seeing colour appearances the consciousness of the person meditating can go through an entire colour scale; thus follow the 'eight stages of overcoming' (*abhibhāyatanāni*) of which ibid. p. 28 speaks (and frequently mentioned elsewhere). This is always about a vision of supernatural appearances which follow in the context of the object chosen as the point of departure of meditation (*kammaṭṭhāna*). A special technical designation for such a *kammaṭṭhāna* is *kasiṇa* (*Aṅg.* I, p. 41f. and others).

The stepladder of the states of consciousness is also constructed in such a way that the point of departure is the consciousness of the elements. Here the person meditating starts from the earth element (*paṭhavī*); after concentrating his consciousness on the earth for a while and remaining in the consciousness of the earth (*paṭhavīsaññā*), he either raises himself immediately to the consciousness of the space ether (in this way, e.g., *Majjh.* III, p. 105ff.) or he passes successively in his consciousness through the stages of the elements of earth, water (*āpo*), air (*vāyo*), fire (*tejo*) in such a way that he successively extinguishes the sensations of earth, water, air and fire in his consciousness. (Thus, e.g., *Aṅg.* V, p. 7, 318, 353 and others.) Fire is followed by (as it were as a fifth aggregate state) the ether element (*ākāsa*): the person meditating raises himself to the consciousness of this element when he moves from the fire consciousness (*tejosaññā*) to the 'sphere of the limitlessness of the space ether' (*ākāsānañcāyatana*). In the next stage (*viññāṇañcāyatana*) he has extinguished even this consciousness of the ether and has only the sensation of the limitlessness of the spiritual consciousness. By leaving even this stage behind, he then faces the next, the 'raising to the sphere of nothingness' (*ākiñcaññāyatana*), facing nothingness. This 'facing nothingness', however, in Buddhism does not at all imply a final state, but only a passage to further stages of consciousness. The person meditating has to extinguish within himself even this sensation of nothingness, and when he has succeeded in this, he abides in the *nevasaññānāsaññāyatana*, in the 'stage beyond conscious and unconscious'. When he then 'no longer has the consciousness of this and no longer the consciousness of that world', he raises himself to the last and highest stage of extinguishing, *nirodha*; this stage, it is said in the texts (*Aṅg*. V, p. 7, 354 and others), is already 'the peaceful, highly sublime (*paṇītaṃ*), the extinguishing of the *saṃskāras* (*sabbasaṅkhārasamatho*), the complete destruction of passion, *nirvāṇa* (*nibbāna*)'.

The beginning of this stepladder of consciousness shows how stages of consciousness touch on the spheres of the individual elements, and this opinion is further supported in Buddhism: the individual spheres of consciousness appear at the same time as particular world spheres (*dhātu*). The terms 'stages of consciousness' and 'worlds' or 'world spheres' blend into each other completely in Buddhism, and everything that the Buddha teaches about different world spheres in such a fantastic manner, refers only to the experiences of the meditating consciousness described above. Thus it does not make any sense at all to criticize and ridicule, as some have done (e.g., Spence Hardy),[2] the Buddhist 'world system' from the standpoint of modern astronomy, for the standpoint of the external consciousness which astronomy assumes towards such things, is not at all that of the Buddha. Everything that appears to modern science as substantial and real, to Buddhists appears extinguished, sunk into nothingness, already in the second stage of meditation. Likewise all spiritual experiences with which the Buddhist disciple meets in these stages of mediation are nothing to the astronomer. By raising himself to certain higher stages of consciousness the person meditating raises himself in the sense of the Buddha to just as many world spheres or world planes. And each of these world spheres has a respective category of beings; we may indeed say from the point of view of Buddhism that it consists in essence of nothing but such spiritual beings. For any materialistic concept is foreign to Buddhism, even with the world spheres we thus have to think of something spiritual, not of something in any way material. In the Buddhist texts themselves this relationship emerges clearly, e.g., in the Saṅkhāruppattisutta of the *Majjhimanikāya* (III, Nr. 120) it is explained that each of the *āyatana*-stages of consciousness has a particular class of deities (*deva*). The person meditating in the respective stage, as it were, enters their consciousness. In this sense the individual stages of consciousness are also distinguished as stages of being (*sattāvāsā*, e.g., *Dīgh*. III, p. 263, *Aṅg*. IV, p. 401). At first there are certain lower elemental beings which embody the consciousness of the respective elementary stage (e.g., the earth consciousness, *paṭhavīsaññā*) in themselves. In the Mahāparinibbānasutta (p. 63, ed. Childers) they are mentioned as beings which take part in the emotions of human beings. Above them are the actual higher hierarchies of gods of which Sanskrit and Pali texts usually distinguish nine. They are (from the bottom to the top) normally enumerated as: 1) the hosts of the four great kings or world protectors (Pali *cātummahārājika devā*), 2) the 33 gods (Pali *tāvatiṃsā*) with Indra (*sakko devānaṃ indo*) at the helm, 3) Yāma-gods, 4) Tuṣita-gods, 5) *nimmānarati* (Sanskr. *nirmāṇarati* 'those who enjoy creative formation'), 6) *paranimmitavasavatti* (Sanskr. *paranirmitavaśavartin*, 'those who reign over the work of others'), 7) the gods of the Brahmā heaven (*brahmakāyikā*), 8) *ābhassarā* (Sanskr. *ābhāsvarāḥ*, 'those radiant like light'), 9) *suddhāvāsakāyikā* ('gods of the pure abodes'). Apart from those mentioned here, there are several intermediate categories which cannot be discussed here. All these beings belong to worlds which are situated above the sensory world, the sphere of sensual desire (*kāmadhātu*), the worlds to which one raises oneself in meditation, in the first *dhyāna* stage. In contrast to *kāmadhātu*, the sensory world, this higher, spiritual sphere which is only to be realized in meditation is called *rūpadhātu*, i.e., 'realm of form' or 'world of forms'. It is in interdependence with the four stages of *dhyāna* and includes the lower hierarchies of gods. (A good overview of the details is in Köppen, vol. I, p. 260f.).[3] Above *rūpadhātu* emerges *arūpadhātu*, the 'sphere of the formless'. Entering this sphere happens with 'raising oneself to the limitlessness of the space ether' and includes the various stages of contemplation designated as *āyatana*. As mentioned above, this sphere, too, has certain divine beings. *Kāmadhātu*, *rūpadhātu* and *arūpadhātu* (cf. *Dīgh*. III, p. 275, *Aṅg*. I, p. 223) are in a way the Buddhist threefold world from which the disciple of the path seeks an exit. He has found it when he has attained the stage called *nirodha* in meditation about which it is said: it is the peaceful, highly sublime, the calming of the *saṃskāras*, the destruction of worldly desire, *nirvāṇa* (*nibbāna*). Here, too, the state of consciousness corresponds to the spiritual sphere: above the three worldly spheres of sensuality, form and formlessness (*kāmadhātu*, *rūpadhātu*, *arūpadhātu*) there rises as the sphere of the highest transcendence *nirodhadhātu* (*Itivuttaka* 51, 73 and others). The disciple enters it when he has risen above all lower stages of meditation and has attained the stage of *nirvāṇa*. It is thus also called the *nirvāṇa* sphere or the *nirvāṇa* element (*nibbānadhātu*), and depending on whether the physical substrates are still present or not, *upādisesa* and *anupādisesa-nibbānadhātu* are distinguished (cf. *Itivuttaka* 44). With his physical death, with the throwing-off of his physicality (*parinibbāna*) the Buddha enters the sphere of the *nirvāṇa* devoid of substance (*anupādisesa-nibbānadhātu*). The *nirvāṇa* sphere is also called *amatādhātu*, 'the immortal sphere (or 'the sphere where death is lost in blissful rapture [*todentrückt*]') (*Aṅg.*, IV, p. 423f., *Itivuttaka* 73 and others) because it lies beyond the spheres where the cycle of birth and death takes place. It is the sphere of that immortal salvation (*amṛta*, Pali *amata*) lying beyond all temporality which the Buddha found under the *bodhi* tree. All those spheres which the disciple touches on in the lower stages of meditation in some way still take part in temporality. Thus the classes of gods which belong to these different spheres and to whose consciousness the person meditating raises himself in the stages of *dhyāna* are accorded different lifespans which are connected with a certain sense of time which is different from that of human beings. For example, 50 human years are only one day (the timespan of day and night) for the *cātummahārājika* gods, 100 human years, one day of the gods in Indra's paradise, 200 years, one day of the Yāma gods, 400 years a day of the Tuṣita gods, 800 years, a day of the *nimmānarati* gods, 1,600 years, one day of the *paranimmita-vasavatti* gods, etc. (*Aṅg.* IV, p. 252 ff.).

For the entire understanding of Buddhism it is important to note the idea that the person meditating raises himself to the consciousness of these different divine hierarchies *through meditation*. In the *Aṅguttara-nikāya* (vol. IV, p. 302), there is a rather remarkable *sūtra* (already mentioned by E. Hardy)[4] where the Buddha describes in a vivid manner how he arrived at an ever clearer vision of those supernatural beings called 'gods' (*deva*) by increasing his clairvoyance through intense meditation practices during the time prior to his enlightenment when he was still a Bodhisattva. Initially, the Buddha says, he could only perceive a shimmer of light (*obhāsa*) in meditation. By increasing his concentration, he raises himself to a higher degree of clairvoyant vision (*ñāṇadassanaṃ parisuddhataraṃ*), and now he also has imaginations of forms and colours, but cannot yet enter into a dialogue with these spiritual beings (which express themselves through these imaginations of form and colour). Further persistent practice brings him to the point where he not only sees the shimmer of light and has imaginations of form and colour, but is able to enter into a dialogue with the divine beings which express themselves through these imaginations (*tāhi ca devatāhi saddhiṃ santiṭṭhāmi sallapāmi sākacchaṃ samāpajjāmi*), but he still lacks the inspiration to realize to which divine hierarchy (*devanikāya*) these beings belong. By continuing his intense meditative strife, he finds the sought-after inspiration. Now he knows to which divine hierarchy the supernatural beings with whom he holds a dialogue belong, but he still lacks the knowledge through which *karma* these beings have brought their development to the respective stage. By a final intensification he then attains even this highest intuition; his clairvoyant vision has reached such a degree that he not only perceives a shimmer of light, not only imaginations of colour and form, holding a dialogue with the divine beings expressing themselves through such appearances, but he also now knows through which *karma* these beings left a certain previous stage of existence and reached their present stage, the length of their life span, what kind of experiences of pleasure or pain constitutes the content of their lives and whether he himself has been in any relationship to those beings in some previous stage of development. The Buddha ends with the hint that only when he had attained this clear, clairvoyant vision with regard to divine beings (*adhidevañāṇadassanaṃ suvisuddhaṃ*) was he able to awaken to the highest, perfect enlightenment of a Buddha.

This description of the *Aṅguttaranikāya* ascribed to the Buddha shows particularly clearly that the 'gods' (*deva*) of Buddhism are something that can only be understood in the context of meditation, something experienced purely in spiritual terms, i.e., something essentially different from dogmatic creations or 'concessions to popular beliefs' (even though the names of these beings are partially borrowed from Brahminical religion). It is correct that in Buddhism the 'gods' play a fundamentally different role than in so-called polytheistic religions, that Buddhism does not know an actual worship of the gods as this word is used in those religions (even though the Buddha occasionally advises adopting an attitude of veneration towards these beings, cf. Mahāparinibbānasutta, p. 14, ed. Childers). But nothing would be less correct than to believe for this reason that the 'gods' had no significance whatsoever in Buddhism. In truth, nothing is so apt to shed more light on the true nature of Buddhism as its relationship with those 'gods'. For this is precisely what is significant and instructive before all else, that Buddhism does not know the dogmatic relationship with 'god' or 'gods' that other religions have, and still carries within itself so clearly the character of a religion in its entire approach to the sacred and supernatural. In another context (see p. 111) we have already discussed the silence on 'god' and its significance. The 'gods', however, who play such a large a role in it and who are so often encountered in all sacred texts, are not beings to whom the Buddhist 'prays' or whom he asks for something, but they are beings, purely spiritual, supernatural beings to whose sphere the disciple of the path *raises himself in meditation.*

It is impossible to grasp the nature of Buddhism as a religion and at the same time its difference from other religions more correctly in any other way than by pointing to this significance of *meditation* and by comparing it with the part which in other religion is played by *prayer.* As prayer forms the heart of the religious life in other religions, for the Buddhist this heart of the religious life is meditation, the meditative immersion into the spiritual, supernatural, into that which to the modern occidental sensibility, appears as a 'nothing'. (And indeed, as we have seen, 'facing the nothing' is experienced in a particular stage of Buddhist meditation.) If we move away from the original teaching of the Buddha presented here so far and take a look at those forms Buddhism has taken as an external religion in different countries of Asia, we find that the entire religious life is nowhere more thoroughly penetrated by meditation than in Tibet. The formula *'oṃ maṇi padme huṃ'* ('*Om* (yes), the jewel (dewdrop) in the lotus, amen' which is 'prayed' there by the faithful in all life-situations does not contain a plea for something towards some cosmic power, but is the simplest, most artless meditation, a *kammaṭṭhāna*[5] through which the devout raise themselves to the Bodhisattva Avalokiteśvara and through him to Amitābha, the Buddha of immeasurable light in a sacred allegory. As strange, even perhaps as ridiculous as these forms, in which in that country the raising to the divine, supernatural connected with the above-mentioned formula occur, may appear to the Western person (cf. Pischel, p. 98; Waddell, op. cit., p. 572; Sven Hedin, *Transhimalaya,* vol. I, p. 324, II, p. 174ff.), on the other hand a certain sublimity in the very form of how, as it were, the entire atmosphere of the country is penetrated by that meditation. Sven Hedin shows a sensibility for this when he says of those words (*oṃ maṇi padme huṃ*) in his book:

> They belong to Tibet, these words; they are inseparable from it: I cannot imagine the snow-capped mountains and the blue sky without them.

> They are as closely connected with this country as buzzing with the beehive, as the flutter of streamers with the pass, as the ceaseless west wind with its howling.[6]

That which appears as nothing to the experience that clings to matter becomes a fact in meditation. On this path of meditation Buddhism thus reaches the point of speaking about 'gods' as actual supernatural beings. (In this context the retention of the term 'gods' has no significance. It has established itself since the Indian *deva* corresponds to the Latin *deus*. Additionally, the term *deva* outside of Buddhism is often close to the common understanding of 'god' or 'gods'. But the 'gods' of Buddhism are much rather to be compared with the angels of the New Testament than with the gods of a polytheistic religion, and thus the usage of some translators, for example, Rhys Davids, to render the word *deva* as 'angel' has some merit.)

How the experience of meeting the gods in the Buddhist sense is immediately connected with meditation, with the individual inner work of the person meditating, is shown by another *sūtra* of the *Aṅguttaranikāya* (vol. IV, p. 262). Here, the disciple, Anuruddha, describes how the appearances of colour through which the gods once manifested for him, formed and re-formed according to his own inner imagination, how these supernatural beings revealed themselves to him in that colour respectively in which he wished to see them.

As meditation leads the human being during his lifetime towards the community and dialogue with the gods described above, he also reaches that community after death, provided that 'right effort' during his earthly life in the Buddha's sense has destined him for this 'good going' (*sugati*), the entering into the bliss of the heavenly world (*svarga*, Pali *saga-loka*). It is in particular the devout veneration of the Buddha which secures this kind of entitlement to the heavenly world (cf. *Dīghanikāya* II, p. 212; Mahāparinibbānasutta, ed. Childers, p. 51, also above, p. 78). These 'heavenly worlds' are nothing but those spheres of the gods described above (p. 162)—thus the world the human being reaches after death is the same as that which he already enters in meditation during his time on earth—and it depends on the level of inner development, the height of consciousness reached in the moment of death, to which divine sphere the human being raises himself in the hereafter (see *Dīgh.* II, p. 212, 250 and especially *Aṅg.* II, p. 129). The human being enters the Brahmā world, one of the highest divine spheres, after death because he has filled all the cardinal directions in his meditation with thoughts of love (*mettā*) for all living beings (*Aṅg.*, ibid.). In this earthly life a meditation suffused with love and compassion for all beings is the path to Brahmā already (thus Mahāgovindasutta, *Dīgha* II, p. 250 and especially Tevijjasutta, *Dīgha* I, p. 249ff.). In this *sūtra*, it is presented as the highest perfection of meditation if the disciple, after passing through all stages of the path and having partaken of all attainments of meditation, lets this mood of love, of compassion, sympathetic joy, equanimity radiate in his inner contemplation across the entire world. One only understands the nature of Buddhist meditation at all correctly if one does not take it as a cold, uncharitable or as a spiritual striving which only serves the individual's personal perfection, but as a striving which serves the entire world or at least 'many beings' for their salvation and blessing. We find this thought—that from the spiritual striving of the disciple who has entered into the paths of the sacred life (*brahmacariya*) blessings radiate for all beings—expressed by the Buddha over and over again in the texts. The thought that the meditation of a saint protects and blesses all beings in the widest vicinity is a general Indian one (cf. the beginning of the *Mṛcchakaṭikā*, translated into German as '*Vasantasena*'). In the Sonadaṇḍasutta (*Dīgha* I, p. 116) it is said of the Buddha that gods and humans are equally drawn to him, and that in the place the Holy One's foot enters no supernatural or demonic beings (*amanusse*) whatsoever cause harm to humans, that by the Buddha's presence, as it were, the spiritual atmosphere is cleansed of all harmful influences. It has already been mentioned (pp. 59, 119) that especially love (*mettā*) in Buddhism is a spiritual power working through suffusion, and it is the gods of the Brahmā heaven who are, as it were, in immediate connection with this suffusion.

By renouncing the world the disciple enters into the spiritual life. After overcoming the first (preparatory) stages of the path he reaches spiritual contemplation and by raising himself from stage to stage in meditation, an *inner development* occurs in which the gods of all spheres participate. This development and the part which the gods play in this is illustrated by a unique and poetic parable in the *Aṅguttaranikāya* (vol. IV, p. 117). It speaks of the Kovidara tree (*pāricchattako kovilāro*) in Indra's paradise and the way in which the gods follow its growth. When they spot the first light yellow leaves (*paṇḍupalāsa*) they look forward to the soon fully developed foliage (*sattapalāsa*) and with the same joy they look forward to, when this moment has been reached, the first signs of the delicate flower buds (*jālaka*), then of the developed ones (*khāraka*), then of the opening blossoms (*kuḍumala*). Then they wait full of excitement for the first half-opened blossoms, and when finally the tree is in full bloom (*sabbaphāliphulla*), they hold a high celebration of joy lasting four god-months, and the flowering tree spreads a radiant light far afield, and its fragrance fills the entire vicinity of heaven. For the gods the disciple treading the path of meditation is such a Kovidara tree developing in progressive growth. When the disciple within himself takes the decision of renunciation, the tree develops its first light yellow leaves; when the disciple brings this decision to execution and enters into spiritual life by renouncing the world, the leaves are fully developed; when he reaches the first stage of meditation (*dhyāna*), the first delicate sign of flower buds has developed, in the second stage of meditation the buds are further developed, and in the third stage they start to open. When the fourth stage of meditation is reached, the flower starts to form, and when finally all sinful passions have been extinguished in *nirvāṇa*, the liberation of the heart and knowledge has been found, the tree in the paradise of the gods stands in full bloom, and one hierarchy of gods announces the joyful event to another, and the jubilations reach up to the gods of the Brahmā heaven.

Elsewhere, too, the gods take an intimate part in the inner life of human beings; in the Mahāparinibbānasutta, for example, in the mourning of the Buddha's death. Before the Buddha enters the great *nirvāṇa*, they flock from all world realms and congregate around him in order to speak to him for the last time. In the same text it is said that the inclinations and decisions of the will of human beings are led by those supernatural beings. The Buddha legend (narrated in Part 1) shows the extent of the part these deities play in the entire career of the Buddha-to-be, how they lead him on all paths, give him the decision to enter the path of renunciation of the world, and greet each of his triumphs, each inner victory with joyful jubilations. This divine lead reaches an important turning point in that moment when the Bodhisattva awakens to a Buddha under the *bodhi* tree. The deities which so far have led him, now bow before him. It is an important idea of Buddhism that the human being in a sense has a more exalted nature than all deities, because only the human being has the opportunity to reach the highest stage of being, that of a world-liberating Buddha. In order to become a Buddha, the gods themselves have to descend from their heavenly spheres to a human birth. Only in a human body can they partake of the highest salvation, the highest perfection. In this sense, a human birth in Buddhism is seen as the ideal birth, as an invaluably high possession, and, as with human beings entering the heavenly world after death, is called the 'good walk' (*sugati*); with the gods conversely becoming human is tellingly called the 'good walk' (*Ittivuttaka* 83: *manussataṃ ... devānaṃ sugatigamana-saṅkhātaṃ*). Without this idea of the interrelationship between gods and human beings a deeper understanding of Buddhism, especially of the doctrine of the nature of a Buddha, cannot be acquired. It is an essential basic assumption of Buddhism that a Buddha, just as he appears as a human teacher among human beings, also works as a teacher of the gods, the Māra-beings etc. among the supernatural beings, and that he, as he appears to human beings as a human being, is taken by each of this class of supernatural beings as one of their own (MPS, p. 28).

Apart from the gods (*deva, devatā*), Buddhism knows numerous categories of lower supernatural beings (e.g., *yakṣa, gandharva* and many more) which play no minor role in the texts (see among others L.V. ed., Lefm., p. 71). We cannot enter into any details here. Only one of these beings should be considered here, because it has a particularly close and important connection with meditation: the being of Māra, the Buddhist tempter, whom we have met several times already in the context of the narration of the Buddha legend in Part 1. To occidental thinking it appears obvious to take this form of Māra as something entirely subjective, as the mere personification of certain inner experiences and challenges of the Holy One. However, this does not correspond to the Buddha's viewpoint. Even Māra's being is only to be understood from the perspective of meditation, and as we have seen, it is distinctive of this meditation in the Buddha's sense that objects which appear to objective observation as nothing or something merely subjective, take on a character of objective external reality, while things that were previously regarded as substantial now appear unsubstantial. It is thus with deliberation that the problem of Māra is discussed here in the context of meditation. It has to be assumed that the Buddha—like meditating saints of other religions and spiritual schools—had a vision of the tempter. In Buddhism Māra stands, in any case, on the same level of reality as the 'gods' who, as we have seen, reveal themselves to the disciple as supernatural beings in meditation in the way described above. In the texts Māra's hosts are also often enumerated among the classes of gods, and Māra himself is called *devaputta*, '[son of] god'. Just as the gods greet the disciple's decision to turn towards the spiritual heights of meditation with joy and take a friendly part in his effort, Māra is the adversary who seeks to, as it were, obstruct the path to those spiritual heights for the person meditating. The story of the Buddha as narrated in Part 1 already showed how through the Buddha's sitting down for meditation under the *bodhi* tree Māra with his hosts is called forth into opposition. The Pali texts say clearly how Māra always presses on the meditating disciple with his whispered suggestions in order to disturb the meditation. Every time the person meditating does not remain in wakeful consciousness, when he does not powerfully overcome those adverse emotional reactions mentioned as hindrances of meditation, Māra wins an opportunity to get at him (*labhati tassa Māro otāraṃ, labhati tassa Māro ārammaṇa; Majjh.* III, p. 94). Of particular importance for the defence against Māra is 'mindful consciousness' (*kāyagatā sati*) to be directed at the body. This is, above all, the reason for the Buddha's continuously repeated admonition to be mindfully conscious which constitutes a Buddhist counterpart to the Christian 'keep watch and pray' (as shown above, Buddhism puts meditation in the place of prayer). The Māra episodes in the canon are numerous and interesting from various points of view. The Mahāparinibbānasutta contains a particularly remarkable one (see above, p. 73f.). There is an entire passage of such episodes in the *Saṃyuttanikāya* (the Mārasaṃyuttaṃ, vol. I, pp. 103–127; cf. also what follows up to p. 135). We cannot enter into the wealth of details here. Of more general significance in this context is again a *sūtra* from the *Aṅguttaranikāya* containing various profundities through which light is shed on the Māra-problem, in particular its relationship with the problem of meditation. Once, in times gone by, it is said there, the gods fought with their enemies, the demons (*asura*). Victory soon inclined to one, soon to the other party. But the gods were safe from the demons when they finally retreated to their divine castle in the north after the unfortunate fight. And the *asuras* were equally safe from the gods in their demon castle in the south. In the same way, it is then said, the disciple is in a safe castle when he has obtained meditation free from sensual desire, where the power of Māra can no longer harm him; and when he has attained the highest stage of extinguishing Māra's power is completely broken. Here, firstly the comparison of meditation with a safe castle into which adverse inner forces can no longer enter, is notable. But it is also not without significance that precisely in this context the battle of the gods with the enemies of the gods, the hostile angels or *asuras*, is mentioned. Of course, this battle superficially only serves as an illustration of the comparison, and the *tertium comparationis* is merely the security offered by the solid castle against the approaching enemies. But we would not understand the Buddha's parables correctly if we were to judge them according to the perspectives of formal logic in this way. These parables, rather, contain the most profound connections in that which apparently serves only for the concrete illustration of the image. And with the parable mentioned here, the deeper thought is that the challenges which the disciple has to survive from the part of hostile inner forces before reaching the safe castle of meditation, are, as it were, a mirror image of those battles which were fought between gods and their enemies, the demons, in supernatural spheres in the beginning of time. (The old Vedic texts, too, frequently mention these battles.)

A common epithet of Māra in Pali is *pāpimā,* which is usually translated as 'the wicked one (*der Böse*).' (In the Sanskrit texts the adjectival *pāpīyān* corresponds to this.) Originally, however, *pāpimā* is a noun and means 'evil' (*das Übel*) (Skt. *pāpman*); a more correct translation would thus be 'Māra, the evil'. If we trace which evil is meant here, we meet with a peculiar double-nature in Māra. It follows that Māra presents himself as the embodiment of really two main evils. On the one hand, Māra is the lord of the senses and representative of sensual desire (*tṛṣṇā,* Pali *taṇhā*) which in Buddhism, as we have seen, is the cause of the malady of the world. In the Kassaka-episode of the Mārasaṃyutta (*Saṃy.* I, p. 115) Māra approaches the Buddha in the form of a peasant (*kassaka*) with a plough and asks him: 'Have you seen the bulls?' The Buddha replies: 'What business are the bulls to you, bad one?' Māra: 'Mine is the eye, mine the colours . . ., mine the ear, mine the sounds, mine the smell . . ., mine the body, etc. (with the rhythmical enumeration of all details common in Buddhist texts). Where do you want to go to be free of me?' The Buddha answers: 'Yours the eye . . ., yours the ear, etc. (follows again the same long enumeration of the sense organs and sense objects). But where, you bad one, there is no eye . . ., ear . . ., etc., you cannot enter.' (Translation [into German] in Windisch: *Māra und Buddha,* p. 104f.)[7] In the sphere of sensuality (*kāmadhātu,* see above, p. 163), it is said, Māra reigns absolute. In this sense, Māra is also called Namuci which was originally the name of a demon of sensuality defeated by Indra, and he is in effect depicted as the god of love with arrows. On the other hand, Māra is the lord of death, i.e., of that power in which for the Buddhist the suffering of the world finds its most immediate and most painful expression. This is also the original meaning of the word *māra* (the word contains the same root as the Latin *mors.* In a different way, though rather unconvincingly, Kern explains the word in *Buddhismus*, vol. I, p. 302).[8] For the Buddhist *Māro pāpimā* corresponds in the old Brāhmaṇa texts to *mṛtyuḥ pāpman* 'death, the evil'. Between the two sides of Māra's double nature there is now a profound connection, for sensual desire (*taṇhā*) as the cause of worldly evil is also that of death in Buddhism. Through desire the human being is tied to the sensual world, in which he is subject to the cycle of birth and death. By overcoming desire he frees himself from this fetter, reaches the place beyond birth and death. The path to overcoming desire, however, is exclusively that path which, as we have seen, a path of *meditation*. Thus also a reflection on the nature of Māra from this perspective leads us back to meditation; it becomes clear why Māra is interested in disrupting meditation and why a meeting with him is particularly experienced in the attempt to raise oneself to meditation.

Even a victory over Māra like the one the Buddha won under the *bodhi* tree does not once and for all keep the tempter away from the sphere of the Holy One. Again and again he seeks an opportunity to come close to him, and the Mahāparinibbānasutta tells us how Māra even in the last hours of the Buddha's life undertakes attempts to reach his aims with the Holy One. Elsewhere, too, the canon is full of episodes which take place between Māra and the already perfected Buddha. Even when meditation has been attained, Māra tries again and again to enter into its circle, and it requires continuous strong exertion by the disciple to defend that which has been won and to remain steadfast in meditation. Thus the Buddha's continuous admonition to strive unceasingly, repeated even immediately before his passing.

The passage on meditation in the *Dīghanikāya* (Sāmaññaphalasutta 64ff.) from which the present discussion initially started, only follows the stages of meditation until the fourth *dhyāna (jhāna)* while the ensuing stages of consciousness and meditation (*āyatana*) are discussed in the Poṭṭhapādasutta and elsewhere. This fourth stage of *dhyāna* or 'contemplation' is of particular importance and nobility in Buddhism. Before his passing, after having raised himself through all stages of consciousness up to the heights of *nirodha*, the Buddha returns backward to the first *dhyāna* stage in order to then raise himself again to the fourth *dhyāna*, and, from this fourth stage of meditation, he then enters the great otherworldly *nirvāṇa*. Everything which in the Sāmañña-phalasutta is listed further as 'attainments' of the path which find their realization already in this visible state of existence (*diṭṭh' eva dhamme sandhiṭṭhikaṃ sāmaññaphalaṃ*) also has this fourth stage of *dhyāna* as its point of departure and prerequisite. It is the stage of complete detachment from all passions, from all concepts of sensory or supernatural objects and all experiences of joy and pain, that state of which it is said that the disciple therein was entirely clothed as if in a spotless white garment from head to toe. From this state emerges everything which the Sāmaññaphalasutta describes as abilities of clairvoyance and higher spiritual power or supernatural perfection (*iddhi*), just like all realizations of Buddhism which refer to that which is usually presented as the dogmatic content of this religion. 'If,' thus it is said in the passage on meditation in the *Dīghanikāya* (SPhS 83),

> the mental element (*citta*) has been thus concentrated, purified and filled with light, free from all impurities and earthly passion, compliant and pliable (*kammaniya*), steadfast and unmoving, then he directs this spiritual element towards the realizing vision (or 'seeing realization', *ñāṇadassana*).

That which presents itself first to his vision is his own body, his own being, which he then sees as if split into a duality: a physical being, constituted by the four elements which is the result of physical heredity (*mātāpettikasambhava*) and which carries the conditions of decay and dissolution in itself, and another one, a principle of spiritual consciousness (*viññāṇa*) which permeates that physical being in the same way as a coloured thread drawn through a pure, stainless, polished eight-sided precious stone;[9] and it is said that he sees this, his physical body, which is subject to decay and traversed by the thread of the consciousness-soul as if *from the outside* like someone who takes a precious stone into his hand and says: this is a precious stone with these particular characteristics, and here a coloured thread has been drawn through it. A prerequisite for the practice of higher abilities is then yet another step which sheds light on the nature of meditation and the supernatural processes which according to Buddhism take place therein. This stage is described in the passage on meditation in the *Dīghanikāya* (SPhS 85, 86) as follows: If the mind has reached that pure, light, passionless and motionless concentration, then, it is further said, the disciple directs the mental element towards the formation of another, spiritual (spiritual-etheric) body (*manomayakāya*) which is furnished with all main and ancillary members and with full sense organs. This spiritual-etheric body, furnished with all main and ancillary members and full sense organs he then draws out of his physical body like a stalk from the leaf-sheath, or like a sword from the sheath, or like a snake from the basket (according to others: pelt), and the person meditating then has this duality of his being in front of him like an external image (SPhS 86). Not only ordinary comparisons are given with these images, but certain Imaginations are described which accompany the process (conceived of as supernatural) of detachment from a spiritual body. These images which are interesting with reference to Yoga techniques were most likely not invented by the Buddha, but are of older origin. The image of drawing out the blade of *muñja* grass from the leaf-sheath (*muñjād iṣīkāṃ*) can already be found at the end of the *Kāṭhaka-Upaniṣad*[10] (in which so much recalls Buddhism). It requires hardly any mention that Buddhism here operates entirely within the sphere of Yoga.

In connection with this problem of the multiple sheaths of being, nesting within each other and extracted from their context through meditation, light is also shed on the Buddhist teaching of the I or Self, which has found its most widely known expression in the Pali work, *Milindapañha*[11] (no longer belonging to the canon) in the dialogue between King Milinda (Menander) and the Buddhist sage, Nāgasena (see Oldenberg, op. cit., p. 299f.,[12] Pischel, op. cit., p. 71).[13] Often, a Buddhist 'negation of the I' is spoken about. It would be more appropriate and correct to speak of a 'non-penetration to the I'. The Poṭṭhapādasutta of the *Dīghanikāya* contains a deeper discussion of the subject, following the above-mentioned problems of meditation (I, p. 195). To start with, a three-fold self (*attā*, Skr. *ātman*) or I is distinguished here: a crude material (*oḷārika*), the physical body, a higher-spiritual (*manomaya*) which corresponds in its attributes to the spirit-body drawn out through meditation (*manomayo sabbaṅga-paccaṅgī ahīnindriyo*) as described in the SPhS, and an even higher one, called *arūpī saññāmayo.* The attribute *rūpī*, 'formed' given to the second of these selves refers to the fact that it belongs to the (supernatural) sphere of form (*rūpadhātu*) which is entered on the first stage of meditation (see above, p. 163f.). The next higher self (*arūpī saññāmayo*, i.e., 'unformed, consisting of consciousness') then belongs, as the term reveals, to the *arūpa* sphere which is entered with raising oneself meditatively to the 'limitlessness of the space ether' (*ākāsānañcāyatana*; see above, p. 160f.). All these 'selves', however, only have a seeming and relative validity in Buddhism and it is the progressive meditation which destroys their respective appearance. The Poṭṭhapādasutta teaches that it is distinctive in meditation that the I which at a certain stage can be taken as substantial, cannot, as it were, be taken to the next higher stage, that it is experienced as insubstantial there (PoṭṭhS 48, p. 199). In the sense of these deliberations the crude material (*oḷārika*) body is taken as the I or Self in the normal state of sensory existence. This concept of I is then experienced as insubstantial when in meditation (from the first to the fourth level) the etheric-spiritual self (*manomaya*) is realized, and this I-concept is in turn destroyed in the *arūpa* sphere. The self or I experienced there also has only the same relative nature. The meditating disciple, at each stage, loses that which on the previous stage he experienced as his I. And now it is quite intrinsic to Buddhism that it does not raise itself above these relative 'selves', does not penetrate to an absolute, highest self or I. Such an I is not denied, but it is only said that everything which is on any level experienced as the I, is not in reality the I. Compare with *Majjh.* III, p. 19 and other passages where it is stated of each of the five *skandhas* that it 'is not the I' (*rūpaṃ anattā vedanā anattā saññā anattā saṅkhārā anatta viññāṇaṃ anattā*). The first three of these *skandhas,* or basic parts of human nature, are relative to the three 'selves', the last two belong to still deeper inner foundations. Thus, even the Buddhist teaching about the I can only be understood correctly on the basis of the meditation problem.

Through this extraction of an etheric-spiritual body 'furnished with complete sense organs' from the physical-material body as described in the passage on meditation in the *Dīghanikāya,* the person meditating has now attained the tool to exercise that which in the same passage of the *Dīghanikāya* (SPhS 87ff.), as everywhere else in the Buddhist texts, is described as supernatural perfections, the phenomena of higher spiritual power (*ṛddhi,* Pali *iddhi, iddhi-pāṭihāriya*). Even in the outer arrangement of the subject the correspondence between this Buddhist passage on meditation and the *Yogasūtra* mentioned everywhere, is revealed again. Just like the discussion of the stages of meditation in the *Yogasūtra* in the third chapter is followed by that of the Yoga perfections or higher powers (*vibhūti*), the passage on meditation in the *Dīghanikāya* proceeds to present as a further attainment won by that process of the path the opportunity to exercise these phenomena of supernatural power (*iddhi*) after the extraction of the supernatural body has been described in the context of meditation. 'If,' it is said there (SPhS 87),

> the mental element (*citta*) has become detached and purified through concentration, free from impurity and earthly passion, compliant and pliable, steadfast and motionless, he leads and guides this mental element towards exercising the various supernatural perfections (*iddhi-vidhāya cittaṃ abhinīharati abhininnāmeti*).

In Buddhism the term *citta*—in the philosophy of Sāṃkhya (and Yoga) that element of thought conceived of as etheric-material—is not to be connected with some naturalist concepts. It only signifies that something spiritual is formed like pliable clay, brought to manifold form and effect by the person meditating. This idea is presented in three parables in the Sāmaññaphalasutta (88): as the potter from well-prepared clay forms pots at will, as the ivory carver and the goldsmiths shape their material at will and form objects of all kinds from it, thus, as it were, the disciple of the path works into the material (made pliable in meditation) of his spiritual body in order to bring forth the *iddhi*-forms, the supernatural phenomena. The rhythmical repetition of one and the same idea in three similar parables appears to want to illustrate the working into the material and nature of the supernatural body (cf. what was said on p. 101 about the rhythm in the Buddha's speeches). If much in what has been previously said was alienating to occidental understanding, the way in which the Buddhist texts speak about these *iddhi* phenomena must now completely appear to occidental feelings as the highest madness, as the insurmountable peak of folly. But here, too, we may recall that remarkable passage in the Pāyāsisutta (*Dīgha* II, p. 329) where Kassapa points out to the nobleman, Pāyāsi who doubts the reality of the supernatural world and supernatural appearances and beings, that this supernatural world could not be seen with eyes of the flesh (*maṃsacakkhunā*) as he imagined it. Only a purification of spiritual vision in lonely, silent, secluded meditation leads to this vision. Similar things are also true for the *iddhi* phenomena. They are processes which, at least initially, are conceived of as taking place in the medium of that subtle spirit-body, not in the sphere of the physical-sensory. The actual folly would only be to take such things as the 'touching of sun and moon' (of which the passage on *iddhi* talks among other things) in a literal, crudely material sense, and to believe the Buddha had actually thought reaching for sun and moon (as material stars) with sensory hands possible. In the above-mentioned Pāyāsisutta (*Dīgha* II, p. 319) it is explicitly stated that 'sun' and 'moon' have to be understood as divine beings of a supernatural world. Thus we are obviously concerned here with certain supernatural visions and Yoga experiences which are deliberately shrouded from the naïve worldly understanding by a grotesque way of expression. In the *Vinayapiṭaka* (*Cullavagga* II, p. 112) we find an important passage where the Buddha admonishes his disciples not to reveal the phenomena of higher spiritual power (*iddhipāṭihāriya*) resting on superhuman laws to the eyes of lay people. In Buddhism *iddhi* was thus seen as something highly exalted, to be strictly withdrawn from profane eyes. The Buddha always denied showing any phenomena to mere curiosity (cf. the Kevaddhasutta, *Dīgha* I, p. 211).

The passage which describes the individual supernatural perfections (*iddhi*, SPhS 87. 88) belongs to those which are repeated frequently, always with the same stereotypical phrasing, in the most diverse parts of the canon. The phenomena listed there can be summarized according to the multiplication of appearance, shutting off of vision, overcoming gravity. This is followed by the above-mentioned strange phenomenon which is described as follows: 'The moon and the sun, those magically powerful, wonder-working stars, he touches and brushes with the hand (*imepi candimasuriye evaṃ-mahiddhike evaṃ-mahānubhāve*), with his body he reaches into the world of Brahmā.' It has already been pointed out that these are entirely supernatural things, that it must be the already mentioned 'spirit-body' to which here a stretching of spiritual antennae towards distant, supernatural worlds, is ascribed. The multiplication of form (which plays an important role in Indian Yoga, cf. *Yogasūtra* IV, 4) equally lies initially in the sphere of this supernatural body, and the same is true for the various appearances of elevation (cf. *Yogasūtra* III, 38), the overcoming of gravity and the feeling of etheric lightness effected by meditation. In *Saṃy*. V, p. 283, it is said that through body-encompassing spiritual concentration and meditation the body of the Tathāgata becomes lighter, more compliant, pliable and radiant. There is a theoretical explanation of the shutting off of vision in the *Yogasūtra* (III, 20). These things play a hardly less important role in Buddhism than in the actual Yoga. In a lengthy passage of the *Saṃyuttanikāya* (the Iddhipāda-Saṃyutta, vol. V, 253–293) a separate comprehensive theory of the subject is developed. All these discussions centre around the doctrine of the four *iddhipādā*, the elements or prerequisites of supernatural perfection: *chando* 'will', *viriyaṃ* 'energy', *cittaṃ*, the mental or thought element, *vimaṃsā* (approximately 'formative creativity'). It is these four elements with respect to which it is said in the Mahāparinibbānasutta and elsewhere that those who allow them to become strong in themselves through meditation, who know to move in them (*yānikatā*), realize, use and master them, also have the power to prolong their life in the physical body beyond its natural length. The more detailed explanations—of which there is no scarcity in the canon (cf. *Saṃy*. V, p. 268)—hardly clarify what is actually meant by these four elements or prerequisites, but at least this much emerges from these explanations: that two of these elements belong to the side of the will, two to the side of imagination. It is clearly stated that they have to form an object of meditation (cf. op. cit., pp. 258, 268), and the path to their realization is none other than precisely the already marked path of meditation, the 'noble Eightfold Path' (op.cit., p. 286). Persistent effort (*padhāna*) has to join meditation; from these two then emerges (brought up from the subconscious) a formative force (*saṅkhāra*) which constitutes that which is the actual effective aspect of these phenomena. (In this sense *Saṃy*. V, p. 258 and others: *chandasamādhipadhānasaṅkhārasamannāgatam iddhipādam*, etc.) The Tathāgata, it is said, masters these elements of supernatural power, for that very reason he is called the Tathāgata (op. cit., p. 257), thus in the sense of Buddhism, they belong to the essential perfections of a Buddha. According to the Iddhipādasutta (op. cit., p. 274), the same is true of all true ascetics and Brahmins of the past and the future. It is further said (p. 257) that all disciples have reached the highest goal of liberation through *iddhipāda*-meditation (which is, as we have seen, eventually identical with that of the Eightfold Path). 'And just as the Gaṅgā in its course is inexorably directed towards the East, turns towards the East, flows to the East, so is also the disciple who meditates the four prerequisites of supernatural perfection turned towards *nirvāṇa*, hastening towards *nirvāṇa*' (op. cit., p. 290). In this sense, these things are considered in Buddhism to be one of the highest attainments of the path (*sāmaññaphala*). They are not the goal, but an appearance which according to the Buddha's teaching occurs with certainty on the path towards the attainment of the goal. Through meditation of *iddhipāda* the fetters which tie the disciple to sensual existence are also cut off (*Saṃy*. V, p. 292).

Apart from that, *iddhi, sensu stricto,* is only one of five or six higher inner abilities usually called *abhiññā* (Skt. *abhijñā*) which are also mentioned in the passage on meditation in the *Dīghanikāya* (where the term *abhiññā* is not used) as further attainments (standing above *iddhi*) of the path which occur when the separation of the etheric-spiritual body from the physical-material has been reached. In the Iddhipāda-saṃyutta the four prerequisites of *iddhi* are also presented as the path towards the attainment of those further spiritual powers (*Saṃy*. V, p. 263ff.). The first of these abilities is *dibbaṃ sotaṃ* (corresponding to the *divyaṃ śrotram* of the *Yogasūtra* III, 41), the 'divine hearing' or clairaudience which is described as a hearing of human (even distant) and heavenly sounds 'in the heavenly, purified tone elements which go beyond human [hearing]' (*dibbāya sota-dhātuyā visuddhāya atikkanta-mānusikāya*; expressed in Pythagorean terms: in the harmony of the spheres). The realization of others' thoughts and stirrings of the heart (*cetopariyañāṇa* = *paracittajñāna* of the *Yogasūtra* III, 19) follows clair-audience. The examples of where the Buddha penetrates the thoughts of others are numerous in the texts (e.g., *Dīgha* I, p. 119, *Aṅg*. III, p. 408, V, p. 160). But this ability especially refers to a realization of the character of others, their disposition and temper, the degree of their freedom from sinful passions, the degree of spiritual concentration attained by them, etc. The abilities in question are elsewhere called *ādesanā-pāṭihāriyaṃ* 'the miracle of information', which, according to Kevaddhasutta 6 (*Dīgha* I, p. 213), means that the disciple is able to see the thoughts and attitudes, concepts and deliberations of another person, and tell him: 'This is what you are thinking, this is what your heart is like.'

The two remaining higher abilities which are mentioned as further attainments of meditation in the passage on meditation of the *Dīghanikāya* (SPhS 93–96) are the memory of previous existences (cf. *Yogasūtra* III, 18) and the divine (or heavenly) eye of clairvoyant vision (*dibbaṃ cakkhuṃ visuddhaṃ atikkantamānusakaṃ*, literally: 'the heavenly eye, the purified one [whose vision] goes beyond human [vision])'. In as far as this latter ability enables seeing supernatural beings, it has already been mentioned. In the passage on meditation of the *Dīghanikāya* it is said how the power of the divine eye serves the seeing of the fates of beings in the different spheres of existence between death and rebirth. This then is already one of the three main higher 'realizations' (*paññā*) of Buddhism, the realization of *karma* and rebirth. The same is true of the memory of previous existences. The discussion of these 'higher abilities' thus already belongs to the subject of the following passage.

d) Third stage of the Path: Realization (*paññā*)

In this section it has to be made clear from the very beginning that the type of realization referred to here has to be understood in the context of meditation, just like the preceding. This realization (*paññā*) in the Buddha's sense is not some combination of the speculating intellect (*tarka*) but the result of a higher clairvoyant vision (*abhiññā*) which can only be attained by 'right meditation' (*sammāsamādhi*), by the kind of meditation which again, in turn, as its necessary foundation, has 'right ethical behaviour' (*sīla*) as described in the first main part [of this book]. If the person meditating has reached the stage of inner purity, lucidity of mind and concentration in the fourth *dhyāna* which is compared with a white garment clothing the disciple from top to bottom, when he has further reached the point where the 'spiritual body furnished with complete organs' (*manomayakāya*) is released from the physical-material body like the stalk from the leaf sheath, and the disciple, as if from the outside, looks onto his physicality shot through by the spiritual principle as if with a thread, then he has in this spiritually woven body the organ for exercising these higher inner faculties (elsewhere called *abhiññā*), out of which three, namely *iddhi*, clairvoyance and the penetration of other people's thoughts, have already been described in the previous section. These are followed by three further abilities which in Buddhism's sense equally rest on meditation. With these the person meditating already enters the area of higher realization, of knowledge. They are identical with the three-fold knowledge the Tathāgata was blessed with under the *bodhi* tree, and through whose attainment he was raised from the Bodhisattva to the Buddha (cf. above, p. 62ff. and *Lalitavistara*, p. 344f., where only the sequence of realizations is different).

The first of these realizations (SPhS 93) is the *memory of previous lives,* i.e., that inner experience which those who have obtained it in different countries and in different periods have described unanimously as a memory of previous existences. In the *Sumaṅgalavilāsinī,* Buddhagoṣa's commentary on the *Dīghanikāya,* we find a remarkable passage in the context of the explanation of the beginning of the Mahāpadānasutta where it is described how this inner experience occurs in different degrees of clarity at different degrees of sainthood. With ordinary ascetics of the different schools, it is said, this memory—if it occurs at all—is only as weak as the glow of a glow-worm; with disciples of the Buddha it is like the radiance of the morning star; with a Buddha who has only found enlightenment for himself it is like the moonlight; and with a world-liberating Buddha the memory of a previous life is as bright as the light of a thousand suns. Once (*Itivuttaka,* p. 99) the Buddha speaks of the true Brahmin as one who not only speaks about all sorts of things of the spiritual domain but who remembers his previous life himself. It is of some importance for the understanding of Buddhism that this memory of a life is first and foremost taken as that as which it clearly reveals itself according to the entire character of the respective section, namely as a meditative experience, not as a dogma.

Instead of tracing this speaking about previous existences, as it is also ascribed to the Buddha (see above, p. 104), back to existing dogmas we should ask whether these dogmas perhaps originated because individuals had the meditative experience in question and described it in their own way. In the context of the theoretical discussion of these things it remains a strange contradiction that Buddhism, which does not penetrate to an I or a Self which our logic demands for the creation of a link between the different existences as the subject which moves from one life to the next, still knows reincarnation, even a memory of previous existences and allows the Buddha to state at the end of many stories: 'at that time (in that previous life) I was this and that person'.

The essence/constitution of the human being is divided into five main components or *skandhas* (Pali *khanda*) in Buddhism: *rūpa* physical appearance, *vedanā* feeling, *saññā* consciousness of perception, *saṅkhāra* subconscious (latent formative forces), *viññāṇa* spiritual consciousness. It is said about all these five basic parts of being that they are 'not the self' (*anattā*; *Majjh.* III, p. 19 and others). The Buddha explicitly refutes the assumption of taking for example *viññāṇa* as the stable essence moving through a series of reincarnations (*Majjh.* I, 38, p. 256ff.; in this context the term *anañña* 'unchanged' has to be stressed: what is refuted is that *viññāṇa* forms a link between the different existences as an *unchangeable I-unit*). While the texts often speak about how this principle of spiritual consciousness leaves the body in death, and how it enters the womb again at birth or conception together with the inner being, in the sense of Buddhism it is not the I. The previous observations (p. 175) have shown that there is a connection between the *skandhas* and that which in meditation extracts itself, as it were, from the whole constitution of the human being as the higher, spirit-body 'selves'. *Oḷāriko attā*, the crude sensual self, corresponds to the physical body (*rūpa-khanda*); *saññāmayo attā* (Poṭṭhapādasutta 39) to the third *skandha* (*saññā*); *manomayo attā* thus probably corresponds to the second *skandha* and it is likely that the split of the overall being experienced in meditation, as if the *skandhas* gained independence in the spirit-body, gave the impetus for the unique doctrine of the *skandhas* so important in Buddhism. It has further followed that none of these 'selves' is experienced as the actual true I, but that the self, found on one level of meditation, is overcome on the next higher level (Poṭṭh. 48) without Buddhist meditation penetrating to an absolute I, and that we have to understand the doctrine of the non-I (*anattavāda*) of Buddhism based on these circumstances.

Thus *memory*—the possibility of penetrating in meditation to that point where the memory awakens: at that time I was this and that person (SPhS 93)—provides the only substitute for the missing I which would create the link between the individual reincarnations. With the ordinary person this memory lies, as it were, in the unconscious and is brought up by meditation from the subconscious (*saṃskāra,* Pali *saṅkhāra*). In the *Yogasūtra,* from which here, too, light is shed on Buddhism, it is expressed directly (III, 18) that the memory of a previous life is brought about by raising the *saṃskāra,* i.e., that which is initially subconscious, to consciousness. In these subconscious formative forces (*saṃskāra*) what is brought along as *karma,* the sum of one's actions in one incarnation, into the later incarnation like a subconscious memory of a previous life, has an impact. Thus if the meditation penetrates into those regions of the subconscious where the supernatural-spiritual nucleus of the later life is, as it were, kept which continues to work as the seed of previous incarnations, the vision of that previous life itself opens itself to the meditation. This is how we can somewhat grasp the nature of this Buddhist memory of previous lives, and it has to be continually pointed out that in Buddhism's sense these things are not something that should be seen as a philosophy and be measured by the yardstick of philosophical thinking, but they are connections which can only be penetrated in meditation as the Buddha penetrated them under the *bodhi* tree.

In the section on meditation in the *Dīghanikāya* (SPhS 93) the memory of a previous life is described in such terms that the person meditating, when he has reached that state of inner clarity in the fourth *dhyāna* and turns his mind towards the memory of previous births (*pubbenivāsānussati*), looks back upon these incarnations as someone who has been on a journey when he has returned to his home village looks back upon his stays in villages on the way and his experiences there. Thus, it is said, he remembers one, several, innumerably many births in eons of world creations, world dissolution or at the climax of eons:

> There (in that birth) I was this and that person, had that name, belonged to that lineage, that caste, lived under such and such circumstances, had these and other experiences of joy and pain, this and that lifespan. From there I came into that other incarnation etc., until I finally reached this earthly life.

(The teaching of the periodical-rhythmically repeating dissolution and recreation of the world in eons (*kalpa,* Pali *kalpo*) stretching across successive time periods is generally Indian.)

In close connection with this realization, which comprises one's own previous life, is the second of the great realizations which refers to the fate of the beings in the cycle of rebirths (*saṃsāra*). If we spoke about previous earthly lives or at least about physical reincarnations in the context of the memory of previous lives, the second realization is about supernatural stages of existence which the various beings enter after death, or between death and a new physical incarnation as a result of their *karma* (Pali *kamma*), the deed of their previous life which determines fate in all spheres of existence. This, too, does not refer to abstract realization, but it is said that the person meditating with the 'heavenly clairvoyant superhuman eye' sees the intertwined paths of all those beings through the various world spheres as if in a picture. (Cf. also Pāyāsisutta, *Dīgha*. II, p. 329.) Just as someone from a high vantage point, the parable states, sees the people wandering across streets and squares, into houses and out again, thus the person meditating sees how all beings walk the 'bad walk' (*duggati*) after the dissolution of the body in death, how they are transported to dark places of torture through evil thoughts, words and deeds, through lack of respect, wrong worldviews and through letting their actions be determined by this view. [He also sees] how they walk the 'good walk' after death and raise themselves to bright heavenly worlds through good thoughts, words and deeds, through worshipping venerable persons, through right worldviews and through correspondence between their deeds and this right view. We have already spoken about this entering into (supernatural) worlds of the gods in the section on meditation (above, p. 169). Those who walk in the right striving thus after death reach that sphere to which in the sense of Buddhism he can already raise himself in this life through meditation. Correspondingly, this entering into the worlds of the gods is granted to all those who on this side have proven themselves in right conduct as disciples of the Buddha (*Dīgha* II, p. 212) and who tread the path of meditation. It depends on the spiritual height they attained in this life, on the degree of their realization and love, which hierarchy of gods (angels) they enter into society with, into social intercourse (*sahavyatā*) with after death (*Aṅg*. II, p. 128f.). In particular the devoted worship of the master, of the Buddha, leads to entering into heavenly realms of bliss of the gods. Those who on pious pilgrimage—thus the Mahāparinibbānasutta—look with a quickened heart upon the places where the Tathāgata was born, where he awoke to the enlightenment of a Buddha, where he set the wheel of the norm in motion, and where he entered the sphere of the great *nirvāṇa*, will, after passing through the gate of death with a tranquil mind, enter into the bliss of the heavenly world (*sugatiṃ saggaṃ lokaṃ*) after the dissolution of the body. This is no eternal bliss, but even though the life of the individual classes of gods is bound to a certain period of time (see above, p. 164), which much exceeds a human lifespan, this sojourn in the spheres of the gods also reaches its end when the respective *karma* has been spent, and at a particular point in time the being in question—if it does not sink into lower spheres (*Aṅg.* II, p. 127)—enters a physical incarnation as a human being. Liberation, the final escape from the cycle (*saṃsāra*) can only be obtained from such a human incarnation (see above, p. 169). The stages through which a physical incarnation occurs form the subject of the third great realization (of which we will speak in more detail below). Thus the 'normal course' of those who walk here in the right striving has been described. Opposed to this is the 'abnormal' or 'downward leading' course (*apāya*) to which the others condemn themselves by their wrong thoughts, words and deeds. It leads to the realms of hell (*naraka* or *niraya*), the shadow realm (*petaloka*), the demon world (*asuraloka*) or into the bodies of animals (*tiracchāna*). The actual places of torture or hells are, even though they have to be conceived by those spiritually realizing (in meditation) as supernatural states (cf. Waddell, *Buddhism of Tibet*, p. 89),[1] described in Buddhism like external places and are classified in detail and their horrors are described in horrible pictures of the most sensual realism. A liminal state is that of the shadow realm (*petaloka*) which can be compared to 'purgatory'. Here are those souls (i.e., in this context: the remainders of supernatural parts of being) of those who have passed on and who have not entered the realms of hell, demons or the animal kingdom, but have also not or not yet ascended to the heavenly worlds. In this sphere they have to cleanse away the impurities attached to them through the sins committed by them in their human body. Through the sensual desires not yet overcome they still return to the domain of attraction belonging to the sensual world (*kāmadhātu*) and there appear as ghost-like beings (*peta*). An entire book of stories about such souls of people who have died is contained in the Pali canon (the Petavatthu in the *Khuddakanikāya*). According to Buddhism, inhuman deeds lead into inhuman spheres after death, into the world of the demons (*asuraloka*) or into the bodies of animals. We have already spoken above about the demons (*asura*) as enemies of the gods (p. 171). Demonic possession (similar to the New Testament) is mentioned in the *Lalitavistara* (and elsewhere; see above, p. 39). The concept of entering into animal bodies is generally Indian and has been taken over entirely by Buddhism. In the *Aṅguttaranikāya* (vol. I, p. 35ff.) it is said that the cases of incarnations in the lower worlds, in the realms of demons and in the animal kingdom are much more numerous than the incarnations in the human world. (In Buddhism a human birth is seen as a particularly precious attainment, see above, p. 169). The 'abnormal course' (*apāya*) thus plays in the sense of Buddhism a much larger role in reality than the good or normal one. Buddhism's decisive perspective is, however, that even in those dark realms there is no lasting (eternal) damnation; the sojourn there can extend over terribly long periods of time (there is no dearth of examples for this in Buddhist narrative literature). But when the evil *karma* in question has exhausted itself, has been consumed (thus the technical term) or processed, the possibility of an incarnation into higher realms, into the realm of human beings, even into the spheres of the gods, is open to the person concerned. When he has attained a human birth, nothing prevents him from even becoming a disciple of the Buddha and thus entering the path which, even if only after many further incarnations, frees him conclusively from the necessity of rebirth.

The third great realization, the *realization of suffering* and its overcoming, presents itself in the sense of Buddhism as the immediate consequence of the Buddhist realizations of repeated lives on earth, of *karma* and the cycle of rebirths (*saṃsāra*) discussed above. This realization has found its well-known expression in the argument from suffering, of the cause of suffering, of the annihilation of suffering and of the path towards the annihilation of suffering. The section on meditation of the *Dīghanikāya* also refers to the phrasing of the argument from suffering—which is assumed to be known—when it (SPhS 98) describes the third great realization (the sixth of the higher abilities elsewhere called *abhiññā* which are obtained through the separation of the spirit body in meditation) in such terms that the person meditating guides his mind in the state of concentration (described above) of the fourth *dhyāna* towards the knowledge of the annihilation of the delusion of earthly passion (*āsava*) and then realizes: This is suffering, this is the cause of suffering, this is the annihilation of suffering, this is the path to the annihilation of suffering. That this 'realization', too, is not speculation, not an abstract value judgement on earthly existence, but the immediate result of meditative vision, is particularly stressed in the section on meditation in the *Dīghanikāya* (SPhS98) and illustrated by a concrete parable: Just as in a mountain lake with clear water, where one can see to the bottom and someone with good eyes perceives shells, pebbles and shoals of fish and says to himself: this is the pure, clear mountain lake, these are the pebbles and shells on its bottom and the shoals of fish which move about in it—in the same way the person meditating realizes, when in pure, sheer meditation he turns his spiritual element which has been freed from all earthly impurity and sinful passion and has become compliant and pliable towards the annihilation of earthly delusions: this is suffering, this is the cause, this is the annihilation of suffering, this is the path leading to the change; this is the earthly delusion, this is the cause, this the annihilation of delusion, this is the path leading to the annihilation of delusion. In realizing this,

> he himself becomes free of the delusion of earthly desire (*kāmāsava*), of the delusion of being in the world (*bhavāsava*), of the delusion of worldly misconception (*avijjāsava*), and by being thus freed he also knows: this is the liberation; extinguished is birth, the sacred conduct has come to an end, the duty has been fulfilled, there is henceforth no return to earthly existence (SPhS 98).

In the Sāmaññaphalasutta this realization is then called the highest of all attainments of the spiritual life that can be reached in this earthly life above which there is none higher or more distinguished.

Because the path of realization finally culminates in the realization of the truth of suffering in the way described, this end, again, joins the starting point, for the same 'truth of suffering' is Buddhism's basic dogma from where, as has been described above, the disciple of the path, too, takes his departure. And yet there is a very significant difference between that point of departure and that which has been reached on that stage of the path just described, and it is important to note this difference. That stage which really precedes the entering of the path—that stage at which all those who call themselves Buddhists who do not become disciples of the path actually remain—is a pious acceptance of a realization found by someone else, by the Buddha, at best a felt, but not yet a realized truth. Even if the impression of that truth perhaps compelled the listener to entering the path, this is not yet a realization in the sense of Buddhism. Only through the path itself, Buddhism teaches, can belief turn into realization. Only by truly treading the entire path described in the preceding sections: by gaining steadfastness in everything which forms the foundations of the path as 'right conduct', by training himself in compassion and selflessness, truthfulness, chastity and austerity, by 'closing the doors of the senses' and remaining in mindful contemplation, by attaining contentedness with fate and a calm, steady external attitude, and then by freeing himself from all that still ferments in himself of earthly passion, purifying the spiritual element in himself to such an extent as to enable him to find in 'right contemplation' the path into his own inner being and thus raise himself gradually from one stage of meditation to the next; by then in meditation looking at his physical existence as if from the outside and extracting the etheric-spiritual body from the material body like a reed from the leaf sheath or the sword from the scabbard and thus gaining the ability of clairvoyant vision; only through these things is the disciple finally put in position in the Buddha's sense to now experience inwardly this 'truth of suffering', from whose mere pious acceptance he had erstwhile departed, as a *true realization*. It may be that our era with its tendency towards one-sided theoretical observation finds it difficult to grasp such differences, but for a true understanding of Buddhism it is of the greatest importance that they are noted. One will then no longer come to the wrong conclusion of seeing an expression of a pessimistic mood of soul in the statement of this 'argument from suffering'. This kind of pessimism was entirely remote from the Buddha—and Buddhism, as we have discussed above—and those who draw their judgement not from hearsay but from the original source texts, will have to admit to themselves in an objective approach that there is not the slightest trace of an actual pessimistic mood in these sources as we meet, for example, in Schopenhauer or Hartmann. The mood of Buddhism is everywhere an unpretentious, calm serenity, not without the expressed awareness (cf. *Dhammapada* 197–200) that the disciple of the path is granted a much higher measure of true earthly bliss than those who remain in worldliness, even if the latter may lack any yardstick for realizing this fact. Not the sentiment of world suffering, but the victory he has won over this suffering, puts the characteristic stamp on the mood of the Buddhist disciple. The 'argument from suffering', however, is nothing but a value judgement which the higher awareness *in the Buddha's sense* has to pass on the world of ordinary awareness. Here, too, Buddhism concurs with the *Yogasūtra* (II, 15) where the phrase is expressed 'for those who realize, everything is suffering'. Buddhism does not turn away from the worldly because in a weighing of the joy and pain of existence (as these terms are understood in their ordinary, worldly sense) the weighing pan of pain sinks deeper (this problem is hardly touched on in Buddhism). It does so because of the seed of death contained in everything worldly, death and impermanence are the true sufferings, that suffering from which even the joys of the heavens of the gods are not exempt. For the Buddha the concept of the non-eternal is inextricably linked with that of suffering. The idea that the non-eternal is suffering (*anicce dukkhasaññā*), it is said (*Aṅg.* IV, p. 51), should always be present in the disciple's thoughts and in his meditation, and equally the additional idea that suffering is not the self, not the true I (*dukkhe anattasaññā*, p. 53). (The connection between the concepts of the non-eternal, suffering and non-self are equally found in the *Yogasūtra* [II, 5] where *avidyā* [*avijjā*], delusion, is declared to be the confusion of the non-eternal, the impure, of suffering and the non-self with that which is eternal, pure, free from suffering and the true I). The Buddhist idea of turning away from the transient, from everything which bears the seed of death in itself, has found its strongest expression in the Buddha legend. This legend essentially treats the same problem as the meditation section of the *Dīghanikāya*, but only in pictures, in a more concrete form. The Buddha reached his experience of the transience of all worldly things, the suffering of birth, old age, sickness and death through deep meditative penetration into his own inner being. The problem of whether we can possibly come to a deeper understanding of the meaning of impermanence and suffering, or in particular understand death even more deeply than the Buddha, can no longer be the subject of this writing which is devoted to a description of Buddhism. It has to confine itself with remarks towards how the Buddha experienced these things and how he had to experience them in accordance with the entire development of time and his own inner development.

Regarding how far the outer argument from suffering with its fourfold structuring—suffering, cause of suffering, annihilation of suffering, path to the annihilation of suffering—follows ancient medical terminology, has already been discussed. We also find the same terminology in the *Yogasūtra*, where the four 'noble truths' of Buddhism correspond to the following *sūtras*: II, 15 the argument from suffering; II, 24 and 17 cause of suffering—only that the differentiation between spirit and matter based on the Sāṃkhya-philosophy is absent in Buddhism—; II, 25 annihilation of suffering; II, 28 and 26 the path leading to the annihilation of suffering. The distinction between the third and fourth truth ('annihilation of suffering' and 'path to the annihilation of suffering'), although perhaps not readily obvious to occidental thinking, again shows the clear practical tendency of Buddhism. The Buddha simply did not want to erect just a theory of the connection between worldly suffering and sensual desire (*taṇhā*), but wanted to show an actual attainable goal of salvation to humanity. He probably knew that it was not easily possible to extinguish *taṇhā* in order to detach oneself from the entanglement of the world. If he wanted to say what he was eventually aiming for, he had to state clearly on which path the fight, necessary for overcoming earthly passion, can be fought to a victorious conclusion. As the explanations above have shown, the entire norm culminates in the 'path' and it was thus self-evident that the 'argument from suffering' which contains the essence of the entire norm has to include a reference to the path of meditation through which, as we have seen, the 'argument from suffering' in turn can be reached. Thus the 'truth of suffering' contains the 'path' and the path again contains the truth of suffering; the theoretical and the practical aspects of Buddhism merge in a perfect circle.

That the argument from suffering really is the essence of the entire Buddhist norm of realization has been expressed in the most unambiguous way by the Buddha. Not in the sense that in the Buddha's opinion all realization as such were contained in it. This is not and cannot be said. The Buddha himself states that he had realized a great deal which he had not revealed because it would not be for the salvation of humanity (see above, p. 106). The consistent answer to the question posed by himself what it was then that he revealed is:

> This is suffering ... this is its cause ... this is the annihilation of suffering ... this is the path to the annihilation of suffering; I have revealed this to you, because it is the prerequisite for sacred conduct, because it leads towards renunciation, to freedom from passion, to the annihilation of the cause, to inner peace, to clairvoyant realization, to awakening, to *nirvāṇa*.

Even though the 'truth' expressed in the Buddhist 'argument from suffering' may contain something most profound, most important for those who take it seriously in the practical sense demanded by the Buddha, from a theoretical perspective the expression of this 'truth' as given in this fourfold formula still appears sparse and in many ways unsatisfactory. An attempt at reaching additional, deeper information by logically analyzing the phrase would not lead to positive results. The Buddha did not give this phrase in order for it to be 'academically' analyzed or speculated on, but in order for it to be penetrated in its depths through meditation (on this, see the previous section). With respect to the 'truth' found by him, the Buddha expressed most decidedly (see above, p. 66f.) that these depths are unattainable for the ordinary intellect and speculative observation (*tarka*). The disciple should allow this 'truth' to affect him in attentive spiritual contemplation (cf. *Saṃy.* V, p. 414 where the Buddha admonishes his disciples to penetrate to the 'truth of suffering' in meditation), and even in the phrasing of the terms this meditative effect has been considered, that effect which finds its expression also in the sound of the words, in the rhythm of the formula in the original texts and which in translation can only be partially reproduced.

Apart from that, the truth found by the Buddha is also expressed in another formula which offers more to theoretical needs than the 'argument from suffering'. It is the *twelvefold formula of conditioned arising* (*pratītyasamutpāda,* Pali *paṭiccasamuppāda*) which in the Buddha legend appears as the original version of the third of the three great realizations attained under the *bodhi* tree, the realization of the cause and the overcoming of suffering, and from which the fourfold 'argument from suffering' etc. is only then deduced. Not only the Mahāyāna text *Lalitavistara* proceeds this way, but even the Pali canon departs initially from that form of the realization of the Buddha given in the twelvefold formula where the experiences under the *bodhi* tree are narrated. Indeed, it is very significant that precisely the first text of this canon, the *Mahāvagga* of the *Vinayapiṭaka,* starts with this twelvefold formula. It thus stands at the helm of the canon, and this outward position corresponds quite clearly to its inner significance and importance. If the fourfold 'argument from suffering', as it were, contains the folk version of the realization found by the Buddha, easily remembered and meditated by anyone, the twelvefold formula of conditioned arising constitutes the 'scientific'—in the sense of those times—phrasing of that realization (cf. p. 100). The writers of the Buddhist texts (or the collectors of the Buddha's lectures) were aware of the fact that the truth of suffering (or the second and third of those four sentences) and the twelvefold formula of the *pratītyasamutpāda* eventually are merely different expressions of the same realization. In the *Aṅguttaranikāya* (vol. I, p. 177) one half of the *pratītyasamutpāda* is equated directly with the phrase of the cause of suffering, the other half with the annihilation of suffering. (The discussion of the path of meditation above similarly showed that the eightfold formula contained in the fourth of the 'noble truths' has to be put in line with the meditation section of the *Dīghanikāya* and how it suggests that which in that section is then described in its full content, cf. *Majjh.* I, p. 301).

The phrasing of the formula has already been given above (p. 62f.). Corresponding to the Sanskrit terms for the twelve parts ['limbs, members'—*Trs. note*] (*nidāna*) of the chain of causal arising (*pratītya-samutpāda*) provided there, following the Sanskrit text *Lalitavistara*, are the following Pali terms 1. *avijjā* delusion (Skt. *avidyā*), 2. *saṅkhārā* the formative forces in the subconscious (Plural of *saṅkhāra* = Skt. *saṃskāra*), 3. *viññāṇa* consciousness (*vijñāna*), 4. *nāmarūpa* name and form (Skt. same), 5. *saḷāyatana* the senses (lit. 'the six realms', Skt. *ṣaḍāyatana*), 6. *phassa* touch (Skt. *sparśa*), 7. *vedanā* perception, 8. *taṇhā* sensual desire (lit. 'thirst', Skt. *tṛṣṇā*), 9. *upādāna* the grasping of the sensual (as fuel of desire), 10. *bhava* being, physical being, 11. *jāti* birth, 12. *jarāmaraṇa-sokaparidevadukkhad-omanassupāyāsā* old age and death, worry and lamentation, suffering, melancholy and desperation (Skt. *jarāmaraṇa-śokaparidevaduḥkad aurmanasyopāyāsāḥ*. The names of the fourth, seventh, ninth, tenth, and eleventh causal parts are the same in Sanskrit and Pali.) The phrasing of the causal formula in the Indian language is: *avijjāpaccayā saṅkhārā* (Skt. *avijdyā-pratyayāḥ saṃskārāḥ*) 'from delusion arise the *saṃskāras*', *saṅkhāra-paccayā viññāṇaṃ* etc. through all causal parts until the twelfth part of the series (old age, death and suffering). The word *paccaya* is linked to the word *paṭicca* (Skt. *pratītya*) in *paṭic-casamuppāda* (*pratīyasamutpāda*) and signifies the causal relationship (the 'origin' in something else). The following observations will reveal that the term 'cause' referred to here is not entirely identical with that familiar to us from our natural sciences and logic. This concept of cause is not about linking the individual 'appearances' within 'existence' amongst each other, but to link this 'existence' itself with something which is not yet 'existence'; one could, in order to come closer to the Indian shade of the term, represent *paccaya* as 'original state', also following a term coined by a German mystic,[2] and thus translate: 'in delusion the formative forces of the subconscious have their original state (originate in), in the subconscious originates consciousness' etc. In the backwards (*paṭiloma*) formula of the *pratītyasamutpāda* (see above, p. 63) the word *nirodha* 'restraint, suppression, annihilation, extinction, overcoming' replaces *paccaya*: *avijjānirodhā saṅkhāranirodho* 'through the annihilation of delusion [is effected] the annihilation of the *saṃskāra*' etc. until the annihilation of suffering. It is often stated: *avijjāyā asesa-virāganirodhā* 'through the annihilation of delusion based on complete freedom from passion'. We may also call the positive (*anuloma*, 'running in the right direction') first formula of the *pratītyasamutpāda* the *formula of becoming* and the negative formula, again following a term coined by a German mystic, appropriately *formula of de-becoming*.[3] The actual meaning and legitimization of these terms will emerge from the following explanation.

Even the Indians, the oldest Buddhists themselves, were aware of the difficulty and metaphysical obscurity of the formula. When once, thus tells us the Mahānidānasutta (*Dīgha* II, p. 55), Ānanda expresses in front of the Buddha that the formula of the *pratītyasamutpāda* now appeared easy to grasp and obvious, the master opposes him:

> Do not speak thus, Ānanda, do not speak thus. Deeply entwined is this *pratītyasamutpāda*, it contains a profound revelation. By not realizing and penetrating this norm (*dhamma*), humanity sinks, entangled in suffering, down to lower stages of being and does not cross the cycle of rebirths.

Explanations of the formula are found in an extremely large number of texts of the Pali canon (and other Buddhist sources), but these explanations (hardly given by the Buddha himself) are mostly little indicative, partially even contradicting each other. In the just mentioned Mahāpadānasutta, the formula itself is transmitted in a variant; the causal chain there is traced back only up to *viññāṇa* and after stating that *nāmarūpa* has its foundation and origin in *viññāṇa*, the question where then *viññāṇa* was founded is answered against all logic: in *nāmarūpa*! There are, however, in those explanations a few valuable and noteworthy aspects, but hardly anywhere do the texts consider the true depths and difficulties of the problem. (De la Vallée-Poussin in his work, *Théorie des douze Causes*, Gent, 1913, has gathered the different Indian attempts at explanation in a manner that deserves our gratitude.) For Western science, too, in as far as it is concerned with research into the Buddha's *teaching*, the *pratītyasamutpāda* contains the most difficult and most contested of all questions, the true main problem. In the following we can only refer to the most important aspects.

It has to be noted from the outset that this formula, too, is not a 'philosophy' in our sense of the word, but that it arose from meditation and should in turn serve meditation. All the same, there is in the individual technical terms—which most certainly were not coined by the Buddha himself but borrowed from existing systems—at the same time a terminological element which cannot be overlooked. For the Buddha, it is about expressing that which in his sense was a higher truth, now also in the form of logical thought. In this respect the twelvefold formula also is of interest for us from the point of view of cultural history, as with it we are confronted with one of the earliest monuments of logical effort, one of the first attempts of humanity to think about problems of existence in an abstract, terminological form. Some of what we are inclined to regard as a logical deficiency of the formula (e.g., the above-mentioned turn of phrase in the Mahānidānasutta) becomes understandable from this point of view. With the beginnings of Buddhism we find ourselves in an era where the ancient mystical-pictorial form of thinking and imagining—of which remarkable remnants are extant for us in the Veda and the ancient *Brāhmaṇa* literature—is seeking for a transition towards a more terminological-abstract form of thinking. (The deliberations on this subject in the beginning of the book, *Die Rätsel der Philosohpie*[4] by Rudolf Steiner deserve more notice than they have hitherto received.) The earliest beginnings of this later form of thinking can be traced back as far as the Veda. The development of the true philosophical systems—that which is here called philosophy is still far removed from our concept of philosophical thinking—is close to the beginnings of Buddhism (see p. 100), i.e., it has to precede them slightly because Buddhism has borrowed its terminology from it. Here, the Sāṃkhya-system, which is also important for the understanding of the *pratītyasamutpāda*, has to be particularly considered. It represents, as it were, the theoretical side of the Yoga system. In more ancient times, particularly in the *Mahābhārata*, it is mostly named together with Yoga, so that, in those days, Sāṃkhya-Yoga did not signify much above 'theory and praxis' (with regard to the relationship of the human being with the metaphysical).

It can now be explained that those terms which correspond to Buddhist terminology were later included in the (theoretical) Yoga system, the *Yogasūtra*, which according to latest research belongs to a much later time than the Buddha. But the Buddha legend already points to a familiarity of the Buddha with that which is called the older Sāṃkhya and the older Yoga. The credit of having established the connections between Buddhism, in particular the *pratītyasamutpāda*, and this Sāṃkhya-Yoga in the correct light, is particularly due to Hermann Jacobi (*Der Ursprung des Buddhismus aus dem Sāṃkhya-Yoga*. Aus den Nachrichten der Königl. Gesellschaft d. Wissenschaften zu Göttingen, Phil.-hist. Klasse 1896, cah. 1).[5] In the following discussion there will be several occasions to return to this connection. Taking the Sāṃkhya-Yoga into account will prove helpful for the understanding of the formula of the *pratītyasamutpāda*. It should, however, not be forgotten that precisely the basic assumption of the Sāṃkhya-system, the duality of spirit and matter, is alien to Buddhism (which does not assume a reality of matter at all), so that the same or at least outwardly corresponding *termini* do not have the same meaning in both systems. Hence the scaffolding of material concepts of the Sāṃkhya system—which initially proves to be a good support for climbing the steep heights of the Buddhist *pratītyasamutpāda*—has to be afterwards taken away if a correct picture of the Buddhist doctrine is to be gained.

If we approach the Buddhist formula with our terms, our thinking, the central part from the fifth to the ninth part initially appears most obvious: from the senses originates touch (*phassa*), from touch sensation (*vedanā*), from sensation sensual desire (*taṇhā*) and from sensual desire grasping the sensual (*upādāna*). Now to the interpreters it always seemed obvious to think that if there is talk of sense organs, sensations, desire etc., there must well be an individual human being organized according to our experience which has those senses and those sensations, develops this sensual desire and does that grasping of the sensual. But in the sequence there follows first *being* (*bhava*, lit. 'becoming'; how this term is to be understood will be explained later), and birth, from which then old age, death and suffering originate as the final part of the sequence. If a fully organized, individual human being then enters existence only in the eleventh part of the sequence it cannot, one should think, have existed before—unless one takes recourse to the doctrine of reincarnation. Thus *bhava* and *jāti* were correlated with a later rebirth caused by sensual desire in one existence. There were even interpreters who subtracted the necessity of spreading the entire formula across three incarnations in order to accommodate the twelve parts in a manner that to them appeared logical (mentioned by De la Vallée-Poussin, p. 36). The original meaning of the formula knows nothing of this. The Buddha sits under the *bodhi* tree and contemplates the origin of worldly suffering (now before his eyes in clairvoyant, meditative vision). He finds the origin of this twelvefold sequence in meditation. Nothing in the sequence directly speaks of reincarnation. It only answers the question: How does *this physical existence* originate in the first place and the suffering connected with it? The term *bhava* which has posed problems for some interpreters and is understood by some as *saṃsāra*, future rebirth and the like, simply means being, thus first and foremost physical or earthly existence. The initial beginning of this physical existence which the human being enters fully only at birth is conception; in this sense we may translate the word *bhava* in the *pratītyasamutpāda* almost as 'conception' (as many interpreters have correctly understood). Only with *bhava-jāti* thus occurs the entrance into sensual-physical existence, and from that follows logically that the preceding stages of the terminological sequence do not at all belong to 'being', to sensual-physical existence yet. The *pratītyasamutpāda,* or at least the first, positive part of the formula (the formula of becoming) is about nothing else but about how something supernatural, which is not yet 'being' in a physical sense, becomes something physically-sensual, becomes 'being', as it were condensing, and how worldly suffering originates in the process. From this then follows that *saḷāyatana, phassa, vedanā, taṇhā* are not yet the senses of a physically organized individual human being, but, at the most, of a supernatural soul-being which only reaches 'being', union with sensual-material existence, at conception (cf. De la Vallée, op. cit., p. 38). In Buddhism this soul-being which prior to conception carries the supernatural elements of being (*skandhas*) in itself is called *gandharva* (Pali *gandhabba*) and it is remarkable that an important *sūtra* of the *Majjhimanikāya* (no. 38) which chiefly deals with the *pratītyasamutpāda* also mentions the *gandhabba* (see *Majjh.* I, p. 265f.) and speaks about how, during the origin of a physical human being, not only father and mother work together but that as a third party, the supernatural soul-being descending from higher worlds, also joins. In the Sāṃkhya-doctrine which has been referred to above p. 194 'the subtle body' or 'inner body' (*liṅga*) corresponds to this Buddhist soul-being. It is woven from the subtle (*sūkṣma*) elements, the sense organs (*indriya,* corresponds to the Buddhism *saḷāyatana*) and the higher elements of being (in Buddhism: *skandha*) up to *buddhi* (cf. Garbe, *Sāṃkhya,* p. 267).[6] In Buddhism, too, there is (as we have seen; see above, p. 174) the idea that such a subtle spiritual body is detached from the sensual-physical body through meditation practices. The big difference between Sāṃkhya and Buddhism however is that those higher elements of being are conceived in Sāṃkhya as woven from a higher, subtle (*sūkṣma*), supernatural-real substance, while the concept of such a substantiality, as of any matter, is alien to Buddhism. The only real thing in Buddhism is becoming, occurring, and this happening has to be thought of as spiritual occurring. Thus *bhava,* if it at all corresponds to that which we call 'being', originally signified 'becoming'. In the sense of Sāṃkhya philosophy the *pratītyasamutpāda* would thus be a descent of a supernatural [being] through a sequence of stages of initially still supernatural, but gradually more and more dense states of becoming down to incarnation in sensual-visible crude matter, in physical existence. Between the individual stages of the *pratītyasamutpāda* and the categories of Sāṃkhya there is now, as Jacobi has demonstrated,[7] substantial correspondence, only that Buddhism does not mention, as Sāṃkhya does, supernatural subtle substantiality, but only a sequence of stages of spiritual events. This is also the reason why 'physical matter' or 'material incarnation' do not form the final part of the sequence, but only the spiritual idea of suffering. For Buddhism *suffering* is the true reality of that which we call physical matter; not the object into which we stumble, but the pain caused by the stumble is what is real for Buddhists. If we become fully aware of this, a juxtaposition of Buddhism and Sāṃkhya no longer holds the danger of misapprehension. We then know that a comparison, a presentation of reciprocal correspondences does not mean an identification but can still prove helpful for the understanding of the Buddhist formula.

The sense organs (*saḷāyatana,* in Sāṃkhyā: *indriya* as elsewhere also in Buddhism) from which we initially started (see above, p. 195) our observations are both in Buddhism and in Sāṃkhya not a physical substance of nerves, but something supernatural (*atīndriya,* see Garbe, op. cit., p. 258). We can thus, in order to remain somewhat comprehensible to the occidental imagination, also speak about the 'superphysical substrate of the sense organs'. In addition to the five known senses *saḷāyatana* ('the six realms') also comprises a sixth inner sense, *manas* (the same in Sāṃkhya, Pali *mano;* cf. *manomaya-kāya,* the 'body woven from *manas,* i.e., spiritual being' of which the SPhS speaks, see above, p. 174). For Buddhism, the senses are thus not only something on the body, but something which already exists in the supernatural being independently before physical incarnation. In this form we also find them in Manu's cosmogony.

The higher element of being, in which the senses 'originate', is called *nāmarūpa,* 'name and form' in the *pratītyasamutpāda.* In the psychology of Sāṃkhya *ahaṃkāra,* the I, literally 'the I-maker' corresponds. For this 'I' is already taken as merely illusionary in Sāṃkhya; it is, as Jacobi defines it (quoted in Garbe, op.cit., p. 248) 'the principle through which we take ourselves as acting and suffering etc., while our self, i.e., our soul, remains eternally free from it'. This highest soul (*puruṣa*) which is the true (transcendental) I in the sense of Sāṃkhya and Yoga is excluded in Buddhism from the realm of that about which we are speaking here. Any other 'I' also is illusory to it, in accordance with Sāṃkhya-Yoga, and we have shown above how this 'illusion of the I' is destroyed stage by stage in meditation. It is thus only consequent if Buddhism chooses a term from this principle called *ahaṃkāra* in Sāṃkhya which expresses the fact that this is not a real I but only the appearance and shadow of the personality, whose unity is, as it were, only simulated by 'name' and 'form', by the external appearance, while in reality these are—like all the other parts of the sequence—spiritual events, processes of becoming.

If the parts of the sequence considered so far were processes of becoming which at least seemingly still belonged to a particular individuality, to an individual soul-being, this appearance of individuality ceases with the remaining parts. *Viññāṇa*, for example, spiritual consciousness, in which 'name and form' have their origin, is already something super-personal. It corresponds to the *buddhi* of Sāṃkhya which in that system is also spoken of as a 'cosmic *buddhi*' (Garbe, op. cit., p. 234). And the same is then also true for *saṅkhāra* and *avijjā*. Consciousness (*viññāṇa*) 'originates' according to the Buddhist sequence of origin in the subconscious where the formative forces (*saṅkhāra*) are at work, which in Buddhism are the 'house builders' who build this house of physicality and suffering; cf. the famous verses 153, 154 of the *Dhammapada*.[8] The term *saṃskāra* (Pali *saṅkhāra*) does not play its chief role in Sāṃkhya, but in Yoga, for in Yoga, in the practical application of meditation, one works into that subconscious and that which was so far subconscious, is raised into consciousness. Correspondingly, the important *saṃskāra*-problem in Buddhism is chiefly illuminated by the *Yogasūtra*. The connection between *saṅkhāra* and *avijjā* (Skt. *avidyā*) as it is expressed in the first phrase of the Buddhist causal sequence also follows from the *Yogasūtra*. In *sūtra* II, 12 it says: 'The (supernatural) residue of *karma* (*karmāśaya* = *saṃskāra*) is rooted in delusion (*kleśa*) ...' but all forms of delusion—I-delusion, passionate love, hatred, attachment to everything earthly—according to II, 4 rest in *avidyā*, (metaphysical) misapprehension. In Buddhism *avijjā*, misapprehension, is usually explained as not knowing the four noble truths of the argument from suffering (e.g., *Saṃy*. II, p. 4). In the conception of Sāṃkhya—alien to Buddhism—which sees in the causal sequence a process of material condensation and which regards the individual parts as woven from a substantiality conceived of as supersensory and subtle, the (supernatural) original matter (*mūla-prakṛti*), which in a school mediating between Sāṃkhya and Vedānta, is identified with *māyā*, cosmic illusion, corresponds to the *avijjā* of Buddhism. Even though such concepts are initially to be kept separate from Buddhism we have to ascribe a super-personal, i.e., cosmic, nature to *avijjā* also in the Buddhist formula of becoming—for the simple reason that the individual personality (in as far as Buddhism acknowledges one in the first place) is only reached with the third part of the sequence from here, with *nāmarūpa*. All the preceding still takes place beyond individual personality. For Buddhism the existence of such a special personality itself is something which is caused by the original misapprehension; it can thus not take place in the individual personality. In the formula of becoming *avijjā* is thus that power of misapprehension which appears as not knowing the truth of suffering where it is reflected in the individual. In the backward-turning[9] *pratītyasamutpāda*, in the formula of de-becoming which in its beginning already presupposes the individual personality, *avijjā* is then immediately that not-knowing of the truth of suffering which occurs in the individual. We may also say: Through the existence of a not-knowing of the truth of suffering at a point in the spiritual which precedes the arising of the individual personality, that very process of becoming was called forth which has led through the different stages of spiritual becoming and formation finally to the suffering of physical existence and earthly birth, and which by the annihilation of that misapprehension has been, as it were, eradicated, brought to a halt again. In the context of the formula we must not at all think in too concrete a form of the fate of the individual personality, of the soul-being etc.; for the Buddhist it initially contains nothing but spiritually-abstract connections between spiritual processes of becoming, processes which (for the person meditating) occur on the secluded heights of spiritual vision. But of course the truth thus seen then has to be applicable in the concrete case of each incarnation or rebirth (in the sense of Buddhism). This does not prevent us from allowing the other interpretation of the formula as well, and to regard *avijjā* as the seed of misapprehension brought into the new incarnation from a previous existence, as the seed of misapprehension which precisely had to bring about this new incarnation according to the law of *karma*. This effective, formative, forming force of misapprehension presents itself in the *saṃskāra* (*avijjāpaccayā saṅkhārā*, also *Yogasūtra* II, 12, see above, p. 198). Just as (according to Yoga teachings) present concepts (*vṛtti*) when they are forgotten, i.e., when they sink into the subconscious, continue to work there as formative forces (*saṃskāra*), any impulse of passion and delusion (*kliṣṭa-vṛtti*, Y.S. I, 5) also leaves its trace in the subconscious and works there like a subconscious memory of existence as formative, forming forces for a future life and fate (Y.S. II, 12). Put briefly, this is also the meaning of the doctrine of *karma* and *saṃskāra* which is also a given in Buddhism. Only the opinion resting on Sāṃkhya which considers *saṃskāra* as supernatural-material (*sūkṣma*), does not hold for Buddhism. In Buddhism these terms are of a purely spiritual kind. But in all contexts *saṃskāra* signifies the invisible, subtler, subconscious from which later that which is perceivable, cruder, conscious, is formed (thus e.g., also when the Buddha teaches that the formative forces [*saṅkhāra*] of physical existence rest in the breath, *Majjh.* I, p. 301).

The next creation of the *saṅkhāra* then is that principle which is already conscious but still super-personal and spiritual, *viññāṇa*. It corresponds, as we have seen, to the (cosmic) *buddhi* of Sāṃkhya which there (not in Buddhism) is seen at the same time as the subtlest form of the development of matter, the first expansion of original matter (Garbe, op. cit., pp. 189, 288). Only from this develops 'name and form', the appearance and shadow of the individual personality, and further the (super-physical) sense organs. Precisely how the (still supernatural) being is brought, as it were, to an immersion into the sensual element is then described by the following parts of the sequence: from the senses develops touch, from touch sensibility, from sensibility sensual desire (*taṇhā*), from *taṇhā* then the grasping of the sensual (*upādāna*, 'the grasping of the fuel'). This, too, is still a process in the supernatural being which just now is on the point of entering physical incarnation through touching the sensual element. This process, however, coincides with that other process which presents itself as the satisfaction of sensuality in the earthly sphere as well. From this grasping of the sensual then arises the entry into physical existence (*bhava*), conception, from conception birth, from birth old age, death and suffering.

It is not without interest how in Tibet on the 'wheel of life' used by the Lamas (printed in Waddell, *Buddhism of Tibet*, p. 108)[10] the abstract terms of the *pratītyasamutpāda* are illustrated in images: *avijjā*, misapprehension, appears as a blind woman; *saṅkhāra*, the formative, forming force, very significantly as a potter modelling clay pots on his potter's wheel; *viññāṇa*, as a monkey; *nāmarūpa*, as a ship crossing the sea; *saḷāyatana*, as a house (the 'empty house' of the senses), in other illustrations, eyes looking through a mask; *phassa*, touch, the kiss of a couple in love; *vedanā*, feeling, an arrow hitting the eye; *taṇhā*, a thirsty person drinking; *upādāna*, the picking of a fruit from a tree; *bhava*, a pregnant woman; *jāti*, a woman giving birth; *jarāmaraṇa*, an old man, in other illustrations, a corpse which is carried to the burial ground. The pictorial illustrations of a later era, of course, do not carry any proof for the terms themselves, but they are not worthless if, as in the present case, they verify the results gained through a different approach. Namely with *saṅkhāra, upādāna* and *bhava* this is of importance.

The formula of becoming thus describes, as if once and for all in the world of spiritual connections, and then also in the case of each individual incarnation (i.e., in the sense of Buddhism: reincarnation) how the supernatural descends to the sensual, the macrocosmic to the microcosmic, the spiritual to the physical and thus to the suffering of birth and death, and how misapprehension with respect to the truth of suffering stands at the point of departure of this case. We may call this the psychological aspect of the *pratītyasamutpāda*. This psychological aspect is complemented by a cosmogonic side. For according to Buddhism, the suffering of old age and death was not always present in the world as it must be present in an era when a Buddha appears in the world (cf. *Aṅg.* V, p. 144). The Buddhist paradise legend of the Agaññasutta (see above, p. 35, footnote and *Dīgh.* III, p. 84ff.) narrates that once in a distant past, when after the passing of the last world era (*kalpa*) an era of world renewal had started, human beings still lived as light beings in paradisiac innocence and bliss in the aerial circumference of the earth in spirit-woven (*manomaya*), radiant bodies. Only when they let themselves be tempted by sensual desire (*taṇhā*) to taste the surface of the earth which then still consisted of sweet cream did they become entangled with the earth element. Through cruder and cruder food gradually crude earthly physicality developed, sexuality (originally non-existent) appeared and in its wake bad deeds of all kinds and the entire painful state of humanity. That which here is described like a Buddhist fall from grace is in a way a cosmological *pratītyasamutpāda;* even though not every part of the sequence may have been recorded, the basic thought—the entanglement from a supernatural state into the earthly element of suffering and death caused by sensual desire—still shines through clearly. In the 'tasting of the sweet cream' is given *upādāna,* the grasping of the sensual. *Upādāna,* significantly illustrated by the Lamas by the grasping of a fruit, is in a way the Buddhist 'biting of the apple', the actual 'fall from grace', in as far as we can speak about something of this sort in Buddhism. We may also say: the *pratītyasamutpāda* expresses in an abstract sequence of terms that which is called the 'fall from grace' in other religions, that which we may also be tempted to call a 'fall into matter'. In this we have to note, however, that the category of matter is alien to Buddhism. Buddhism also does not really speak of 'sin', only of *misapprehension,* not knowing. That which from a different point of view may appear as a 'fall from grace into matter' for Buddhism is a *fall through misapprehension into suffering*, a fall which repeats itself in each individual incarnation (reincarnation). Just as we should not identify the positive *pratītyasamutpāda*, the formula of being, with the 'fall from grace', but can compare the two, the Buddhist equivalent of 'salvation' appears to be given in the negative or backwards *pratītyasamutpāda*, the formula of de-becoming which leads from the annihilation of delusion through all the individual parts up to the annihilation of suffering and death. That which has been distinguished above as the psychological and the cosmogonic aspects of the *pratītyasamutpāda* is eventually identical. For in the immersion into one's own inner being the meditating Buddhist finds in the secret of the arising of his own personal existence at the same time the secret of the entire arising and passing of the world. One has not understood the *pratītyasamutpāda* if one does not see how incarnation, the arising of the world and the arising of suffering and death really coalesce. (In *Aṅg*. II, p. 23, e.g., it is said in a remarkable way that the arising out of the world [*lokasamudaya*], the dissolution of the world [*nirodha*] and the path which leads to the dissolution of the world [*lokanirodhagāminī paṭipadā*] have been realized and revealed by the Tathāgata.) The reversal, too, of the great cosmic processes, the suspension of the suffering of the world, can only occur if the *human being* destroys in himself misapprehension, penetrates to the realization of the truth of suffering, and even the gods have to be born as human beings in order to find liberating realization. The continuation of the formula (already mentioned above, p. 141f.) expresses beautifully how in suffering itself lies the power which can bring a human being to find the path of de-becoming which leads him out of suffering and dying after he has descended the path which leads into suffering and dying to the lowest point. Here it is said how from suffering springs belief, from belief blessing, from blessing joy, from joy tranquillity, from tranquillity wellbeing, from wellbeing spiritual concentration, from concentration the true visionary knowledge [realization] and from here on the renunciation of the world, freedom from passion and finally liberation (*vimutti*) and the awareness of liberation (*Saṃy*. II, p. 31, 32).

With this, our discussion has reached a point which will be discussed in more detail in the following section.

e) Fourth stage of the path: liberation (*vimutti*)

The goal of the 'path' described in the previous section is called 'liberation' (*vimutti*) in Buddhism. Just as ethical behaviour (*sīla*) should serve to prepare and carry right meditation (*samādhi*), and as this meditation is the means and preliminary stage for the attainment of higher abilities, especially higher knowledge (*paññā*), these higher abilities and this knowledge themselves are nothing which the Buddhist seeks for their own sake, but they merely form a passing stage, a preliminary stage and a means for the attainment of that which beckons as the lofty goal for the disciple who has in right striving followed the path to the end, to *liberation*. The previous observations have shown how through the realization of the truth of suffering in the sense of Buddhism this purification of the soul is immediately effected which finds its concluding climax in liberation and the 'awareness of liberation' (*vimuttasmiṃ vimuttaṃ iti ñāṇaṃ*; SPhS 98, *Dīgha* I, p. 84). This liberation is thus no unconsciousness, but a state of highest awareness. The liberated person, it is always said, knows he is liberated, liberated from the 'power which binds all beings'[1] (as we may say following the phrase of a great poet which has been mentioned before and which is not unsuitable for a characterization of Buddhist striving), i.e., liberated in the sense of Buddhism from the power which keeps beings bound in *saṃsāra*, in the cycle of reincarnations, the continuous painful repetition of being born, ageing and dying. In the 'wheel of life' of the Tibetan Lamas (printed in Waddell, *Buddhism of Tibet*, p. 108) this 'power which binds all beings' is depicted as a horrible demon who holds the beings of the different spheres of existence with his claws and with the teeth of his terrible jaws. These spheres of existence—the world of the gods, demons, human beings, animals, purgatory and hell—are on the inner area of the wheel (or circle), on the outer circumference the twelve parts of the causal sequence are illustrated in the above-mentioned pictorial description. The Buddha, however, having found the liberation from *saṃsāra*, sits outside the circle on a lotus throne in quiet meditation. The 'power which binds all beings' symbolized in such stark images by the Buddhists is in the sense of the truth of suffering (*Vinaya* I, p. 10f.) *taṇhā*, sensual desire which aims at the continuous renewal of sensual existence (*ponobbhavikā*) and which according to the 'formula of becoming' (*pratītyasamutpāda*) 'originates' in delusion (*avijjā*) which is precisely the not-knowing of the truth of suffering. The goal of liberation (*vimutti*) striven for by the disciple in persistent wrestling is thus the annihilation of sensual desire (*taṇhakkhaya*) which according to the 'formula of de-becoming', the backward *pratītyasamutpāda*, is reached through the 'annihilation of delusion in perfect freedom from passion' (*avijjāya asesavirāganirodha*). In the sense of Buddhism this annihilation is, as the addition mentioned already suggests, not possible through mere imagination, presumption or philosophical conviction, but only if the path of meditation which requires much self-denial and which departs from moral purification in 'right conduct', passes through the supernatural perfections (*iddhi*) and higher realization (*paññā*) and which may possibly reach the goal only after many incarnations, is truly followed. The process which then happens during this 'liberation' is, as it is described in the 'formula of de-becoming' (see above, p. 190) in detail, such that through the annihilation of delusion the formative forces (*saṅkhāra*) are destroyed which spin the *karma* and which, across the different supernatural intermediate links of the causal sequence, finally build the sensual form of existence, the house of suffering.

When the *saṃskāras* (*saṅkhāra*) are destroyed, all those intermediate links of the sequence, the (supernatural) substrates (*upadhi*) of physicality, one after the other, the *skandhas* (*khandha*) are annihilated or prevented from further entering into existence; from the annihilation of the subconscious formative forces follows the annihilation of the (supernatural) substrate of external consciousness (*viññāṇa*), from this the annihilation of the personal (*nāmarūpa*) and the substrate of the sense organs (*saḷāyatana*), from this the annihilation of touch (*phassa*) and sensation (*vedanā*), and from this the annihilation of the 'power that binds all beings', of sensual desire (*taṇhā*). With this, the 'grasping of the fuel of the sensual' (*upādāna*) is abolished and with it the precondition for another 'being' or physical existence (*bhava*), for birth, old age and death. 'Uprooted is the desire for existence, annihilated the one that leads to existence, there is henceforth no rebirth' (*ucchinnā bhavataṇhā khīṇā bhavanetti n'atthi dāni punabbhavo*) thus the formulaic verse recurring in numerous passages of the canon. According to the *pratītyasamutpāda* the essential process in 'liberation' is thus that *saṃskāra*, the builder of the house, is destroyed and with this the axe is put to the root of existence. The technical term for this 'annihilation' in the 'formula of de-becoming' and everywhere else in the phrasing of the sacred texts is *nirodha* ('suppression, annihilation, reversion, cancellation, overcoming' etc.); this term *nirodha* at the same time is the true main term in which Buddhism and Yoga meet. As in Buddhism, the actual final goal in Yoga is the annihilation (*nirodha*) of *saṃskāra* (*Yogasūtra* I, 51) and in this also lies the actual key to the understanding of the path of Yoga as well as that of Buddhism—that it is about working down into those depths of the subconscious, of *saṃskāra*, in meditation (*samādhi*). Together with *saṃskāra* that factor is annihilated which is the true effective force in the Buddhist power of fate (cf. *Yogasūtra* II, 12), in the *karma* (Pali *kamma*), the 'deed', so that 'annihilation of the *saṃskāras*' thus practically coincides with the 'annihilation of *karma*'. This is the reason why the goal of liberation for Buddhism is also called the 'annihilation of any *karma*' (*sabbakammakkhaya*; e.g., *Aṅg.* II, p. 24). Any essential characteristics and designations of 'liberation' which follow from the discussion so far appear summarized in that formula which often reoccurs in the texts (e.g., *Aṅg.* IV, p. 423, V, pp. 320, 322, 354, 355, 358 and others): 'this is the peaceful (*santaṃ*), highly exalted (*paṇītaṃ*), the calming (i.e., cancellation) of all *saṃskāras* (*sabbasaṅkhārasamatho*), the dissolution of all substrates (*upadhi*, i.e., of the substrates of the individual personality or the *skandhas*, *sabbūpadhipaṭinissaggo*), the annihilation of sensual desire (*taṇhakkhayo*), the freedom from passion (*virāgo*), the annihilation of all causes (*nirodho*), *nirvāṇa* (*nibbāna*, the 'extinguishing'. *Nirvāṇa* is first and foremost the participle 'extinguished, blown out', from the root *vā* 'blow').' In the West the Buddhist goal of liberation has become most widely known under this latter name. The question of what should be understood by *nirvāṇa* (*nibbāna*) has already been largely answered in the above discussions. It is simply that exalted goal which the Buddhist has in mind and which will perhaps be reached soon, or perhaps only after many incarnations in intense wrestling, 'for the sake of which sons from noble families go from home into homelessness (*agārasmā anagāriyaṃ pabbajanti*), the highest fulfilment of the holy life' (*anuttaraṃ brahmacariyapariyosānaṃ*) as one of the most often recurring formulas of the sacred texts says (e.g., MPS, p. 60 ed. Childers; *Aṅg.* III, pp. 70, 399 and others). Is that goal for the sake of which 'sons from noble families go from home into homelessness', is liberation, *nirvāṇa*, 'nothing'? That this question, so much debated in the West, in Buddhism's sense cannot be affirmed already follows very clearly from the just mentioned formula, which appears especially in conversion narratives, whose stereotypical continuation says that the convert reaches and realizes that exalted goal, the 'highest fulfilment of the holy life' *already in this visible near-side world*, in the 'visible order of things' (*diṭṭhe dhamme*). *Nirvāṇa* is thus a positive state which can be experienced by the disciple in the visible near-side world, still in his physical body and in this sense the texts often speak about this 'worldly *nirvāṇa*' (*diṭṭhadhammanibbāna*, e.g., *Aṅg.* IV, p. 454). Elsewhere this state is presented as the highest state of health (*ārogyaṃ*, e.g., *Majjh.* V, p. 511) and just as sensual pleasure (*kāma*) is compared with a big, deep swamp, anger and despair with a sheer abyss, *nirvāṇa* is compared with a gentle, lovely pasture (*samo bhūmibhāgo ramaṇīyo, Saṃy.* III, p. 109). That it is a *positive* state is particularly said in that important passage at the beginning of the Pali canon (*Vinaya* I, p. 5) where the Buddha hesitates to reveal the norm found by him to the world, [the norm] which is 'deep, difficult to see, difficult to realize, peaceful, exalted, unattainable to rational thinking (*atakkāvacara*), subtle, only to be known by wise people'. (cf. above, p. 66). He sees the actual difficulties in the *pratītyasamutpāda* (see above, p. 192f.) and in that which forms, as it were, the culmination of the teaching, in *nirvāṇa*. Devoted to sensuality is humanity, he says, and would thus be unable to grasp this 'place which is difficult to see' (*duddasaṃ idaṃ ṭhanaṃ*)—i.e., *nirvāṇa*—correctly. Buddha's disciple, Sāriputta, speaks about *nirvāṇa* as bliss (*sukha*) and when he is challenged on how one could speak of bliss where there was no longer any perception (*vedayita*) he replies: in that is precisely the bliss, that there is no longer any perception (*Aṅg.* IV, p. 415), and in the following it is explicitly described how this bliss of *nirvāṇa* is reached through the stepladder of the states of consciousness discussed above. That this 'absence of perception' does not mean total unconsciousness already follows from what has been explained above (p. 202), for the knowledge of liberation, the awareness of *nirodha* (*nirodhasaññā*) as it is also called (*Aṅg.* V, p. 111) is clearly present in the state of liberation. Those who have attained this state also know—it is always said: 'This is the peaceful, exalted, etc., the annihilation of sensual desire, *nirvāṇa*.' In so far as Buddhism knows such a 'near-side' *nirvāṇa*, a *nirvāṇa* which is experienced in this physical body—we even find the phrase: 'to touch the immortal sphere (*amata-dhātu*) with the body' (*Aṅg.* III, p. 356)—the question whether *nirvāṇa* in the sense of Buddhism is 'nothingness' cannot be affirmed, and this fact has by and large always been known and respected in Western scholarship. The crucial point of the problem, however, is not touched by this. Certainly, it has been said—and Childers, who in many ways deserves credit for his ascertaining of Buddhist terminology, has defended this opinion under the entry '*nibbānaṃ*' with great eloquence[2]—*nirvāṇa* is already experienced as positive bliss in this life by those who have reached the stage of a saint or *arhat*. Such near-sided *nirvāṇa*, he thought, is thus equivalent to *arhat*-hood; but since, as we have seen, the seed for reincarnation is destroyed in *nirvāṇa* the *arhat* only has to complete the span of his life in the physical body; when the 'substrates', the *skandhas*, then fall away at his physical death, at the so-called *parinirvāṇa* (*parinibbāna*), the remaining is 'nothingness', complete annihilation ('extinction', 'cessation of being'). According to this view there would thus be a double *nirvāṇa*: a this-sided *nirvāṇa* = *arhat*-hood, and the otherworldly *nirvāṇa* (*parinirvāṇa*) = complete annihilation, eternal death, which begins with the death of the *arhat*. The goal 'for the sake of which sons of noble families go from home into homelessness' would thus—in the sense of this opinion—indeed be nothingness, eternal death, only that this nothingness is not realized at the same time as the attainment of the stage of *nirvāṇa* or *arhat*-hood, but only with the physical death (while other beings who are less advanced than the *arhat* face a repeated existence in future reincarnations). It would certainly be out of place to contradict this opinion brusquely and prematurely. For from the point of view of occidental thought, occidental worldviews and logic, it can be understood very well. But the question is whether the conditions of this occidental thinking apply to Buddhism, and this question has to be negated. It is indeed expressed very clearly that *nirvāṇa* is the annihilation of worldly existence, of 'being' (*bhava*; *Aṅg*. V, p. 9: *bhavanirodho nibbānaṃ*) and according to the *pratītyasamutpāda* the same *bhavanirodho* follows also from the 'annihilation of sensual desire' (*taṇhakkhaya*) which forms an essential component of *nirvāṇa*. Even when the texts speak about the *nirvāṇa* which is attained during one's lifetime, they always attach the comment that the respective person consciously knows: 'destroyed is birth, completed the sacred path, fulfilled the duty, there is no need for further life in this world' (*khīṇā jāti vusitaṃ brahmacariyaṃ kataṃ karaṇīyaṃ nāparaṃ itthattāya*).[3] Thus even in the sense of Buddhism it cannot be denied that in *nirvāṇa* the axe is put to the root of being in the world, of physical existence. To our materialistic occidental thinking, for a kind of thinking which can precisely grasp any reality only in physical existence, in 'being', the *parinirvāṇa* which follows the this-sided *nirvāṇa* thus doubtlessly means nothingness. But even from the previous discussions (see above, p. 196f.) it emerges clearly that Buddhism takes an entirely different stance vis-à-vis the question of reality. Although *bhava* corresponds to our 'being' or physical existence, Buddhism calls it differently; it only speaks about 'becoming' (this is the original meaning of *bhava*), it does not see in this an absolute reality of a 'being', but only a relative reality of 'becoming', a process of becoming. And all parts of the causal sequence, as we have seen, are essentially only processes of becoming, and with regard to reality or non-reality *bhava* is in no way ahead of the other parts of the causal sequence. (This is precisely why the *pratītyasamutpāda* is so difficult to understand in European terms, because one always believes one should have to presuppose a physically organized being in which 'misapprehension' is present, to which 'consciousness', 'the senses' belong, which experiences 'touch', 'sensation', 'desire', which acts the 'grasping of the sensual' etc., while in Buddhism these terms are quite independent spiritual beings, independent of a physical individual, they are connected amongst each other in a supernatural, spiritual way, and their reciprocal linkage only reveals the secret of physical existence ['being' or 'becoming'] and its roots in an extra-physical and super-physical sphere.) For Buddhism, reality is in the spiritual connections of a supernatural process, the so-called 'laws' (*dhamma*), not in that which we call matter. Such a connection exists, e.g., between the different reincarnations of an individual being, although Buddhism does not speak about any material link, be it ever so shadowy, between the different incarnations which would be perceivable by the sensory intellect. We are touching here upon the true secret of Buddhism, a secret which will remain eternally unfathomed as long as we persist under the spell of sensory-material thinking. And in the same secret is rooted the problem of *nirvāṇa*, that 'place' (*ṭhānaṃ*) of which the Buddha says that it is so difficult to be seen by humanity devoted to sensuality and finding its pleasure in the sensual (*ālayarāma ālayarata ālayasammudita*; *Vinaya* I, p. 4, 5). In this description we have often talked about the fact that the Buddha did not see it as his task to construct philosophical theories for such transcendental problems. They were to be penetrated in meditation, experienced in meditation. It is explicitly stated that the disciple should wait in meditation until *nirvāṇa* descended upon him (*Aṅg.* IV, p. 111f.): '*jhānaṃ upasampajja viharati ... okkamanāya nibbānassa*'), and the description of the path of meditation in the *Dīghanikāya* on which the entire discussion above was based, is essentially about how the path outlined there finally leads to the awareness of liberation, to *nirvāṇa*, through the various 'attainments' of discipleship. This state itself is then (*ibid.*) called the highest of all attainments of spiritual striving, 'above which there is none that is higher or more exalted' (SPhS 98). In this sense, *nirvāṇa* is to the disciple of Buddhism the highest of all realities. In the sense of Buddhism it is then entirely meaningless for this reality whether the shadow of the earthly personality simulated by the connection of the *skandhas* continues to exist or whether the above-mentioned 'substrates' (*upadhi*) fall away at physical death. From the standpoint of Buddhism nothing is more incorrect than the view that through the continued existence of these substrates a reality could be guaranteed to the state attained which would be revoked when the substrates fall away. This profound difference between *nirvāṇa* (= *arhat*-hood, i.e., highest attainable stage of being) and *parinirvāṇa* (= complete annihilation) construed by occidental scholars based on this condition, is entirely alien to Buddhism, not even the slightest hint of it can be found in the texts. Just as little as *parinirvāṇa* (Pali *parinibbāna*)—at least in the original Buddhism—implies a higher stage beyond *nirvāṇa*, as little does it express *toto genere*, a different idea from *nirvāṇa*. The verb *parinibbā* (noun *parinibbāna*) simply means the death of someone who has attained *nirvāṇa* in this life (thus something like that which in the Brahminical religion is called the 'death of the liberated'), the falling away of the 'substrates'. The reality of *nirvāṇa* itself is in no way affected by the falling away of the substrates. Depending on whether these substrates still exist or not, *saupādisesa-nibbāna* and *anupādisesa-nibbāna* is distinguished, but no statement of the Buddha suggests that *nibbāna* itself was something essentially different in the two cases. For the reality of *nirvāṇa* it is altogether meaningless whether the 'substrates' continue to exist or not. It is self-evident that materialistic thinking which sees the only possible reality in that which Buddhism calls *bhava* has to take the 'substrateless' *nirvāṇa*, the cancellation of *bhava* as nothingness. But this type of thinking does not need to penetrate to '*nirvāṇa*' (or *parinirvāṇa*) in order to face 'nothingness'; it essentially faces nothingness in the context of everything else Buddhism can say otherwise; for even all the gods and supernatural worlds, for this Western materialistic thinking all the 'supernatural perfections' and 'higher realizations' of Buddhism are nothing, are empty delusions (just like this materialistic thinking itself is empty delusion for Buddhism). Buddhism, too, knows a 'facing nothingness'. But this 'facing the sphere of nothingness' (*ākiñcaññāyatana*) is not experienced in *nirvāṇa*, but at an earlier, lower stage of the inner path (see above, p. 160f.); it only constitutes a certain stage of meditation, a passing experience made in meditation from which the person meditating then raises himself in order to ascend to other, higher states of consciousness, and the highest stage for which Buddhism coins a name is indeed *nirodha* or *nirvāṇa* (*nibbāna*). The Buddha turned away from the teaching of Ārāḍa Kālāpā[4] for whom this 'facing nothingness' (*ākiñcaññāyatana*) was the highest stage of inner uplifting, because this stage did not appear to be a satisfying goal for him (see above, pp. 54, 58). Even immediately before his passing the Buddha passed twice (in ascending and descending direction) through that 'sphere of nothingness' but he then found entry into substrate-less *nirvāṇa* not from here, but from the fourth stage of *dhyāna*, the point of departure for all supernatural perfections (see above, p. 176f.). It is thus important to note that for Buddhism 'nothingness' is in no way the coveted last and highest goal, but only a passing experience; that the soul in its meditative struggle has to work itself towards this sphere of nothingness and face it, but only in order to raise itself from it again and to ascend to higher spiritual spheres. The yearning of those who in the sense of Buddhism 'go from home into homelessness' is thus no 'yearning for nothingness'. For the 'yearning for nothingness' which results from weariness of existence Buddhism has also coined a term, it is called *vibhavataṇhā* (in *Ittivuttaka* 49 – in contrast with other opinions which may appear possible – explicitly defined as the desire of those who long for not-being after death as the highest and thus miss their goal), and this *vibhavataṇhā* is already rejected by the Buddha as ignoble and not leading to the goal of liberation in the sermon of Benares (*Vinaya* I, p. 10, *Saṃy.* V, p. 421). Buddhism sees in this weariness of existence, that yearning for not-being, merely a sensual desire turned into its negative, which is put on the same level as other kinds of sensual desire, with the desire for sensual pleasure (*kāmataṇhā*) and the desire for physical existence (*bhavataṇhā*) and which, like these kinds of 'thirst', works as a hindrance to true liberation. It is thus a complete misunderstanding of Buddhism to regard the teaching of the Buddha as a gospel of world nausea or weariness of existence. It is not 'yearning for nothingness' which is the feeling governing the disciple of Buddhism, but a yearning for the eternal, or, in the sense of the negatively framed Buddhist phrase: *a turning away from everything which is not eternal.* (*Majjh.* II, p. 263: *Yad aniccaṃ taṃ nālaṃ abhinandituṃ nālaṃ abhivadituṃ nālaṃ ajjhosituṃ* 'that which is not eternal is not worth finding pleasure in it, not worth being greeted, not worth turning towards'). The actual suffering which Buddhism tries to overcome is impermanence and everything impermanent is held as painful (expressed with the utmost determination in *Majjh.* III, p. 20). Consequently *nirvāṇa*, liberation, in the sense of Buddhism is an escape from the realm of impermanence, from all those (sensory and supernatural) spheres of 'being' in which the cycle of rebirth (*saṃsāra*) occurs, those spheres which are summarized as *kāmadhātu, rūpadhātu, arūpadhātu* (see above, p. 162f.). By entering the substrate-less *nirvāṇa* the Buddha thus also disappears for all those deities who still partake of the earthly, who belong to the above-mentioned lower spheres of the supernatural (see above, p. 163). In a wider sense, everything which Buddhism designates as *bhava* belongs to these three spheres (Mahānidānasutta, *Dīgha* II, p. 57: *kāma-bhavo, rūpa-bhavo, arūpa-bhavo*). The sphere beyond *kāmadhātu, rūpadhātu* and *arūpadhātu*, disconnected from *saṃsāra* which is entered in *nirvāṇa*, the exalted sphere of eternal liberation, is called *nirodhadhātu* or *nibbānadhātu* in Buddhism, the '*nirvāṇa* sphere' or the '*nirvāṇa* element', and it is said about the saint who has attained *nirvāṇa* in this earthly life that he dissolves into the 'substrate-less *nirvāṇa* element' (*anupādisesāya nibbānadhātuyā*). The phrase *amata dhātu*, the 'immortal sphere' or 'sphere disconnected from death', is also often used in the sacred texts (e.g., *Aṅg*. IV, p. 423f., where *amata dhātu* and *nibbāna* are identified with each other, similarly *Saṃy*. V, pp. 139, 232 and others), and in numerous passages *nirvāṇa* is called *amṛta* (Pali *amata*), i.e., the immortal (or 'immortal salvation'). The Buddha puts his decision to reveal the truth found by him in the following words: 'Opened is the gate to immortality for them, those who have ears to hear, believe' (*Vinaya* I, p. 7). In the *Sumaṅgalavilāsini*, in his commentary on Poṭṭhapādasutta 34, Buddhagoṣa talks about the 'great *nirvāṇa* disconnected from death' (*amata-mahānibbāna*). The passage which talks about a 'touching the immortal element with the body' has already been mentioned (*Aṅg*. III, p. 356). With all this it is clearly expressed that *nirvāṇa* constitutes that sphere where the Buddhist yearning for escape from the sphere of impermanence and death finds its eternal satisfaction. In the sense of the parable from the Sāmaññaphalasutta mentioned above (p. 186f.) this *nirvāṇa* element, this sphere which is disconnected from death (*amata dhātu*) is, as it were, the crystal clear, sheer and pure mountain lake in which all earthly realities, 'suffering' in the sense of Buddhism, are only visible like shells and pebbles at the bottom of the pure water surface by those who see, who have attained liberation (*Dīgha* I, p. 84). To materialistic thinking this 'crystal clear lake' may appear like nothingness. But Buddhism is precisely as far removed as anything can be from the conditions of this kind of thinking; for Buddhism this crystal clear lake, this 'nothingness' is the highest reality, the sphere of the immortal, eternal (*amata dhātu*). One must not, however, amalgamate this 'immortality' of Buddhism with the idea of a continued existence of anything personal (i.e., in the sense of Buddhism with *bhavataṇhā*). Thus the question whether the Tathāgata continued to exist after death is among those which the Buddha declined to answer (see above, p. 108f.). It rests on the assumption of a kind of thinking away from which it was the Buddha's entire effort to break human beings. Everything connected with the appearance and shadow of the individual personality faces the most complete imaginable annihilation in *nirvāṇa,* and that even in the 'this-sided' *nirvāṇa* experienced in the physical body, and any materialistic-personally tinted hopes of immortality are refuted more decisively in Buddhism than in any other religion. The *nirvāṇa*-element, it is said, acts indifferently towards anything personal, it is sublimely superior to it and remains untouched by it: 'Just as all streams of water of the earth and the air empty themselves into the great sea, and the great sea still does not become fuller or emptier, in the same way this *nirvāṇa*-element (*nibbāna-dhātu*) never becomes emptier or fuller even if ever so many disciples enter into the substrate-less *nirvāṇa*-element.' (*Aṅg.* IV, p. 202, *Udāna,* p. 55). Just as in the comparison with the mountain lake it is the crystal purity, in the sea parable it is infinity, it is indifference towards everything earthly-personal which is the *tertium comparationis.*

It immediately suggests itself to connect the Buddhist *nirvāṇa* with that which is called the merging with the *brahman* etc. in Brahminical religion and mysticism (cf. on this question Oldenberg, *Buddha,* p. 334 of the 5th ed.). In this context the term *brahma-nirvāṇaṃ* 'the extinguishing (blowing away) in *brahman*' can be found in the sense of union with the highest deity. There is hardly any doubt that with reference to coining the technical term '*nirvāṇa*' (*nibbāna*) Buddhism has been hardly more creative than with other terms, but that it has borrowed it from an existing Brahminical terminology. The only particularity of Buddhism—from an external point of view—is in the mere omission of *brahman,* i.e., in something purely negative. This omission of the word *brahman* is related to the inmost nature of Buddhism. If the Buddha had searched for any kind of designation for a deity, a highest divine source of the world, dozens of terms would have suggested themselves to him in the Brahminical armoury. Nothing could have suggested itself more immediately to him as an Indian than to speak in this terminology. He did not speak like that. It has already been discussed that this aversion of the Buddha to harness the 'final reasons for existence', the 'divine source of all existence' into word and term does not have to be taken as a denial of such a primal source (see above, p. 112; Oltramare in his writing, *La Formule Bouddhique des douze causes,* Genève 1909, p. 49,[5] very pointedly calls this aversion of the Buddha as '*son antipathie naturelle pour le finalisme*'). The Buddha wanted to avoid theoretical laziness that would be content with a word or a term when from his point of view only the true experience in meditative effort is of any value. The entire Buddhism is geared towards this practical knowledge in meditative experience, and this aspect is particularly valid in the context of the *nirvāṇa*-problem. 'Remain steadfast in meditation, my disciples' (*jhāyatha bhikkhū mā pamādattha*) thus the Buddha's admonition, 'so that later you may not be seized by regret' (*Aṅg*. III, p. 87). Indian philosophy shows particularly clearly how theoretical systems have a preference for starting from the most general, abstract and empty terms and are particularly unlikely to be at a loss for words for the designation of the final and highest, the 'primal source of all being'. But the Buddha's path is no path of rumination, speculation or combination, but of immediate meditative experience, and such an experience can—in the sense of all those who teach such paths—only approach the inside of things by gradual penetration, without, at any point, including the final secrets of existence.

For all these reasons the talk of the highest things, like *brahman*, *ātman*, etc., in which Brahminical philosophy and mysticism delighted and which in our opinion is so monotonous and tiresome, found no place in the teaching of the Buddha. The word *nirvāṇa*, 'extinguished, blown away', means something different in Buddhism, and that is initially simply the fact that the fire of desire, passion, delusion is extinguished (cf. *Jātaka* I, p. 61).[6] Thus the same pictorial image which is present in the technical term *upādāna* 'grasping the fuel', i.e., grasping the sensual, is also the basis of the word *nirvāṇa*. In the sermon at Gayā (*Vinaya* I, p. 34), the Buddha speaks about how everything is on fire, all the sense organs are on fire, and with them all perception mediated by the sense organs, everything is stricken by the fire of passion, hatred, delusion, of the suffering of impermanence. By turning away from the senses, it is further said, the disciple reaches liberation and the awareness of liberation. This fire through which everything was ablaze is then extinguished, blown out (*nirvāṇa*). With this, the Buddha points to the practical demand on which everything depends, which is the condition of everything else which in the sense of Buddhism cannot be dug out but only reached by fulfilling this practical demand. It corresponds to the entire basic character of Buddhism that the word *nirvāṇa* in a way only provides the negative, and that the positive behind it (in contrast to Brahminical custom) is only rarely hinted at, only in dark suggestions, i.e., always only in such a way that it cannot give rise to the delusion that a final and highest was to be once and for all put in certain terms. Such an obscure suggestion of a positive, a sublime sphere of eternal liberation, an infinity disconnected from death, is already present in the above-mentioned terms *anupādisesā nibbānadhātu* and *amatādhatu*, and it is especially present in the Buddha's words:

> There is, O disciples, the realm (*āyatana*) where neither earth, nor water, nor fire, nor air, where neither the sphere of the limitlessness of the space ether, nor the sphere of the infinity of consciousness, neither the sphere of nothingness (*ākiñcaññāyatana*), nor the sphere beyond conscious and unconscious, where there is neither this world and not that world, where there is neither sun nor moon; there, I tell you, is no passing, no leaving and no staying, no exit and no return, no basis, no development, no support: that is the end of suffering (*Udāna*, p. 80).

> There is, O disciples, something which is not born, did not become, was not created, which did not arise from the formative forces; if there was not such an unborn, un-become, uncreated, no escape could be invented for that which is born, has become, is created, has arisen from formative forces. (*Udāna*, p. 80, *Itivuttaka*, p. 37.)

That realm which is nothingness for all those ways of conceptualizing that cling to matter as that which is real, in these words is explicitly described as a most exalted reality, a realm of being above the realm of becoming, while Buddhism sees only a *becoming (bhava)*, i.e., something impermanent, nothing real in the highest sense in that which is real existence for materialistic conceptualization. We may also say that Buddhism transfers existence into the transcendent while it only accepts a becoming and passing in the empirical. In Buddhism meditation fulfils the purpose of raising the transcendental again to an empirical (in a higher sense) level.

A difference between the Buddhist *nirvāṇa* and 'nothingness' in materialistic thinking which should not be overlooked also lies in the fact that this 'nothingness' is immediately certain in the same way to everyone as physical death, to the greatest sage or philanthropist of humanity just as to the villain and idiot, while *nirvāṇa* in the sense of Buddhism can only be gained through persistent inner effort and usually only after many incarnations by someone who has progressed to the highest state of being, as a sublime prize of victory for those who have freed themselves through the highest inner conquests from the 'power that binds all beings'. Untiring, vigorous effort, not quietism is the base line of true Buddhism. 'This norm, O disciples, is a norm for those who make a vigorous effort, not for the quietist' (*āraddhaviriya-ssāyaṃ bhikkhave dhammo, nāyaṃ dhammo kusītassa, Aṅg*. IV, p. 232) says the Buddha, and even with his last words before his passing he admonishes his disciples to hold on to intense efforts.[7] The sacred texts speak about cases where particularly talented individuals who are predestined for spiritual progress immediately find liberation through the powerful impression of the Buddha's words. But the norm is still that the disciple has to continue his intense wrestling through many incarnations before he finally reaches the goal. In Buddhism four stages are distinguished according to the stage of approximation to the goal: 1. *srotāpanna* (Pali *sotāpanna*), 'one who has entered into the stream (of spiritual development)', the disciple who has entered the path; 2. *sakṛdāgāmin (sakadāgāmi)* 'one who will return once', i.e., who still has one reincarnation before him, who will reach the goal in the next incarnation; 3. *anāgāmin (anāgāmi)* 'one who will not return', who will attain liberation in this life; 4. *arhat (arahā)*, the saint who has reached the goal of liberation and is freed from the necessity of future incarnations. In the Pali form *arahaṃ* the latter word is also one of the usual epithets of the Buddha (in the common formula SPhS 40, *Dīgha* I, p. 62, see above, p. 124). As far as both possess the liberating knowledge to its full extent, the Buddha and the *arhat* are equal. The difference between Buddha and *arhat* lies in the fact that the latter has found the liberating knowledge (*bodhi*) as a follower of the Buddha while the former found it of his own accord. Furthermore, if the former has the gift of revealing the liberating knowledge to the world and if he uses this ability, he is called a 'perfect Buddha' (*samyaksasaṃbuddha,* Pali *sammāsambuddho*), in the other case he is called *pratyekabuddha* (Pali *paccekabuddho*), 'one who has awakened for himself'. A being who is predestined by the *karma* of the world to attain Buddhahood in the future is called *bodhisattva* (Pali *bodhisatto*). The term *bodhisattva* is already present in the earliest Buddhism, but it has received a remarkable elaboration in the later mystic-esoteric Mahāyāna teachings. The Buddha legend, which was imparted here following a Mahāyāna text, may provide a certain idea of these teachings. It has already been emphasized that the main elements of the Mahāyāna teachings are already present in a seminal state in the original Buddhism. Old Pali texts already speak about the Buddhas of previous world eons, and the prerequisites for an appearance of a Buddha and the possible eras for an appearance of a Buddha are precisely determined. An era in which a Buddha arises for the world is called a 'blessed era' (*bhaddakappa*). In the Mahāpadānasutta of the *Dīghanikāya* six predecessors of the latest Buddha are mentioned by name: Vipassī (Skt. Vipaśyin), Sikhī (Śikhin), Vessabhū (Viśvabhū), Kakusandha (Krakucchanda), Konagamana (Kanakamuni), Kassapa

(Kāśyapa), and the biography of one of them, the Buddha Vipassī, is told. According to the teaching of Buddhism each Bodhisattva passes through a sequence of stereotypical experiences in that life in which he reaches the liberating knowledge, *bodhi*; the development to a Buddha takes place in a career which is set once and for all and legitimized by the laws of the world. Therefore, the biographies of all Buddhas agree in all their main points, the only differences are in certain details. Each Buddha, for example, finds the liberating knowledge under a different kind of tree, and the lifespan of a Buddha is different according to the general lifespan of human beings in the world era in question (*Dīgha* II, p. 4).

The Buddha of the future world era who is now still residing in the Tuṣita heaven as a Bodhisattva (see above, p. 36) goes by the name of Maitreya (Pali Metteyo), 'the loving one'. This name contains the suggestion that according to the Buddhist doctrine a great world teacher will appear in a future (still distant) world era whose mission it will be to reveal love (*maitrī*, Pali *mettā*) to humanity, to bring to the fore love among beings. According to the doctrine of Buddhism this love can only be realized on a high stage of being, it is in close, intimate connection with that which is presented in the sacred texts as the highest goal of the 'path,' as liberation. In the same way that low sensual love (*kāma*) and passionate love (*rāga*) are regarded as a fetter, as a delusion (*āsava*) effecting the binding of the soul, thus belonging to the 'power which binds all beings', a love which is high, all-penetrating and cosmic, the sublime emotion of friendship* towards all beings is regarded as a power which frees the heart, the soul from all fetters—*cetovimutti* 'liberation of the heart'. According to the sacred texts liberation (*vimutti*), the true goal of Buddhism, to which this last section is

*It is of little consequence whether the term *maitrī*, Pali *mettā* (from *mitra, mitto* 'friend') is translated as 'love' or 'friendship'. The yardstick given in this context is always the feeling of a mother for her child (cf. *Suttanipāta* 149, 150); similar passages also frequently in the *Lalitavistara*). This feeling however is not merely friendship but precisely that which we call love. Therefore, the translation 'love' is to be preferred. This does not mean that we have to identify the Buddhist *maitrī* with the 'Christian love', the **ἀγάπη** of the apostle Paul. **ἀγάπη** is the Christian, *maitrī* is the Buddhist love; between **ἀγάπη** and *maitrī* the same difference of shades of sensibility holds as between Christianity and Buddhism in general. Even so, *maitrī* is the term in whose context Buddhism appears to approach Christianity most closely. [In order to preserve the distinction from romantic love *maitrī/mettā* are generally translated as 'loving kindness' in contemporary works on Buddhism. *Trans. note*] devoted, has two sides: *paññāvimutti* 'liberation of knowledge' and *cetovimutti* 'liberation of the heart'. The former has to be understood as liberation through knowledge, at the same time a going beyond knowledge in a higher state of consciousness (cf. *Aṅg.* IV, p. 452); the latter is the liberation of the heart from all passion which causes bondage to sensual existence—that which was already called 'cutting the knots of the heart' in the ancient Upanishads. 'The liberation of the heart and liberation of knowledge which is already free from delusion, attained through the annihilation of delusion in visible existence' thus *nirvāṇa* is called in numerous passages of the canon (e.g., *Aṅg.* III, p. 119). It is now a significant concept of Buddhism that love—which is not a sensual love—the feeling of friendship with all beings (*maitrī, mettā*) acts as such a 'liberation of the heart' which purifies away everything that binds the soul to low sensuality. This concept finds its expression in the fact that *cetovimutti* 'liberation of the heart' appears almost as a standing attribute of *mettā* in the sacred texts. According to Buddhism this heart-liberating love does not require any external activity in order to be effective, but works spiritually-supernaturally like a magic power through mere emanation or like a rain which swells all streams, pouring blessings over all beings (in this sense the beautiful parable *Aṅg.* I, p. 423). It is always said that this love which emanates from the heart penetrates all cardinal directions and how the heart, the soul itself, expands into infinity, filling the entire world with thoughts of love (thus e.g., *Dīgha* II, p. 251; *Majjh.* I, p. 297, 351; II, p. 207; *Aṅg.* II, p. 129 and others). The same is said about three further inner states: of compassion (*karuṇā*), sympathetic joy (*muditā*), equanimity (equanimity particularly towards everything impure and evil, *upekṣā*, Pali *upekhā*); these are therefore, like *mettā*, called the 'immeasurable' (the *Yogasūtra* [I, 33] also speaks about the soul-purifying effect of these four sentiments); they are also called *cetovimutti* and outwardly equated with *mettā* in the texts. In actual fact it is possibly *karuṇā*, compassion, which is most emphasized in Buddhism, and it is not without significance that *mettā*, love, appears woven into the name of the *future* Buddha. That Buddhism—despite the external equation of the three inner states in the texts—seems to have a certain sensibility for the fact that *mettā*, love, 'is the greatest among them' is possibly shown most beautifully in section 27 of the *Itivuttaka* (p. 19f.; first noticed and translated by Pischel), where *mettā* is presented as something which is highly exalted above all external work and action: as the light of the moon eclipses the radiance of the stars, thus the text, or as the sun rising in a cloudless sky in autumn, at the end of the rainy season, chases away all darkness and sparkles and glows and shines, and like at the end of the night, at daybreak, the morning star shines and rays forth, in the same way 'love, the liberation of the heart' eclipses all outer work and actions belonging to the lower sphere and 'sparkles and glows and shines'. The *mettā* of Buddhism thus does not belong to the realm of outer action, but to that of supernatural action, of meditation, and it is (*Aṅg.* V, p. 360) literally listed among the stages of meditation. The mere concentration on thoughts of love leads to the high heavens of the gods, to Brahmā (*Aṅg.* II, p. 129) and truly experienced *mettā* immediately provides—as the attribute *cetovimutti* already conveys—liberation in so far as it is the liberation of the heart. That the essential characteristic of liberation—the annihilation of earthly *karma*—also takes place in this kind of liberation is also explicitly stated in the sacred texts: in *mettā cetovimutti*, heart-liberating love, an area is entered where earthly actions and their consequences are not taken along, the limitlessness of the spiritual (*cittaṃ appamāṇaṃ*) where the four 'immeasurable sensibilities' (*appamaññā*) lead, extinguish and annihilate all earthly *karma* belonging to the finite sphere, and which frees from the compulsion* of a return into physical existence (*Aṅg.* V, p. 300). It is in this sense that the texts also speak about 'immeasurable liberation of the heart' (*appamāṇā cetovimutti, Majjh.* I, p. 291): by raising himself to this sublime, all-penetrating, exalted world-love the disciple enters the immeasurable sphere, *nirvāṇa*).

---

*A Buddha's or Bodhisattva's earthly incarnation does not occur under the compulsion of an individual karmic necessity, but is a deed of free love.

Notes

Foreword

1. Edmund Hardy (1852–1904), a senior Indologist at the University of Bonn which Beckh visited in the summer of 1903. Hardy had published four major books on Buddhism before writing *Buddha* for Sammlung Göschen and was an expert on Pali texts. The small introductory work was published posthumously in 1905 as Hardy had died in 1904. For an appreciation of his life and work, see T.W. Rhys Davids, *Professor Edmund Hardy*, Journal of The Royal Asiatic Society of G.B. and Ireland, 1905, pp. 213–5. Hardy's *Buddha* is recorded in Beckh's bibliography and there is little doubt that Beckh met him personally in 1903.
2. The series started in 1889 with publishing classical works of German literature. Emil Daniel's *Das Kriegswesen der Neuzeit* appeared in three volumes, 1911–13. For an overview of the publishing concern, see *Georg Joachim Göschen: sein Verlag*, Walter de Gruyter, 1935, and the *Gesamtverzeichnis (der) Sammlung Göschen*, De Gruyter, 1930, with recent reissues. The former study indicates that at the period of Beckh's involvement with Tibetan texts the company, joining forces with Walter de Gruyter, was facing hard decisions regarding its policy on publications and pricing.
3. Two of the early growing-points for Neo-Buddhism can be found in the life and scholarly work of Karl Eugen Neumann (1865–1915) and the publications of Paul Dahlke (1865–1928). For Theosophy, see René Guénon, (2004). *Theosophy: history of a pseudo-religion.* translated by Alvin Moore, Jr. Hillsdale, Sophia Perennis, NY. For the romantic image of Tibet there is Donald Lopez, (1999). *Prisoners of Shangri-La: Tibetan Buddhism and the West. Tibetan Buddhism and the West* (Reprint ed.). Chicago: University of Chicago Press. Among the Professors of Indology between 1900 and 1916 included within Beckh's bibliographical review here, Joseph Dahlmann S.J. (1861–1930) shows the strongest commitment to Roman Catholicism. A commitment to Lutheran-Evangelical principles was upheld by Heinrich Friedrich Hackmann (1864–1935), Professor of the History of Religion in the University of Amsterdam when Beckh's *Buddha und seine Lehre* was published.
4. Beckh's prize-winning doctorate was published by Verlag C.H. Beck, München, 1899. The text is currently online.
5. Regina Schult, *The Village in Court*, Cambridge University Press, 1994.
6. Beckh's career in the law began as *Rechtspraktikant* in 1898, then as *Amstanwalt*. He is found to be trying criminal cases around München at the

turn of the century. His position has often been described as 'Assistant Judge' in English books.

7. Published 1907, *Abhandlungen der Königlich Preußischen Akademie der Wissenschaften*, Berlin. Dr Katrin Binder points out that Beckh's 'Habilitation' in the following year established his Professorial status with the obligation to teach as a *Privatdozent.*
8. *Udānavarga. Eine Sammlung buddhistischer Sprüche in tibetischer Sprache. Nach dem Kanjur und Tanjur mit Anmerkungen herausgegeben.* Verlag Georg Reimer, Berlin.
9. *Verzeichnis der tibetischen Handschriften – 1. Abteilung, Kanjur,* in *Die Handschriftenverzeichnisse der Königlichen Bibliotek in Berlin, Bd. 24.* Verlag Behrend & Co, Berlin, 1914. The book is still a principal source for the study of Tibetan texts today with reprints and online texts readily available.
10. See note 3 above. K.E. Neumann is celebrated today as a leading pioneer in the translation of Buddhist Pali texts into German, including the *Majjhimanikāya* in three volumes. A critical edition of Neumann's translation was issued by Paul Zsolnay Verlag, Wien, 1957.
11. Recorded explicitly in Beckh's essay, '*Steiner und Buddha (Neubuddhistische Geistesströmungen und Anthroposophie)*', 1931. Beckh wrote up the talk he had given by invitation for a group of academic Neo-Buddhists in 1931 and it was intended for publication within their *Zeitschrift für Buddhismus.* It was never in fact published, but the Sütterlin MS. was typed out and the typescript kept safe by Gundhild Kačer-Bock.
12. *Hermann Beckh. Leben und Werk,* Urachhaus, Stuggart, 1997. English translation by Alan Stott, *Hermann Beckh. Life and Work,* Anastasi 2016, with added resources.
13. Relevant details on the biographies of both F. Rittelmeyer and E. Bock are found in Rudolf F. Gaedeke, *Die Gründer der Christengemeinschaft. Ein Schicksalsnetz,* Philosophisch-Anthroposophischer Verlag am Goetheanum, Dornach, 1992. With Hermann Beckh, both F. Rittelmeyer and E. Bock took up the leading role in the new Priests' Seminary for The Christian Community in Stuttgart, December 1922. What is not generally appreciated is that neither Rittelmeyer's work as a Lutheran Pastor, with a D.Phil. on Nietzsche and epistemology, nor Bock's basic Lutheran training plus a Lic. Theol. and some knowledge of classical languages were in any way comparable to the academic standing and capabilities of Hermann Beckh who had turned down a personal request from the Prussian *Kultusminister* C.H. Becker to take up a position as *außerordentlicher Professor* in Berlin. G. Kačer-Bock, op. cit., 111 ff. Becker himself held a D.Phil. in Arabic from Berlin.
14. Ibid., the first section of Part II. See also the collection of personal memories and tributes translated and collated in *Hermann Beckh and the Spirit-Word,* Anastasi, 2015. Michael Bauer was based at this time in Beckh's home town

Nürnberg, leading the Anthroposophical Group. In 1910 M. Bauer introduced Fr. Rittelmeyer to R. Steiner and Anthroposophy. At the founding of the new society at Christmas 1912 Bauer accepted a position on the Executive Committee with Dr Carl Unger and Marie Steiner. There can be little doubt that Beckh took part in the meetings of the Nürnberg Group in 1914. Else Kraus is found as a leading member of the Berlin Group at this time. For an overview of the Anthroposophical Society in Germany, 1910–16, see Helmut Zander, *Anthroposophie in Deutschland,* 2 Bände, Vandenhoeck & Ruprecht Verlag, Göttingen, 2007.

15. G. Kačer Bock, op cit., 128.
16. H. Beckh, *Steiner und Buddha,* op.cit.
17. For Beckh's experience as a student at the Maximileaneum, see G. Kačer-Bock op.cit., Section 1 Part 2: Beckh's own autobiographical observations. For his alienation from the Stuttgart community, see Rudolf Meyer *Zum Geleit,* introduction to *Indische Weisheit und Christentum: Gesammelte Studien,* edited by Lic. Robert Goebel and Rudolf Meyer. Stuttgart: Verlag Urachhaus 1938, quoting Emil Bock: 'Professor Beckh was in our midst like the guest and messenger from a completely different world-order. In some things he did not quite fit into the world as it is around us.' Translation by A. Stott.
18. G. Kačer-Bock. Op. cit., 144.
19. Note for example, Germany's first large-scale use of poison gas as a weapon occurs when 18,000 artillery shells containing liquid xylyl bromide tear gas are fired on the Imperial Russian Army on the Rawka River west of Warsaw during the Battle of Bolimów, 31 January, 1915.
20. When discussing Buddha's teaching in Part II of the text here, Beckh immediately introduces the concept of 'homelessness' in connection with suffering on the very first page, referring to the *Sāmaññaphalasutta* 41, the second sutta of the *Dighanikāya.*
21. *Steiner und Buddha,* trans. Alan Stott, op. cit.
22. In 1882 the Theosophical Society established its headquarters on Huddleston Gardens on the south bank of the Adyar river. Inside, the main hall of the new building prominently displayed a symbol of Buddhism beneath Hinduism, and the symbol of Theosophy beneath that of Freemasonry. See *The Golden Book of the Theosophical Society, 1875–1925,* The Theosophical Publishing House, Adyar, Madras, 1925.
23. The second battle of Ypres, 22 April–25 May 1915; the battle of Loos, 25 September–15 October 1915.
24. The principal lectures are collected and translated in R. Steiner, *From Buddha to Christ,* Anthroposophic Press, 1978.
25. *Boeddha en zign Leer,* Ultgeverij Christofoor, 1992, adds numerous Buddhist photographs. Japanese edition, 342-2 Iwami blue, paperback Bunko.

Part I: The Buddha

Introduction

1. Jan Jakob Maria de Groot (1854–1921), *The Religious System of China, its Ancient Forms, Evolution, History and Present Aspect, Manners, Customs and Social Institutions Connected Therewith*, 1892–1910. See also *The religion of the Chinese* (The Hartford-Lamson Lectures on the Religions of the World. Macmillan 1910).
2. Letter from Lucerne, July 9 1859.
3. Lehmann, Edvard, *Der Buddhismus als indische Sekte als Weltreligion*, Mohr, Tübingen, 1911.
4. Beckh refers to Ernst Windisch, *Buddhas Geburt*, Leipzig 1908, in his Bibliographical Review (at the end of this volume).

B. The historical Buddha

a) The course of his life

1. Rudolf Otto Franke, *Dīghanikāya*, Vandenhoeck und Ruprecht, Göttingen, 1913.
2. Beckh's bibliography here refers to the 1881 Berlin edition of *Buddha. Sein Leben, seine Lehre, seine Gemeinde*, and also to the 5th edition, Stuttgart and Berlin, 1906. [The page numbers do not correspond to the 1st edition. *Tr. Note*].
3. In January 1900.
4. Thomas Rhys Davids, *Early Buddhism*, Archibald and Constable, London, 1908.
5. Ernst Windisch, *Buddhas Geburt*, Leipzig, 1908, mentioned in the Bibliographical Review.
6. Louis Étienne J.M. de la Vallée-Poussin, *Bouddhisme, Opinions sur l'Histoire de la Dogmatique*, Gabriel Beauchesne, Paris, 1909. Mentioned in the Bibliographical Review.
7. p. 140 in the English translation by William Hoey, *Buddha: his Life, his Doctrine, his Order*, Williams and Norgate, London and Edinburgh, 1882.
8. Ed. T. W. Rhys Davids and J. E. Carpenter; William Stede, for the Pali Text Society, H. Frowde, London, 1886.
9. Probably Trübner & Co., London, 1878, or perhaps the earlier edition published by JRAS, Vols 6 & 7.

b) The Buddha as a human being and spiritual teacher

1. Heinrich Kern, *Der Buddhismus und seine Geschichte in Indien*, German translation by H. Jacobi, Otto Schulze, Leipzig, 1882.
2. The phrase is addressed to God the Creator in the celebrated Old High German Wessobrunn Prayer, c. 790. Beckh may have seen the sole sur-

viving manuscript when he was in Munich. Full text, English translation and notes in Charles C. Barber, *An Old High German Reader*, Blackwell, Oxford, 1964.

3. The outdoor bronze statue of Amida (Amitābha) Buddha, c. 1252 CE.
4. Richard Pischel, *Leben und Lehre des Buddha*, Teubner, Leizig, 1910, recorded in Beckh's Bibliographical Review. Beckh makes a particular point of expressing his admiration and gratitude with respect to Pischel (his supervisor in Friedrich Wilhelms University in Berlin) in his Foreword to his own Dissertation on Kālidāsa's *Meghadūta*, 1907.
5. In his bibliography Beckh refers to the edition by Eugène Burnouf: Imprimerie Nationale, Paris, 1852.
6. Not listed in the Bibliographical Review. Beckh may have consulted the English translation by Rhys Davids and Hermann Oldenberg in *Sacred Books of the East*, Vol. 20, Oxford, 1885.
7. From the *Saṃyuttanikāya* 5.
8. The extended sea-parable forms most of the Uposathasutta in the *Udāna* (5.5).
9. In the Bibliographical Review Beckh acknowledges the work of Émile Senart on the *Mahāvastu*. The principal Sanskrit edition was issued by Senart in a series for the *Société Asiatique*, Paris, 1882, 1890, and 1897.
10. From the *Vinayapiṭaka*, Mahāvagga, Pali, PTS, Vol 1, p. 40. The text was published by Oldenberg in 5 vols, 1879–83.
11. The opening words of the Pāpavarga in the *Udānavarga*.
12. Mahāparinibbānasutta 6.7.
13. Poṭṭhapādasutta 4.
14. Beckh's Bibliographical Review, with a similar comment, refers to the Jesuit, Josef Dahlmann, *Buddha, Ein Kulturbild des Ostens*, Berlin, 1898.
15. Max Walleser (1874–1954), Professor in the *Institut für Buddhismuskunde*, Heidelberg.
16. The Leipzig *Theologische Literaturzeitung* remained in contact with Beckh's later work and published very positive reviews of his *Von Buddha zu Christus*, 1925, and *Indische Weisheit und Christentum*, 1938.
17. The original 108 volumes held in the *Königliche Bibliothek*, Berlin, had been indexed and considered by Beckh in 1914.
18. A frequent phrase found, for example, in the *Itivuttaka* 3.5.10.
19. Presumably Beckh is referring to the monumental Burmese Chaṭṭha Sangāyana edition.

Part II: The Teaching

A. General Viewpoints. The Truth of Suffering and the Path

1. I. Kant, *Vorlesungen über Psychologie*, Verlag Ernst Günther, Leipzig, 1964 reprints the 1889 edition which Beckh may have used.

2. *Muṇḍaka-Upaniṣad* 1.1.8.
3. See Hermann Jacobi (Professor of Sanskrit at the University of Bonn), *The Date of the Philosophical Sūtras of the Brahmans,* Journal of the American Oriental Society, Vol 31, No. 9, pp. 1–29.]

B. The individual stages of the path

a) Faith (*saddhā*) as a prerequisite of the path

1. *The Saṃyutta-Nikāya of the Sutta Piṭaka.* Edited by Léon Feer. London: Pali Text Society, 1884–1898, 5 vols.
2. Also known as the Mahāsihanādasutta; in the *Dīghanikāya,* PTS ed., op. cit.

b) First Stage of the Path: Right Conduct (*sīla*)

1. i.e., the *Majjhimanikāya,* PTS, op.cit.
2. In the *Dīghanikāya* op. cit.
3. In the *Vinayapiṭaka,* op. cit.
4. See Patrick Olivelle, Suman Olivelle, *Manu's Code of Law,* Oxford University Press, USA, 2005, which includes a survey of the older texts available to Hermann Beckh.
5. In Vol. 1 of the PTS *Vinayapiṭaka,* op. cit.
6. In the *Khuddakanikāya,* PTS.
7. Both are located in the *Dīghanikāya.*
8. R. Pischel, *Leben und Lehre des Buddha,* Leipzig, 1910, op. cit.; Eng. tr. B.H. Kapadia, Villabh Vidyanagar, 1965, op. cit.
9. In the *Khuddakanikāya,* op. cit.

c) Second stage of the path: meditation (*samādhi*)

1. At an early stage of his work with Rudolf Steiner and anthroposophy Beckh was looking for possible parallels between 'etheric' and 'akashic'.
2. Robert Spence Hardy, *The Legends and Theories of the Buddhists compared with History and Science,* Frederick Northgate, London, 1881. Beckh also records two other publications by Spence Hardy in the bibliography here: *Eastern Monachism,* London, 1850, and *A Manual of Buddhism,* London, 1853.
3. Karl Friedrich Köppen, *Die Religion des Buddha,* Berlin, 1857, new edition 1906. The page reference concurs with the first edition.
4. Edmund Hardy, *Der Buddhismus nach älteren Pali-Werken dargestellt,* Münster, 1900, appears in Beckh's bibliography here.
5. Pali: literally 'place of work'.
6. Sven Hedin, *Trans-Himalaya,* Vol 2, 1909, p. 205.
7. Ernst Windisch, *Mara und Buddha,* Leipzig, 1895.

8. H. Kern (p. 302) is in agreement with Beckh that Māra is cognate with Lat. *malus*, but goes on to argue that the word is also related to Skr. *marīci* 'shining' or 'ray of light' echoed in classical Greek by the verb *marmairo*, to flash or sparkle, a view that Beckh's philology could not accept.
9. Sāmaññaphalasutta 84 in the *Dīghanikāya*. Beckh later returned to this image in *Vom Geheimnis der Stoffeswelt, Alchymie*, R. Geering, Basel, 1931, p. 19. English translation in *Alchymie*, Temple Lodge, forthcoming.
10. The penultimate verse: 'as the arrow-maker strips the reed', S.P. Swami and W.B. Yeats, *The Ten Principal Upanishads*, Faber & Faber, London, 1937.
11. Beckh could consult the text as included in the Burmese edition of the *Khuddhakanikāya*. There was also the English translation by Rhys Davids for Sacred Books of the East, *The Questions of King Milinda*, Vol. 35 (1890) and Vol. 36 (1894). Reprint by Dover Publications, 1963.
12. William Hoey's translation, 1882, op. cit., pp. 258ff.
13. English translation by Kapadia, 1965, op. cit., pp. 84ff.

d) Third stage of the Path: Realization (*paññā*)

1. L. Austine Waddell, *The Buddhism of Tibet*, W.H. Allen & Co., London, 1895.
2. With '*Urstand*'—the original state or condition of Adam—Beckh is probably recalling the extensive use of the term in Jakob Böhme's, *Mysterium Magnum*, e.g., 26.53 where we find the relevant observation that '*sein* (Adam's) *rechter Urstand ist im Nichts*'. The term represented much earlier Patristic Greek and Latin words.
3. *Entwerden*—found in Meister Eckhart, Tauler and Jakob Böhme.
4. R. Steiner, *Die Rätsel der Philosophie*, Siegfried Cronbach, Berlin, 1914. Later editions and their English translations show some changes. Beckh also had access to the original serial publication of Steiner's *Welt- und Lebensanschaungen im neunzehnten Jahrhundert*, (Berlin 1901) on which the 1914 edition is based.
5. pp. 43–58.
6. Richard Garbe, *Die Samkhya-Philosophie, eine Darstellung des indischen Rationalismus nach den Quellen*, H. Haessel. Leipzig, 1894.
7. In *Der Ursprung des Buddhismus*, 1896, op. cit.
8. Beckh is probably referring to the text by M.V. Fausböll as noted in his bibliography, which appeared in a second improved edition, Luzac & Co., London, 1900, or possibly the earlier Latin and English translations. Verse 153: 'I, who have been seeking the builder of this house (body), failing to attain Enlightenment (*Bodhi nana* or *Sabbannuta nana*) which would enable me to find him, have wandered through innumerable births in samsara. To be born again and again is, indeed, *dukkha*!' Verse 154: 'Oh house-builder! You are seen, you shall build no house (for me) again. All your rafters are broken, your roof-tree is destroyed. My mind has reached the uncondi-

tioned (i.e., *Nibbana*); the end of craving (*Arahatta Phala*) has been attained.' *The Dhammapada: Verses and Stories*, Translated by Daw Mya Tin, M.A. Edited by Editorial Committee, Burma Tipitaka Association Rangoon, Burma, 1986.

9. *Entwerden* as discussed earlier by Hermann Beckh where it is referred also to its use in 'German mystics', i.e., Eckhard, Tauler and Jacob Böhme.
10. London, 1895, op. cit.

e) Fourth stage of the path: liberation (*vimutti*)

1. From J.W. von Goethe, *Die Geheimnisse. Ein Fragment.* Beckh resists the temptation to add the second half of the couplet 'Freed, the human being who overcomes himself.'
2. R. C. Childers, *A Dictionary of the Pali Language*, PTS, London, 1875 as noted in Beckh's bibliography. The entry for *nibbāna* begins on p. 265.
3. This often repeated Pali phrase occurs for example in the Cūlataṇhāsaṅkhayasutta, verse 2, within the *Majjhimanikāya.*
4. Here and previously Hermann Beckh uses the Sanskrit form of the name, as found in the *Lalitavistara*, and alludes to Lefmann's (1902) edition in the bibliography. 'Ārāḷa Kālāma' appears in Pali texts.
5. Paul Oltramare, *La Formule Bouddhique des Douze Cause, Son Sens Originale Et Son Interpretation Théologique, Mémoire pub. à l'Occasion du Jubilé de l'Université*, Genève, 1909.
6. Ed. V. Fausböll, PTS, Vol. 1, 1877.
7. Mahāparinibbānasutta 6.7.

Bibliographical Review

Herman Beckh 1916

It is in the nature of such an abbreviated work as this that out of a wealth of literature stretching beyond sight only the most significant may be selected for a broader circle of readers.

In the first place one may call to memory the works which have given shape to the basic principles of the scientific research into the Buddhist religion through their transformative diligence in the publishing of Buddhist texts. Among such editors there may be mentioned here:

Burnouf for the Saddharmapuṇḍarīka,
Fausböll for the *Dhammapada* and *Jātaka*,
Fourcaux for the Tibetan *Lalitavistara*,
Senart for the *Mahāvastu*,
Cowell for the *Divyāvadāna* and *Buddhacarita*,
Childers for the Mahāparinibbānasutta,
Oldenberg for the *Vinayapiṭaka*,
Lefmann for the Sanskrit text of the *Lalitavistara*.

The greatest credit for the editing of texts and research into Buddhism is in general due to T.W. Rhys Davids, the founder of The Pali Text Society. The vast majority of texts which stand in the first rank of the important Pali canon for research into the teachings of the Buddha have been made accessible for co-operative expertise through the lucid and reliable editions of Rhys Davids and his colleagues.

The first major work on Buddhism was the book by Eugène Burnouf, *Introduction à l'Histoire du Bouddhisme Indien* (Paris 1844, new edition 1876). This includes a rich and learned collection of material, while at the same time the spiritual problems of Buddhism recede into the background. Much the same is true of the books by R. Spence Hardy, *Eastern Monachism* (London 1850) and *A Manual of Buddhism* (London 1853); V. Vasilyev, *Der Buddhismus, Part 1: General Overview* (translated from Russian by Schiefner, St. Petersburg 1860) remains a fragment. The book provides a valuable and still indispensable overview today of the various schools and disciplines of northern Buddhism for the specialized researcher. The author does not have a similar understanding for Buddhism as religion.

The book by Karl Friedrich Köppen contains the first comprehensive account of Buddhism, *Die Religion des Buddha*, Berlin 1857 (new edition 1906); second volume *Die lamaische Hierarchie und Kirche*, Berlin 1859 (new edition

1906). Given that research today [1916] has also substantially progressed in many ways, one still finds a number of things in this book which in later works are not equally taken into account. The author's spirited manner of composition, even with its numerous subjective idiosyncrasies, still works its charm today. The account of Tibetan Buddhism in the second volume on the whole has not been superseded to this day.

An all-embracing account is provided by the book by Heinrich Kern, *Der Buddhismus und seine Geschichte in Indien*, 2 vols. (German translation by Jacobi, Leipzig 1882, 1884). Monasticism and church are treated with particular attention to detail here, and also the connection of Buddhism to Yoga is pointed out. The subject is briefly summarized in Kern's, *Manual of Indian Buddhism*, Strasburg 1896 (also with an outline of Indo-Aryan philology and the study of ancient history).

T.W. Rhys Davids, whose name has been already mentioned as the founder of The Pali Text Society, first concerned himself with Buddhism in the book, *Buddhism*, London 1877, which has passed through numerous editions since then; later in *Buddhism, its History and Literature*, New York, 1896.

The book, also well known in wider circles, by Hermann Oldenberg, *Buddha. Sein Leben, seine Lehre, seine Gemeinde*, Berlin, 1881, 5th ed. Stuttgart and Berlin 1906, has developed the perspective of modern science to the highest degree. It displays the older Buddhism according to the Pali sources. The profound contrast between Indian and modern Western thinking and feeling is thereby brought out with full impact. The book by Edmund Hardy, *Der Buddhismus nach älteren Pali-Werken dargestellt*, Münster, 1890, is concerned with the editing and processing of the same range of sources. The small book, *Buddha* (new edition, Leipzig, 1905) published by the same author in the Sammlung Göschen also contains many indications.

Josef Dahlmann, *Buddha, ein Kulturbild des Ostens*, (Berlin, 1898) reaches unsuccessful results with the appraisal of Buddhism in connection with Brahmanism, yet the book (based on lectures), spiritedly and grippingly written, and also well adjusted, does reach out to the consideration of the deeper problems of Buddhism. Added to the array of short accounts of Buddhism is H. Hackmann, *Der Buddhismus*, 3 parts, Halle, 1905, 1906, in which the development of Buddhism in various lands is dealt with.

The volume published by Richard Pischel, *Leben und Lehre des Buddha*, Leipzig, 1910, in the collection 'Aus Natur und Geisteswelt', is distinguished through its straightforward and sound scientific approach. Of a different kind is the enthralling account in the book by Eduard Lehmann, *Der Buddhismus als indische Sekte, als Weltreligion*, Tübingen, 1911, for which a Danish book (*Buddha*, Copenhagen, 1907), provides the foundation. In addition, from Rhys Davids and his spouse there has appeared in recent times the short accounts: J.W. Rhys Davids, *Early Buddhism*, London, 1910; Mrs Rhys Davids, *Buddhism, A Study of the Buddhist Norm*, London (no date).

L Austine Waddell, *The Buddism of Tibet or Lamaism*, London, 1895, is concerned with Tibetan Buddhism. The book is not a strong philological work, but brings together a rich collection of factual material and includes much that is generally of importance for the understanding of Buddhism. With Albert Grünwedel, *Mythologie des Buddhismus in Tibet und der Mongolei*, Leipzig, 1900, one comes to know Buddhism, as also with Waddell, above all in its pictorial representations, which in many instances are of a significance not to be underestimated for the understanding of the spiritual problems.

Max Walleser first of all discussed the philosophical side of Buddhism in detail in the book, *Die philosophische Grundlage des älteren Buddhismus*, Heidelberg, 1904. Through the translation of little known Māhāyāna texts (Mādhyamikaśāstra and Prajñāpāramitā) Walleser formed the basic foundations for further scientific research into Buddhist philosophy.

The spiritual problems of Buddhism have found a notable detailed discussion in the book by Louis de la Vallée Poussin, *Opinions sur L'Histoire de la Dogmatique*, Paris, 1909. (From the same author there is the ongoing publication, *Bouddhism, Études et Matériaux*, London, 1898, which includes further treatises. One of the especially important individual problems for the overall understanding of Buddhism is considered with the text, *Théorie des Douze Causes*, Gand 1913, which contains a wealth of material, and about which also monographs have been published by Oltramare and other authors.)

Not to be forgotten in this context is the service for research into the spiritual problems of Buddhism by the already mentioned English scholar, Childers as editor of texts through the knowledgeable analysis of technical terms of Buddhism in his Pali dictionary (R. C. Childers, *A Dictionary of the Pali Language*, London, 1875). It befits this modestly dressed research in the form of a dictionary when on the whole it does not penetrate to the ultimate depths, but to what has been worked on in Buddhism to the greatest degree of surety.

While in German research the historical problems and the teaching of Buddha have been largely set in the foreground, French research has already focused its attention for a long time also on the Buddha legend, the narration of the history of Buddha's life as this is given in the pictures of the myth and the mysticism of the sacred texts, especially within the so-called northern Buddhism. The book by É. Senart, *Essai sur la Légende du Buddha*, Paris, 1882, aroused much sensation in its time. Even if the import of the pictures and myths, and also a great deal of external material has been superseded—his theory of Buddha as sun-hero, which is still close to Kern, would scarcely find an adherent in our later times; nevertheless the book does contain a wealth of ingenious details and notes interesting problems whose profound meaning has eluded many. Regarding the Buddha legend, the two treatises by Ernst Windisch are relevant: *Mara und Buddha* (Leipzig 1895) and *Buddhas Geburt* (Leipzig 1908), which contain a good deal that is important and valuable for the overall understanding of Buddhism.

In close company with the stimulating problems associated with the Buddha legend there is the research on the hypothetical connections between Buddhist and New Testament texts, especially the Luke Gospel and later apocryphal testaments. First, Rudolf Seydel sought to demonstrate Buddhist influences on the Christian gospel in his book, *Das Evangelium Jesu in seinem Verhältnis zur Buddha-Sage und Buddha-Lehre* (Leipzig 1882). Seydel moderated his viewpoint in the later text, *Die Buddha Legende und das Leben Jesu nach den Evangelien* (Leipzig, 1884, 2nd edition Weimar, 1897). Still more circumspect is G.A. von den Bergh van Eysinga, *Indische Einflüsse auf evangelische Erzählungen*, Göttingen, 1909. Recently the issues have also been taken up in the book by Richard Garbe, *Indien und Christientum*, Tübingen, 1914. Through all this research the impression will be confirmed that it is impossible to emerge beyond supposition on the conjectured Indian influence on Christian texts or, also, on the Christian influence on Indian texts; and that for secure scientific results underpinnings for both are lacking. That profound connections between Buddhism and Christianity (especially Luke's Gospel) truly exist should not thereby be denied at all. However, the attempt to trace back both connections on the grounds of some or other direct, external influence or borrowing proves to be more and more unsuccessful. For any unprejudiced observer, a connection between, for example, the story of Simeon in Luke's Gospel (2:25–35) and the Asita story of the Buddha legend is without doubt existent, and to express this as meaningless is out of the question. It is only right to say that this connection lies in the depths and for the time being it must appear hopeless to wish to shed light on it with the means of external scientific research. Consequently, this book also refrains from making a closer approach to the—after all interesting—problem of the Christian-Buddhist parallels.

For information on the history of Buddhist literature, M. Winternitz, *Geschichte der indischen Litteratur*, 2 vols, 1st half Leipzig, 1913, is advisable. As an introduction to the characteristic endeavour to acquire a foundation for a modern world-outlook or religion as pursued in recent times there are the writings of Paul Dahlke: *Buddhismus als Weltanschauung* und *Die Bedeutung des Buddhismus für unsere Zeit*, Breslau 1912.

Additional Bibliographies

Heimo Rau 1958

Some works of newer research may be adduced. Collections of source material are available which directly assist the further penetration of the reader into the texts: Moritz Winternitz, *Der ältere Buddhismus nach Texten des Tipitaka*, Tübingen, 1929; Ernst Waldschmidt, *Die Legende vom Leben des Buddha in Auszügen aus dem Sanskrit, Chinesischen übersetzt*, Berlin, 1929; Nyanatiloka, *Das Wort des Buddha. Eine systematische Übersicht der Lehre des Buddha in seinen eigenen Worten*, 3. Aufl., Konstanz, 1953; Gustav Mensching, *Buddhistische Geisteswelt. Vom historischen Buddha zum Lamaismus*, Darmstadt, 1955; Helmuth von Glasenapp, *Der Pfad zur Erleuchtung. Grundtexte der buddhistischen Heilslehre*, Düsseldorf, 1956.

A whole series of accounts of the life and teaching of the Buddha was published after Beckh's book, among others: Alfred Hillebrandt, *Buddhas Leben und Lehre*, Berlin, 1925; Helmuth von Glasenapp, *Die Weisheit des Buddha*, Baden-Baden, 1946, and *Buddha. Geschichte und Legende*, Zürich, 1950; Max Ladner, *Gotamo Buddha. Sein Werden, Seine Lehre, seine Gemeinde. Dargestellte an Hand des Pali-Kanons*, Zürich, 1948.

Among the overall accounts of Buddhism may be highlighted: Johannes Witte, *Buddhismus in Geschichte und Gegenwart*, Leipzig, 1930; Helmuth von Glasenapp, *Der Buddhismus in Indien und im fernen Osten. Schicksale und Lebensformen einer Erlösungsreligion*, Berlin, Zürich, 1936; Edward Conze, *Der Buddhismus. Wesen und Entwicklung*, Stuttgart, 1955; Georg Grimm, *Die Lehre des Buddho*, published in a new edition, 1957.

Regarding the art of early Buddhism one may compare: William Cohn, *Buddha in der Kunst des Ostens*, Leipzig, 1925; Ernst Waldschmidt, *Buddhistische Kunst in Indien*, Berlin 1932; Anil de Silvia-Vigier, *Die Buddhalegende in der Kunst*, Köln, 1955; Heimo Rau, *Die Kunst Indiens*, Stuttgart, 1958.

For the question of the relationship between the West and Buddhism: Hans Haas, *Bibliographie zur Frage nach den Wechselbeziehungen zwischen Buddhismus und Christentum*, Leipzig, 1922; Hermann Beckh, *Von Buddha zu Christus*, Stuttgart, 1925; Georg Grimm, *Buddha und Christus*, Leipzig, 1928; H.W. Schomerus, *Buddha und Christus*, Halle, 1931.

Katrin Binder 1958–2016

Beckh's summary of the literature on Buddhism is thorough and detailed. In many respects, the works he lists still stand as definitive. H. Rau's update for the 1958 Freies Geistesleben edition also lists a number of well-known and valuable texts. Here, I concentrate especially on works accessible to an English language reader.

A useful point of departure for an overview of the most important current works is Heinz Bechert & Georg von Simson (ed.), *Einführung in die Indologie. Stand, Methoden, Aufgaben.* Darmstadt: Wissenschaftliche Buchgesellschaft, 1979. Here we find listed:

– useful for practical purposes: Nyanatiloka, *Buddhist dictionary,* rev. Eng. ed. Colombo, 1972 and more recent editions.
– on Indian Buddhism: A.K. Warder, *Indian Buddhism,* Delhi, 1970.
– Bechert & Simson assert that the standard work on ancient Buddhism is still É. Lamotte, *Histoire du Bouddhisme indien, des origins à l'ère Śaka,* Louvain, 1958, 'which portrays the development until the first cent. CE (i.e., before the development of the Mahāyāna) in detail and reliably'. p. 117.
– for a popular German introduction: H.W. Schumann, *Buddhismus,* Olten, 1996.
– Frauwallner's seminal, *Die Philosophie des Buddhismus* was published with commentaries in 1969. Latest edition, Akademie Verlag, 2010. English translation by Lodro Sangpo, 2010.

Regarding publications that touch on subjects scrutinized by Hermann Beckh, the following may be listed:

W. Kirfel, *Symbolik des Buddhismus,* Stuttgart, 1959
R.G. Welbon, *The Buddhist Nirvāṇa and its Western interpreters,* Chicago, 1968.
E. Waldschmidt, *Die Überlieferung vom Lebensende des Buddha,* 2 vols., Göttingen, 1944–48
A. Bareau, *Recherches sur la Biographie du Buddha,* 3 vols., Paris, 1963–1971
B. Mukherjee, *Die Überlieferung von Devadatta, dem Widersacher des Buddha,* München, 1966.

For critical appraisals of earlier scholarship regarding the sources on the life of the Buddha, one may refer to D.L. Snellgrove's article in *Bulletin of the School of Oriental and African Studies* 36 (1973), 399–411

An aid to the Pali canon for German readers exists in H. Hecker, *Der Pali-Kanon, ein Wegweiser,* Hamburg, 1965.

For general reading, the following works have continued the tradition of up-to-date introductions to the life and teaching of the Buddha:

Peter Harvey, *An Introduction to Buddhism,* Cambridge: CUP 2013 (2nd rev. edition).
W. Rahula, *What the Buddha taught,* New York: Grove/Atlantic (1959, 1974 rev. and enlarged edition).
Bhikku Bodhi, *In the Buddha's Words: An Anthology of discourses from the Pali canon,* Somerville: Wisdom Publications 2005.

Bhikku Bodhi, *The noble eightfold Path, Way to the End of Suffering*, BPS 1984, with later editions.
Paul William, *Mahayana Buddhism, The doctrinal foundations*, Routledge 2008 (2nd Ed.).
Gombrich, R., *Theravada Buddhism*, Routledge 2006 (2nd ed., first 1988)
Rupert Gethin, *The Foundations of Buddhism*, OUP 1998.
Tenzin Chogyel, *The Life of the Buddha*, Penguin Books.

Hermann Beckh: Later Works regarding Buddhism

'Anthroposophie und Wissenschaft. Aus Buddhistischen Palitexten,' *Die Drei*, 4. Jg, Nr. 3. 57–65, 1924. English translation (E.), 'Anthroposophy and Knowledge. From Buddhist Pali Texts: Buddha's Relationship to Earthly Destiny,' in *Hermann Beckh, Collected Articles* (forthcoming). (CA = Collected Articles)

Maya—Das Weihnachtsmysterium im Indischen Blütengarten,' *Die Christengemeinschaft*, (CG) 1. Jg., No. 9, Dez. 1924. 254–58, 1924. E. 'Queen Maya: the Christmas Mystery in the Indian Flowergarden', CA.

'Von Buddha zu Christus', Verlag der Christengemeinschaft, Stuttgart, 1925. *Christus aller Erde*, Bd. 10. Heavily condensed as *From Buddha to Christ*, Floris Books, 1956 (trans. Alfred Heidenreich). Complete Ed. *From Buddha to Christ* (Tr., A. Stott, ed., K. Binder), Temple Lodge Publishing 2019.

'Die Sittlilche Forderung bei Moses und bei Buddha', CG 1925. Eng. 'The Moral Demand with Buddha and With Moses', CA.

Der Hingang des Vollendeten – die Erzählung von Buddhas Erdenabschied und Nirvana (Mahāparinibbānasutta des Pali-Kanons), übersetzt und eingeleitet, Verlag de Christengemeinschaft, Stuttgart, 1925. 2 Aufl. Herausgegeben von Dieter Lauenstein, Verlag Urachhaus, Stuttgart, 1960. Eng. *The Passing of the Perfected One*. Temple Lodge Publishing, forthcoming.

'Buddhas Hingang mit Proben aus dem Palikanon,' *Die Drei*, 5. Jg., 12. Heft, March 1926. Slightly re-edited in *Aus der Welt der Mysterien, sieben Aufsätze*, Verlag von Rudolf Geering, Basel, 1927, pp. 88 ff. Eng. 'Buddha's Passing with Excerpts from the Pali canon', in *From the World of the Mysteries* (forthcoming).

'Scheidendes Licht', *Anthroposophie*, March, 1926. Eng. 'Light of Departing,' CA (forthcoming).

Vom Weltanblick des heutigen Buddhismus,' CG 3. Jg. Nr. 3, June 1926, 94–96. Eng. 'Buddhism in the World Today,' CA (forthcoming).

'Neo-Buddhist Streams of Spirituality and Anthroposophy,' CA, 2017. Original typescript, unpublished, 'Steiner und Buddha. Neubuddhistische Geisteströmungen und Anthroposophie)', composed 1931 for Zeitschrift für Buddhismus.

Himmel und Nirvāna in den Religionen der alten Völker. Ein Fragment aus dem Nachlaß', nine essays in *Indische Weisheit und Christentum,* herausgegeben von R. Goebel und R. Meyer, *Theologie und Kultus,* Heft 9, Verlag Urachhaus, Stuttgart, 1938 (posthumous). Eng. with separate titles CA.

Glossary

Katrin Binder

Ādibuddha	'original' Buddha
ākiṃcanyāyatana (Pali ākiñcaññāyatana)	the sphere of nothingness
amṛta (Pali amata)	nectar of immortality, nectar of eternal salvation
aparigraha (Pali apariggaha)	non-attachment, non-concern for worldly things
apsara	heavenly damsels
arhat	saint; one who has reached the final spiritual stage through the Buddha's teachings
asura	demon, evil spirit
aśvattha	the sacred fig tree
atarka avitarkāvacara (Pali atakkāvacara)	beyond normal thinking, beyond logic, philosophy and speculation
ātman (Pali attā)	self, true self
avidyā (Pali: avijjā)	ignorance
āyatana	stage of meditation
bhava	being; lit.: becoming
bhikṣu (Pali bhikku)	mendicant monk
bodhi	knowledge, liberating realization, enlightenment, higher consciousness
bodhisattva	a being destined to become a Buddha
brahmacarya	the sacred life, the life of a Brahmin, chastity
buddhi	understanding, the mind
cetovimukti	liberation of the heart

citta	the brain, the cognitive faculty
deva	god, deity; angel
dhāraṇā	concentration
dharma, (Pali dhamma)	the norm, the doctrine
dharmacakrapravartana	setting the wheel of the norm in motion
dhātu	sphere
dhyāna (Pali jhāna)	meditation; stage of meditation
duḥka (Pali dukkha)	suffering
gandharva	class of spiritual beings
guru	spiritual teacher
jarāmaraṇa	old age and death
jātaka	story about a previous life (of the Buddha)
jāti	birth
kāma	sensual pleasure, love
kammaṭṭhāna	meditation exercise
karma (Pali kamma)	lit. 'deed'; the deeds of a past life; the law by which the deeds of a past life influence a present life
karuṇā	compassion
kāya	the physical, the body, a body
kṣatriya	the caste of the warfaring nobility
mahāpuruṣa	'a great being', a person of superior qualities
Maitreya	the future Buddha
maitrī (Pali: mettā)	unconditional love, loving kindness
manas	the mind
manomayakāya	a spiritual-etheric body
Māra	the evil one
Māyā	Name of the mother of the Buddha; cosmic illusion

muditā	sympathetic joy
naivasaṃjñānāsaṃjñāyatana	the sphere beyond conscious and unconscious
nāmarūpa	name and form
nimitta	'sign', a certain apparition in meditation signalling the success of the practice
nirodha	mastery over, suppression
nirvāṇa (Pali nibbāna)	liberation; lit.: 'blowing away', 'extinguishing'
Pali	the language of the (Southern) Buddhist canon of the Hinayāna
parinirvāṇa (Pali: parinibbāna)	physical death of a person who has attained liberation (*nirvaṇa*) in this life
paryaṅka (Pali pallaṅka)	a seated position for meditation, the 'lotus pose'
prajñā (Pali paññā)	knowledge, realization
prajñāvimukti	liberation of and through knowledge or realization
pratītyasamutpāda	the law of conditioned arising
pratyēkabuddha	a Buddha who has awakened for himself, i.e., who does not teach the norm
ṛddhi (Pali iddhi)	supernatural powers, powers acquired through meditation and/or austerities
ṛṣi	sage, wise man, seer; esp. those of the mythical ancient past and endowed with supernatural powers
ṣaḍāyatana	the six senses
saddhā (Skt. śraddhā)	faith, the prerequisite of entering the path
samādhi	contemplation, spiritual meditation
sammādiṭṭhi	right view in faith, the first stage of the path
sammasamādhi	right contemplation

sammasati	right mindfulness
saṃsāra	the cycle of birth and rebirth
saṃskāra (Pali saṅkhāra)	the formative forces
saṃyakṣasambuddha	a perfect Buddha, a Buddha who teaches the norm
sattva	purity, pure; the purification of the soul
satya (Pali sacca)	truth
śīla (Pali sīla)	right conduct; the first stage of the path
skandha	the five principal parts of the human being
sparśa (Pali phassa)	touch
śramaṇa (Pali samaṇa)	ascetic
stūpa	memorial temple, temple to house relics of the Buddha
sugati	'the good walk', the good path or way, where people who follow the doctrine go after physical death, the path towards the possibility of gaining enlightenment in a future incarnation
tapas	austerities; self-mortification; the 'heat' or spiritual power resulting from such mortifications
tathāgata	one 'having gone thus', someone having gone the 'good path', a Buddha
tripiṭaka (Pali tipiṭaka)	'three baskets', the Buddhist canon and its three parts — *vinaya* (monastic rules), *sutta* (sūtra — doctrinal texts), *abhidhamma* (commentaries and additional material)
tṛṣṇā (Pali taṇhā)	lit. 'thirst', sensual desire
upādāna	'grasping the fuel', satisfying sensual desire
upekṣā (Pali uppekkhā)	equanimity (in the face of evil)
vedanā	feeling

vibhavataṇhā	desire for being
vimukti (Pali vimutti)	liberation
yakṣa (Pali yakkha)	supernatural being
yoga	'yoke'; Indian spiritual practices
yogī, yogin	a follower of yoga